Penguin Education

International Marketing Strategy

Edited by H. B. Thorelli

Penguin Modern Management Readings

General Editor
D. S. Pugh

Advisory Board
H. C. Edey
R. L. Edgerton
T. Kempner
T. Lupton
B. J. McCormick
D. G. Marquis
P. G. Moore
R. W. Revans
F. J. Willett

International Marketing Strategy

Selected Readings

Edited by H. B. Thorelli

Penguin Books

Penguin Books Ltd, Harmondsworth,
Middlesex, England
Penguin Books Inc, 7110 Ambassador Road
Baltimore, Md 21207, USA
Penguin Books Australia Ltd,
Ringwood, Victoria, Australia

First published 1973
This selection copyright © H. B. Thorelli, 1973
Introduction and notes copyright © H. B. Thorelli, 1973
Copyright acknowledgements for items in this volume
will be found on page 358

Made and printed in Great Britain by
Richard Clay (The Chaucer Press) Ltd,
Bungay, Suffolk
Set in Monotype Times

This book is sold subject to the condition that
it shall not, by way of trade or otherwise, be lent,
re-sold, hired out, or otherwise circulated without
the publisher's prior consent in any form of
binding or cover other than that in which it is
published and without a similar condition
including this condition being imposed on the
subsequent purchaser

Contents

Abbreviations 9
Introduction 11

Part One
Success Formula:
Harmonizing Structure and Strategy 21

1 H. B. Thorelli (1972)
 International Marketing: An Ecologic View 23

Part Two
Inter-Nation Interface:
The Fusion of Politics and Economics 41

2 UK White Paper (1970)
 UK in the EEC: Shot Heard Around the World of Marketing 43

3 A. Stoutjesdijk (1970)
 LDC Regional Markets: Do They Work? 47

4 J. A. Ramsey (1970)
 East–West Business Cooperation: the Twain Meet 58

5 M. W. Duncan (1970)
 Union Carbide: a Case Study in Sales to Eastern Europe 64

6 M. S. Massel (1965)
 Non-Tariff Barriers as an Obstacle to World Trade 71

7 Business International (1969)
 Antidumping Rules in the European Community 83

Part Three
Local Environment:
Public Policy Sets the Scene 87

8 C. D. Edwards (1969)
 The World of Antitrust 89

9 E. M. J. A. Sassen (1969)
 Ensuring Fair Competition in the European Community 104

10 L. E. Preston (1968)
    Market Control in Developing Economies 116

11 H. B. Thorelli (1968)
    The Guarded Capitalism of South Africa 129

Part Four
Market Structure: Demand Analysis and Market Resource Base 133

12 G. Katona, B. Strumpel and E. Zahn (1971)
    The Sociocultural Environment 135

13 W. T. Anderson, Jr and L. K. Sharpe (1971)
    The New American Marketplace: Life-Style in Revolution 146

14 H. A. Lipson and D. F. Lamont (1969)
    Marketing Opportunities and Marketing Infrastructure in the Less Developed Countries 154

15 R. Moyer (1968)
    International Market Analysis 162

16 L. T. Wells, Jr (1968)
    A Product Life Cycle for International Trade? 180

Part Five
Marketing Strategy: One-Up on the Marketing Mix 193

17 W. J. Keegan (1970)
    Five Strategies for Multinational Marketing 195

18 P. Stone (1969)
    The Massive Market for Simplicity 204

19 P. R. Cateora and J. M. Hess (1971)
    Pricing in International Markets 209

20 Business Week (1965)
    When Cruzeiros Spiral – Think Dollars 222

21 J. K. Ryans, Jr (1969)
    Is It Too Soon to Put a Tiger in Every Tank? 227

22 Y. Ikeda (1970)
    Distribution Innovation in Japan and the Role Played by General Trading Companies 237

Part Six
Small Business and International Marketing 245

23 J. K. Sweeney (1970)
A Small Company Enters the European Market 247

24 Business International (1970)
Alternative Ways to Penetrate a Foreign Market 257

25 OECD (1964)
Basic Considerations in Connection with the Establishment of Export Marketing Groups 261

26 Business Europe (1968)
How Schick Sharpened Dull Sales Techniques to Cut into German Market 270

27 G. Beeth (1972)
Distributors – Finding and Keeping the Good Ones 273

Part Seven
Global Marketing in the Multinational Corporation 281

28 W. J. Keegan (1971)
Headquarters Involvement in Multinational Marketing 283

29 P. d'Antin (1971)
The Nestlé Product Manager as Demigod 290

30 R. J. Aylmer (1970)
Who Makes Marketing Decisions in the Multinational Firm? 301

31 J. S. Shulman (1969)
Transfer Pricing in the Multinational Firm 312

Part Eight
**The Marketing Plan:
Marketing and Economic Development** 323

32 R. D. Buzzell (1968)
Can You Standardize Multinational Marketing? 325

33 H. B. Thorelli (1972)
The International Marketing Plan: a Checklist Approach 340

34 P. F. Drucker (1958)
Marketing and Economic Development 349

Further Reading 356

Acknowledgements 358

Author Index 361

Subject Index 365

Country Index 373

Company Index 377

List of Abbreviations

CACM	Central American Common Market
EAEC	East African Economic Community
ECSC	European Coal and Steel Community
EEC	European Economic Community
EFTA	European Free Trade Area
FTO	Foreign Trade Organization
GATT	General Agreement on Tariffs and Trade
IFC	International Finance Corporation
LAFTA	Latin American Free Trade Area
LDC	Less Developed Countries
MAGHREB	Maghreb Common Market
OECD	Organization for Economic Co-operation and Development
UDEAC	Central African Customs and Economic Union
UNCTAD	United Nations Council on Trade and Development
VAT	Value-Added Tax

Introduction

The blooming importance of international marketing

International trade is blooming as well as important: trade between nations is growing at a rate of 10 to 12 per cent per year, or at more than twice the rate of world production. The value of world exports now is about 300 billion (300,000 million) dollars a year. In addition, the output of goods and services by multinational companies abroad and marketed abroad or in other countries has been variously estimated at 200–300 billion. By comparison, the total annual output of all underdeveloped countries has been estimated at around 350 billion dollars.

Some countries are vitally dependent on international commerce. Holland, for instance, derives more than 40 per cent of its gross national product from world trade and the Scandinavian countries between 20 and 30 per cent. Traditionally, the USA among Western industrialized countries has been least dependent on international trade, which accounts for only some 5 per cent of GNP. Nonetheless, due to the magnitude of the American economy, this modest share is sufficient to make the USA rank second to the EEC among the largest trading partners of the world. Furthermore, American dependence on international commerce will increase greatly in the next few decades, due to accelerating depletion of domestic national resources and vast growth in luxury imports, reflecting individualization of consumption in affluescent economies. Growing international economic dependence in America will also stem from the geometrical progression of technology which simply makes it impossible for any single nation to keep on top in all fields. The original development of steel oxygen technology, miniaturized TV and supersonic transport in other nations are cases in point.

By 1980 international marketing will be even more pervasive than it is today. By that time all business firms may be divided into two classes: globetrotters and globewatchers. Globetrotters are those who engage in export, import or production abroad. An increasing proportion of all firms, this group is likely to set the pace in most of the economies of the world. Those who elect to stay at home will needs be globewatchers; that is, they will have to face up to increasing competition with overseas firms in their own home market. Even such a trite local venture as the village barbershop will have to follow international fashions on hair colors and hairdos, or face the prospect (hair-raising as it may be) of extinction. Indeed, globewatching in general has great merit: by observing marketing in other cultures the executive (or the student) frequently gains a better understanding of marketing in his *own*.

With the reader in mind

This being a book on marketing, we have attempted to keep the customer in mind. We envisage two groups of readers: seasoned executives and university students of business. The manager should find the book integrated and comprehensive enough to hold its own, whether he personally is a globetrotter or a domestic executive sizing up the international scene. The book also caters to the business student looking for a single concentrated source on international operations. In academic curricula focused on marketing or international business, this collection of readings should find its prime use as a fairly rich supplement to any textbook.

It should be evident, then, that we are assuming some practical or theoretical familiarity with marketing management and at least the rudiments of international trade policy and theory. While the book does specialize on international marketing our selections have been made in full awareness of the fact that in international operations, more than elsewhere, marketing is inextricably intertwined with other management functions. Let it not be forgotten: in nine cases out of ten international business begins with export or import, and the lifeblood of the international firm is marketing abroad.

The treatment here differs from most other books of readings in international marketing. This collection has an integrative framework to both guide and stimulate the reader – and to ensure a useful selection of readings. The overall theme is the adaptation of marketing strategy to the special requirements of international market structures, as outlined below and detailed in Part One. In contrast to other books of readings which deal with differences in domestic operating conditions (comparative marketing), this collection focuses on *international marketing*. It is more analytical than descriptive – we feel that descriptive material, in these fast-moving times, ages rapidly. To promote integration of materials we have edited and abbreviated a great many selections. In this manner, too, it has been possible to include a greater number and range of contributions within the paperback format. We have also minimized incest by overlap – too many articles are making the rounds of the readings books. By digging further, we are able to present here many valuable contributions not elsewhere reprinted. Finally, in an unorthodox twist, we have resorted to excerpts from books and monographs when no suitable articles were at hand. In this manner we have dealt with international pricing, for instance, a vital problem area paradoxically left out of most other international marketing collections.

The level of generalization aimed at is that of the practically oriented and analytically interested executive, as well as of the university student contemplating a career in international marketing at home or abroad. We are avoiding the extreme of generality as found in some background writings on cultural anthropology and international economics as well as the opposite extreme of specificity as encountered in the export-manual type of discussion of bills of lading and letters of credit. The watchword is managerial pragmatism based in sound theory.

Our purpose, then, is to provide an analytical framework in international marketing rather than specific answers for the concrete situation. The objective is to help the reader define the problems he is likely to encounter in international marketing, bearing in mind that defining the problem is the single most important prerequisite to solving it. The executive and the student have a characteristic in common: they are looking for impulses to stimulate their own thinking rather than for a set of patent medicines allegedly curing all maladies. The present collection is intended to meet this need. It should enable the reader to make his own diagnosis of differences and similarities in market structures around the world, and it provides guidelines for the planning of appropriate marketing strategies.

The book should be equally relevant whether the reader (or his company) be European or American, a national of an industrialized or of an industrializing country. If a majority of the selections stem from American sources it is simply because thus far most of the best writings on international marketing have appeared in the United States. We have tried, however, to avoid items looking at the world as a kind of enlarged Yankee playground.

Success formula: harmonizing structure and strategy

Ultimately, the whole field of marketing revolves around a single key question: how to adapt marketing strategy to the prevailing market conditions (i.e. the market structure). Whoever has the answer to this question carries the key to success. In domestic marketing it takes no great discerning skills to see that the marketing of ladies' fashion goods differs from that of Coca-Cola, which in turn differs from the marketing of petro-chemicals or productive equipment for industry. But to note such gross differences is not enough. They are of little interest to a hosiery manufacturer trying to find a niche next to twenty other hosiery manufacturers all catering to the same general market. The rise and fall of firms and brands about which we read daily in the financial pages shows that even subtle variations in strategy may spell the differences between failure and success in the marketplace.

The principal distinction between domestic and international marketing is that as you move from the former to the latter the problem of harmonizing (or 'matching') strategy and structure takes on two *additional* dimensions. One set of complications is encountered in the interface between nations: tariffs, quotas and invisible trade barriers, xenophobia, currency problems, East–West embargoes, UN sanctions and other manifestations of nationalism and international politics. The second array of complications stems from the very fact that one deals with two or more *markets* on the international scene. Market structures for a given product may vary appreciably from one country to the next due to such factors as differences in values, styles of life, economic development, government regulation of business, and political stability. The scale of operations apart, Coca-Cola can be successfully marketed in almost the same way in New York and Bombay, but this clearly is not the case with beef hamburgers. The free auto markets of Europe differ drastically from the rigidly regimented ones in most Latin American countries. Superciliously, an economist may tell you that the differences between domestic and international operations are only a matter of degree. Remind him that so is a difference between normal body temperature and one five degrees above (or below).

Unfortunately, marketing as a discipline has not yet developed to the stage where we have scientifically validated prescriptions about what marketing strategies to apply under given market conditions. This does not mean that it is not worth our while to think about international marketing in a systematic way. On the contrary, the very absence of scientific laws on the subject makes an analytical framework for our thinking all the more desirable. To develop such a framework is precisely what we are attempting in Part One of this book.

Homogenization and heterogenization of demand

One of the most perplexing questions in international marketing is to what extent the emergence of multinational markets (EEC, LAFTA, etc.) and the rapidly increasing communication across national borders will result in greater homogenization (standardization) or greater heterogenization (differentiation, fractionalization) of demand. The corresponding issue for the international marketing strategy planner is whether to capitalize upon (and promote) sameness with its attendant economies of scale, or on individualized demand which frequently offers a set of profitable niches or sub-markets somewhat removed from the hazards of head-on competition. Again, this issue has not received the attention it deserves in the literature.

Part Five is addressed largely to this question. We observe that people have assumed too uncritically that the EEC and similar creations would result overnight in total regional homogenization. This is far from the case. Studies made by the European Commission have consistently revealed amazingly wide – and persisting – disparities in price on products ranging all the way from refrigerators to detergents as between the common market countries. While this is a reflection of the fact that mobility of economic resources is still far from perfect and that distribution structures and trade margins vary considerably inside the community, there is, of course, a long-term trend towards equalization at work. Some implications of these developments are seen in our first selection, pertaining to the effects of UK joining the EEC. Part Five makes additional points concerning multinational homogenization of demand by income and life style groupings and about likely future cyclical developments alternating between homogenization and heterogenization of markets.

Tribalism in the global village

We hear a great deal about Spaceship Earth and the Global Village. And indeed strong technological and cultural forces are pulling the peoples of the world together. Satellite communications are revolutionizing business communications and, via television, enabling everyman to be on the scene – in real time – in almost any corner of the world. Transatlantic passage is already requiring less than a working day; in a couple of years it will take only half of one thanks to supersonic transport. Worldwide computer hookups at this very moment are vastly simplifying the coordination of global concerns; the impact of this single development we have probably only begun to understand. Study and vacation abroad are almost as commonplace to the middle class today as the sojourn at a domestic resort of yesterday.

The links of technology and culture across national frontiers do suggest the nascency of One World. Paradoxically, in the midst of these forces of fusion, man has spawned fission: since the last world war at least forty territories have become independent nations, an increase of at least one-third in the number of suboptimization centres in economic development and international politics. Paradoxically, too, after the first decade of American leadership of the free world, nationalism has gone rampant everywhere. This is most obvious, and psychologically understandable, in the case of the less developed countries. But the LDCs have no monopoly on nationalism, as witnessed by the policies of a de Gaulle or the writings of a Servan-Schreiber, the restrictions on foreign capital investment in Sweden and Japan, the immigration laws of Switzerland and, lately, the restrictive international economic policies of a somewhat disillusioned United States, itself plagued by balance-of-payments problems. The causes of economic nationalism are many. Common markets and customs unions notwithstanding, in one form or another it will be with us for quite a while.

Economic tribalism is at the root of international dislocations at the level of diplomacy as well as that of international marketing by private firms. Parts Two and Three are intended to provide a basis for a deeper understanding of this situation, as well as of the constraints – and opportunities – it presents to the international marketer.

The challenge of international marketing

A modern marketing system is indispensable to the smooth functioning of an industrialized economy. Mass production would indeed be inconceivable without mass distribution. Customer-oriented marketing is not likely to lose in importance in post-industrial society as that is portrayed in the article on the American market in Part Four. A major challenge of international marketing among developed nations in the future will be to effectuate the exchange of styles of life from one culture to another which will doubtless constitute a cardinal element of the coming individualization among increasingly sophisticated consumers.

Marketing can also play a key role in economic development of industrially backward countries, although this is not yet generally realized. Thus it is that marketing development has been almost completely neglected in UN and other assistance programs. This is because we have accepted too uncritically the notion that in the LDCs you have to start with heavy industry, and you have to have socialist or other autocratic governments, willing to suppress private consumption. Indeed, in this view marketing is really a sort of parasitical activity encouraging waste of scarce resources. Reality is precisely the reverse: *only* if marketing is given at least as much emphasis as heavy industry, agriculture and education can nations hope to achieve the twin goals of rapid economic progress and internal political freedom. The key is the *motivational* effects of modern marketing, which results in a dramatic transformation of attitudes towards work, achievement, savings, family planning and consumption.

Beginning twenty-five years ago, Sears, Roebuck in Latin America has provided an excellent example of a multinational marketing organization rendering a powerful contribution to local economic development. It does this in many ways, by:

1. Fostering thousands of local suppliers.
2. Introducing new concepts of quality and, not least, of *quality standards*.
3. Introducing consumer credit.
4. Emphasizing big volume and low margins (the reverse is traditional in less developed countries).
5. Introducing the notion of one-stop shopping.
6. Providing consumer information on an unprecedented scale.
7. Substituting same-price-for-all for wasteful and discriminating haggling.
8. Emphasizing that the customer is king. He is not the means of either merchants or governments.

As indicated by Peter Drucker in Part Eight, perhaps the most important effect of Sears' operations in Latin America has been that of shaking up the established ultraconservative department and specialty stores. These local operators have rapidly adopted – or even carried further – many of these progressive policies, resulting in the overdue arrival of some real competition for the favors of the consumer. Old-time distribution *was* parasitic and static in outlook. Modern marketing is a prime vehicle of development.

There is enormous challenge in international marketing. From a business point of view, it generally offers greater uncertainty than domestic marketing, but the risks are not necessarily much greater. On the contrary, they may often be reduced by an 'international portfolio' approach. The payoffs are often greater than at home precisely because the international marketer brings something new to the situation abroad. From a personal point of view, it offers the satisfaction of contributing to the quality of life and to local economic growth, it broadens our horizons, and, last but not least, it teaches us valuable lessons about how to handle international competition as well as regional and special-group marketing problems in domestic markets.

The plan of the book

This collection of readings is somewhat unique in the number of contributions included in a compact volume, as suggested above. To bring this bounty together, all the while minimizing overlaps, it was necessary to excerpt and edit several items. Such an approach was possible only due to the outstanding cooperation of participating authors.

Beyond seeking coverage for relevant areas of subject matter, the selection of readings in the central parts of the book has been guided by two principal concerns. We have tried to provide an integrated mix of survey-type, conceptually oriented articles with quite specific contributions oriented to particular markets or firms. We have also included in each of those parts at least one item on the EEC and one on the less developed countries. It seemed preferable to give these two vital and different areas of the world some special treatment, rather than to follow the law of least resistance encountered in collections with one stray article on each of a dozen countries.

The general scheme is as follows:

Part One deals with the harmonization of market structure and marketing strategy as the key to success in international operations and provides an analytical framework for the parts to follow.

Part Two emphasizes the close linkage between politics and economics in international relations and seeks to project the implications of major developments in this interface between the nations to international marketing.

Parts Three and Four deal with market structures. Part Three deals with the role of public policy in regulating market structures and practices in different countries. Part Four is concerned with international demand analysis and the identification of marketing opportunities. It also deals with the differential availability of market data, transportation facilities and other aspects of marketing infrastructure.

Part Five is focused squarely on the harmonization of marketing strategy and market structure. Product, pricing, promotion and distribution strategies in different environments are given special emphasis.

Part Six looks at international marketing from the point of view of the small or medium-sized company, concentrating on factors to consider in going international and means of gaining a foothold abroad.

Part Seven is concerned with the problems of coordination of marketing operations in the large multinational corporation.

Part Eight pulls the threads of the book together. The marketing plan is viewed as the practical means by which market structure and strategy may be harmonized. What is involved in international marketing planning is analysed both at the conceptual level and in down-to-earth, checklist fashion.

Part One
Success Formula:
Harmonizing Structure and Strategy

As stated in the introduction, marketing management ultimately faces only one key question: how to adapt the marketing strategy of the firm to the prevailing market conditions (or: market structure)[1]. There are no easy answers to this question. (If there were, marketing professionals might as well pack their bags.) Yet neither executives nor academicians in the field should lose sight of this overriding problem. Whatever he does, the marketer's success ultimately depends on his ability to bring his strategy into harmony with the surrounding market structure.

To be able to attune the two, one needs a good understanding of the concepts of strategy and structure, and some kind of model of how they interact. Reading 1 seeks to provide such a framework for analysis. It does this by applying an ecologic view. This ecologic approach to problem-solving in international marketing provides the theme for the book. Later sections will hopefully demonstrate that this is a valuable analytical tool as well as a stimulus in creative market planning. At the end of the book the reader should be able to use – and adapt – this approach for his own purposes.

1. Buyers naturally face the analogous question, although the answers, due to the partial divergence of seller and buyer interests, are apt to be somewhat different. Buyer strategy in general, and consumer strategy in particular, is an underdeveloped area in marketing.

1 H. B. Thorelli

International Marketing: An Ecologic View

A Reading originally written for this collection.

At least three dramatically different views of marketing are being applied today. The oldest of the current marketing concepts is producer and seller oriented. It is based on the standard that 'we sell what we make'. This beautifully simple notion derives directly from the industrial revolution: the economies of scale realized in mass production were so great that consumers were more than glad to accept the offering as specified by the producer. This philosophy is still prevalent in many firms dominated by engineering minds, or by the type of sales management which feels that there is something amiss with customers who fail to see the beauty of its product. A variant of the same theme is practised in the socialist world: 'planners know better what is good for the people than consumers themselves.'

In affluent and 'post-industrial' society with hectic competition between products as well as brands and inhabited by increasingly finicky consumers, the production-oriented idea of marketing has obvious shortcomings. In the fifties, the customer-oriented marketing concept was developed in the United States. In this view, the needs of the customer rather than those of the factory should define the offering (product, price, image, service, etc.) of the firm in the marketplace. The standard is now, 'we make what we sell'. Customer orientation has since been adopted as the keynote of business policy to varying degrees in most industrialized Western countries.

Certainly, the customer-oriented philosophy of business has great merit. It has called attention to the fact that ultimately firms exist not for their own aggrandizement but to serve the public. It has led to a virtual explosion of marketing research in both theory and practice, such research being the prime vehicle of identifying consumer needs. It has also stimulated much-needed integration of product planning, sales, pricing, advertising, market research, service and other marketing-related activities in thousands of firms. Without doubt, consumers as well as business have been – and are – beneficiaries of this process.

Railroads at bay

Yet this concept of marketing has at least one major shortcoming. This may be illustrated by one of the examples often quoted in the discussion of producer- versus customer-oriented marketing, i.e. the ailing railroad industry in America. It has been said that the prime reason for the demise of railroad companies has been their producer orientation: they saw themselves only in the business of running trains. Had they but been customer-oriented, so the argument runs, they would have seen their business as that of meeting the transportation needs of the population. Ergo, when buses, trucks, and planes emerged on the scene the railroads should have rushed into these new forms of transport. Superficially, the argument is plausible indeed. But it completely neglects one critical question of entrepreneurship: What are the things we are very good at, and what are the things we are not very good at? Now, there is nothing that prompts us to believe that railroad managers are particularly good at running airlines or trucking companies. Indeed, sociological studies suggest that most railroad executives would lack the flexibility and flair that would be required. Nor is there much evidence that the great physical resources (fixed assets) of the railroads would become much better utilized by the addition of, say, airline operations.

The logic of the situation suggests an entirely different tack. Faced with a long-term decline in the demand for their services, alert railroad managers might more reasonably have asked themselves the question: are there any customer wants we might be good at satisfying besides the need for railroad transport? This would have led them to recall that between 1830 and 1900 American railroads received grants of federal and state lands aggregating the land mass of France to stimulate expansion of the iron roads. These vast domains in large part are still owned by the railroads. What could be more natural than investigating, stimulating and exploiting the needs of an expanding and affluent population for community developments, recreational facilities and industrial parks on these lands? The prospect should be especially attractive in that a by-product of these activities would be the generation of additional railroad traffic. And, let it not be forgotten, real estate development is something railroad management *has* to be good at. Until recent years, however, what had been done by the railroads to develop outlying territories owned by them was unimpressive, with a few notable exceptions.

We have developed the railroad case in some detail because it also illustrates the emerging third approach to marketing: what we prefer to call the ecologic view of marketing. Under this view the marketer's standard becomes: 'we market what customers need *and* we are good at'. By taking into account both client needs and own resources the ecologic marketing concept in effect combines the producer-oriented and the customer-oriented points of view in a way that yields more meaningful conclusions than those which might be reached by either of the older approaches. Hence the notion of real estate development as a natural extension of American railroads.

Marketing is an interactive process

The ecologic view of marketing provides the theme and outline of this book. It is also an approach to theory by which we can improve our understanding of international marketing. Most importantly, it provides a framework of analysis of direct utility to practical decision-makers. In view of its treble significance, the approach will be developed in some detail.

In common with biological organisms every human being and every company is dependent on its environment for survival. Neither nature nor human civilization are in the end eleemosynary institutions. No one is self-sufficient. The interdependence of the company and its setting stems from the incessant drive towards specialization, or division of labor as the prime means of survival in a world of scarce resources. In effect, what happens in the process of interaction is that the company is obtaining the support of the environment by disposing of some of its differential advantage – or conversely, procuring resources from other organizations where they enjoy a differential advantage. The process of exchange is manifested by a perennial stream of transactions.

The environment consists essentially of a series of input and output markets (for labor, capital, productive equipment, raw materials, end products, etc.) in which the company must transact. For long-term survival the customer market is of paramount significance, as in the end satisfying customer needs is the *only* reason for the environment to provide the wherewithall (sales revenue) on which company existence depends. This observation is often made to establish the importance of marketing. What is far less clearly realized is that it also establishes that increasing *customer satisfaction* automatically becomes a key objective of any company with the will to grow.

An ecologic model of the company interacting with its environment is displayed in Figure 1. There are four critical and inter-

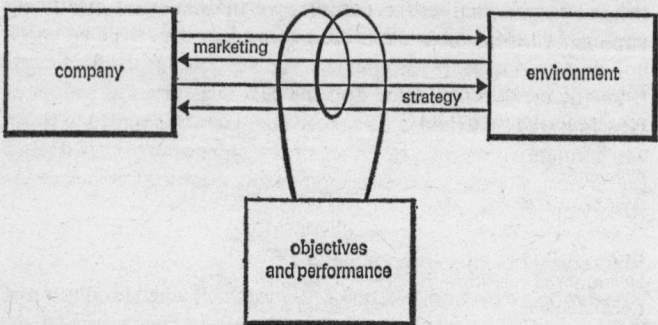

Figure 1 Ecologic view of marketing

dependent parts in the system: the company, the environment, the marketing strategy governing the interplay between the two, and the objectives at which the strategy is aimed (or, the other side of the coin: the performance actually achieved). Each part actually represents a set of factors or variables distinguishing one marketing situation from another.

The ecologic approach to marketing postulates in effect that a company trying to meet its objectives in a certain environment (market structure) should expect to find some marketing strategies a lot more workable than others. As we are not claiming that there is a single best solution for every situation, it should not be surprising to find several strategies coexisting in a given market environment.[1] This is still a far cry from saying that any random strategy might work. And the more we are able to specify the variables composing each of the four parts of the system, and their likely impact in a given situation, the more adept we shall become in zeroing in on superior strategies. This analytical job is that of the practitioner as much as of the theorist. A point of

1. It would lead off the path to discuss in detail the reasons why several strategies may be viable in a given case. They include the fact that different marketing instruments may serve in either a substitute or complementary relationship to each other, time lags in the interaction process, and the existence of 'slack' in both company and environment.

departure is provided by Figure 2, which displays a representative selection of variables for each part of the model.

Company characteristics

Our discussion of details in the model is confined to variables of general significance to the planning of international marketing strategy. Clearly, in a given case some variables will be more

Figure 2 **International marketing ecology: representative variables**

Company	Objectives
Aggregate size	(Performance criteria)
Size of local operation	Survival
Resource profile	Growth
Headquarter relations	Customer satisfaction
Local domain:	Data feedback
product span	Differential advantage
territorial extension	Profitability
mode of operations	Sales volume
customer groups served	Productivity
Organization structure	Local v. global
Marketing strategy	*Environment*
Product	Layers:
Intelligence and promotion	1. Market structure
Channels of distribution	2. Local marketing environment
Price	3. International environment
Post-transaction service	See text for further specification
Trust	

important than others and some factors not even mentioned here may be of special relevance. Too, different dimensions of a given variable may be significant in different situations. In considering the role of the *aggregate size* of an international company, for instance, one might have in mind available export capacity in the mother country in thinking about International Nickel, or the ability of the concern to absorb losses in a new venture abroad during a build-up period (Toyota automobiles in Germany in 1970–72), or the strengths and weaknesses of being a large multinational corporation (Unilever, Siemens) versus a small specialty outfit (a maker of paint sprayers, let us say) interacting with the environment in an LDC such as Peru.

That the *size of the local operation* in a given country is a strong determinant of what strategies may be pursued is beyond doubt. This is also true of the *resource profile*, notably the proportion of fixed to total assets, cost structure, manpower skills, patent position, degree of liquidity and other sources of competitive advantage or disadvantage. In listing *headquarter relations* we are primarily thinking of the degree of centralization of decision-making about marketing strategy (Readings 28–30). As an illustration; a few years ago a large American drug maker required that any local price changes be approved by the New York office. When the Venezuelan government invited bids on behalf of public hospitals the company lost out to a nimbler German competitor whose local management was permitted to make price concessions on the spot.

We come next to the *local domain*. This is an extremely important part of company characteristics. Indeed, together with the set of objectives, the domain defines the mission of the local operation (Thorelli, 1968, p. 76). Every company, every organization may be defined in terms of the four domain dimensions: product span, territorial extension, mode of operations, and customer groups served. Note that the 'product' marketed may be a service (dry-cleaning). Territory covered may be confined to a few cities in an LDC, while being nationwide in Britain. The local mode of operations may range all the way from the most modest (marketing a few units through an export agent in the mother country) to the most ambitious (a fully integrated production-marketing operation supplying both the local market and exporting to other countries, see Reading 24). Customer groups served may be distributors, industrial buyers, or end consumers, or specialized subgroups of these. Each clientele will require a more or less unique strategy.

The local domain may be viewed as the niche which the company has carved out of the total environment of a given country. The niche may be quite specifically defined (Volkswagen in America) or it may cover an entire spectrum of products and activities (Nestlé in France). Any domain is likely to change over time, if for no other reason than that the environment is in an incessant flux. In planning for company growth, eco-man (the ecologically-oriented manager) will seek to obtain common economies – or, more fashionably, *synergy* – between old operations and new. Can any of our existing resources (managerial skills, plant facilities, etc.) be utilized? Does the new product logically supplement the existing assortment? Can the existing sales organization handle the new product? Can we promote it to our existing customers? To capitalize on common economies is especially important in the development of small and medium-sized operations, the paradoxical circumstance notwithstanding that it may be more difficult to find synergistic opportunities in small operations than large.

Our last set of company characteristics is *organization structure*. Of prime significance here is the structuring approach – does the organization setup emphasize product, territory, functions or customer categories? In other words, which dimension of the domain is given priority in shaping the organization? Frequently of equal importance is the allocation of decision-making authority, in other words, the degree of decentralization within the local operation.

The company characteristics discussed here are of special relevance to company strategy. Taken together, they define a profile of the company which largely determines the types of strategies it is capable of pursuing in the short run. In the long run, environmental change will reflect itself in adjustments in strategy which ultimately result in changes in company characteristics. If there is no adaptation, the organization will not survive. Conversely, in the pursuit of company objectives aggressive management may deliberately change company profile and/or strategy in order to affect, or capitalize upon, desirable changes in the environment.

Objectives

The domain defines the nature of a local operation, but says nothing specific about its intended objectives or actual performance (results). Every firm has a set or a hierarchy of goals, more or less clearly perceived. The goal set of an ecologically-oriented marketer would include the objectives listed in Figure 2. Any two objectives may be partially overlapping, partially conflicting. Clearly, too, the relative priorities of individual goals will change from time to time.

Of the objectives, *survival* and *growth* would seem self-explanatory. *Customer satisfaction* occupies a key place in ecologic management, as such satisfaction provides the ultimate rationale for the existence of the business. Ecologic marketing requires a great deal of *data feedback*, to establish customer needs, to measure their satisfaction, to keep track of competition, and to forecast changes in the market and in the marketing environment.

To ascertain that the company is in tune with its environment the maintenance of an orderly information flow becomes a natural strategic objective among others. This environmental intelligence operation may take the shape of a Management Information System or simply of personal contacts, analysis of sales data and other less formal means. In a going concern marketing research and feedback from distributors and salesmen should provide key elements of feedback, whatever other ingredients may be.

Relative to competition any firm has a set of *differential advantages* (and disadvantages), deriving from its resource profile, niche and objectives. This differential advantage in the ability to meet customer needs may take any number of forms, such as cost leadership, specialization on a certain clientele or function, high quality, reliable delivery, outstanding service. Like a capital asset differential advantage is subject to constant change: at any given time the firm is either adding to it or in the process of using it up. If nothing else, environmental developments inevitably will cause shifts in the differential advantages and disadvantages of competing firms. To identify and maximize differential advantage (while trying to reduce attendant disadvantages) is a major entrepreneurial challenge.

In the ecologic view of the market economy *profitability* can no longer aspire to be the end-all of business activity. It becomes an objective among others, though still critically important as the vehicle of ensuring survival and growth. As we have said elsewhere, the modern corporation is not in business to earn profits but earns profits to stay in business (Thorelli, 1965, p. 250). *Sales volume* (and, similarly, *market share*) is an important gauge of viability and growth. Sales growth is typically correlated with profitability; it is also clear that sales increases are sometimes bought by companies at the expense of profitability. *Productivity* is viewed here as a measure of saleable output relative to the total input of resources, i.e. as an expression of internal efficiency. It is almost tautological to say that increased productivity is an objective of all economic organizations.

In international business operations it becomes necessary to make a distinction between *local* and *overall* (global) objectives of the company. In most international concerns top management makes a deliberate effort to harmonize these objectives (see, for example, Readings 31, 32). Due to such factors as nationalism among governments and a tendency of local managers to overemphasize the significance of their particular operations one must expect to find varying degrees of suboptimization in international marketing. Suboptimization simply means that some of the achievements of a local operation occur at the expense of overall achievement of the concern, such as an increase in sales in country A of high-cost goods made in an inefficient local plant rather than of low-cost goods imported from efficient facilities at headquarters. While perhaps worth striving for complete synchronization of local and global goals is hardly a realistic proposition.

The spelling out and periodic redefinition of objectives is a critical part of international marketing planning.

Strategy and structure defined

The key challenge in marketing being to adapt the marketing strategy of the firm to the market structure in which it operates, it behooves us to define these concepts. *Market structure* refers to all relevant characteristics of the marketplace surrounding the firm, notably consumers, middlemen, competitors and the product (offering) with which the market is identified. Important consumer characteristics include their number, income distribution and geographical dispersion as well as the values and attitudes determining their needs and behavior. The same variables apply to distributors and dealers in addition to their classification by size and functions performed. Competing firms may be analysed in similar terms. Additionally, their profiles of differential advantage and disadvantage are of special interest. So are their strategies; from the viewpoint of firm A the strategies pursued by competitors B–Z constitute a part of market structure, at least in so far as the strategies of B–Z are beyond the immediate influence of A.

Several characteristics of the product (offering) itself are among the determinants of market structure. Physical size and weight of the product may place territorial limits on the market. High unit price may preclude its distribution through such channels as supermarkets, drugstores and kiosks. A custom-made product faces a different market from a highly standardized one. A complex product, or one requiring special service, will typically have specialized or even exclusive distribution. The markets for industrial products are different from consumer markets, and consumer durable goods markets have little in common with those of foods or household supplies. In many markets the product life cycle represents an important structural feature (Levitt, 1965 and Thorelli, 1967; see also Reading 16). These illustrations could be extended further.

Marketing strategy on the other hand is the approach, or the stance, that the firm adopts in order to cope in the market structure. Ecologically, strategy is the means of harmonizing corporate resources, domain and objectives with environmental opportunity at acceptable levels of risk. In starkly simplified language market structure may be likened to an arena, while marketing strategy would be the play staged by the home team. Properly conceived, marketing strategy capitalizes on the differential advantages of the firm, while protecting it from unwholesome effects of its differential disadvantages.

The marketing strategy of the firm is reflected in the so-called marketing mix, that is, the particular combination the firm makes of the marketing instruments, notably product, intelligence and promotion, distribution, price, service and trust (Figure 2). Note that marketing strategy is a concept going far beyond the marketing mix. Marketing strategy is what makes the elements of the mix work in a coordinated fashion, as a whole rather than as disparate parts. Strategy is a qualitative concept, related to the idea of intermesh and the German notion of Gestalt. To build a house we need a materials mix of bricks and boards, mortar and nails. But without a strategy for putting them together we would more likely wind up with a big pile of rubble than with a house. Strategy is a scheme or a recipe for applying the means to reach the end in view. Classical marketing strategies include high price–high quality (Rolls-Royce autos), low price–mass volume (Ford's old model T), multi-channel distribution of a standard product with globally homogenized promotion (Coca-Cola). Clearly, the high price and the high quality of Rolls-Royce cars fit like hand in glove; the marketing instruments reinforce each other. We may, however, also observe that these instruments to a fair – but always limited – extent may substitute for each other. Rather than to introduce an improved model of our product we may prefer to increase our advertising or to cut price. Yet as time goes by an increasing number of customers will generally switch to the improved models introduced by competition no matter how much we increase promotion or cut price.

The marketing instruments constituting integral parts of Marketing Strategy in Figure 2 are generally well-known from domestic marketing and do not need redefinition here. Their international implications are developed in some detail in later readings, and especially in Part Five. Only three points need emphasis here. In the context of strategy 'product' refers to the specific variant or offering of a firm (Coca-Cola) rather than the generic product characteristics of interest in discussing the market structure in which it is being sold (soft drinks). Commercial intelligence – arranging for data feedback about market structure and broader aspects of the environment – is of special significance in international marketing (Readings 15, 24, 28, 33). 'Trust' has been included for several reasons. In consumer markets it builds store and brand loyalty – especially in the LDCs. That faith in the integrity and reliability of the other party is often a prerequisite to transactions in industrial marketing is familiar to every supplier and purchasing agent. Due to intercultural differences, time lags in communicating, inability to control the other party and lack of personal contact trust is a critical ingredient in international marketing strategy. None have realized this more clearly than the Japanese, who have made a heroic and immensely profitable effort to transform prewar international distrust into a strong faith in the quality of their wares and the seriousness of purpose in their commercial dealings.

Environmental structure

Three layers of environment of interest to the international marketer were identified in Figure 2. These environmental layers reappear in diagram form in Figure 3. A firm engaged only in

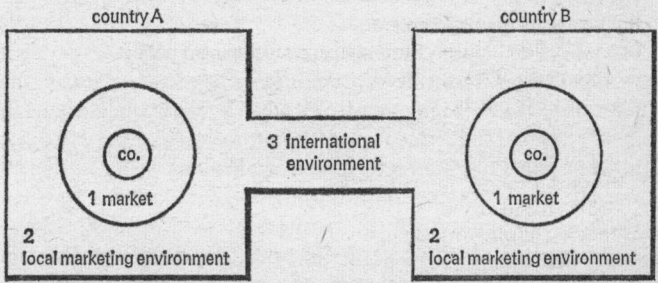

Figure 3 Layers of environment in international marketing

domestic marketing may largely confine its attention to the domestic market structure. The international environment is largely irrelevant (at least short-term) and managers generally have acquired an ingrained sense of the local marketing environment as part of growing up in it. The situation is drastically different – and more complex – in international operations. Not only must differences and similarities in two or more market structures be recognized: the international marketer must also be aware of the local marketing environment abroad and of salient aspects of the interface between his own country and those others in which his company wishes to operate. Indeed, his ability to see the strategic implications of developments in these two broader layers of the environment will frequently spell the difference between success and failure in multi-national marketing. Once again, the ecological view of the field points to the importance of commercial intelligence and environmental scanning in international operations.

Representative variables in the different layers of the total environment are listed in Figure 4. Market structure has been

Figure 4 Market structure and environment: representative variables

1 Market structure
Consumers
Distributors
Competitors
Product
    (for details, see 'Strategy and structure defined' section)

2 Local marketing environment
Government stability
Predictability of public policy
Economic development, stability, and development policy
Government controls:
    competitive practices
    state marketing bodies
    health and safety
    product labeling, standardization
Local business culture
Marketing infrastructure:
    data availability
    market research agencies
    advertising media, agencies
    transportation facilities

3 International environment
Relations between countries A and B
Tariffs
Non-tariff barriers
Currency controls
Transportation costs

discussed earlier. The figure also gives a sample of typically important variables in the broader environments. Their relative significance will differ from case to case, and frequently other variables than those mentioned here will be of even greater importance. The identification of relevant factors and the evaluation of their likely relative impact is an important challenge to the international marketer. The successful accomplishment of this task is a logical prerequisite to the design of strategy. In the *local marketing environment* lack of government stability and predictability of public policy – and attendant risk – is generally of less immediate concern in Western democracies than in the LDCs. Degree of economic development is an important determinant of market potential. Economic instability – engendered, for example, by excessive dependence on one or a few commodities in export trade or high rates of local inflation (Reading 20) – often means extra risk. Aspects of development policy of key interest include government outlook on the role of marketing and consumer products in general, import substitution policy, local ownership and minimum local value-added tax regulations. In the same league are inducements to or restrictions on entry into certain trades.

Government rule-making for domestic marketing is critical in any country. The role and nature of antitrust, consumer protection, and unfair trade practices legislation, as of health, safety, labeling and standardization requirements and of the direct government engagement in marketing activities (food distribution, agricultural export boards, etc.) varies enormously and somewhat unpredictably around the world (Part Three readings). It is a sobering reflection that in most countries at least some products are subject to some form of price control. Such control may not always be governmentally administered – prices may be set by local cartels too powerful to overcome. Other aspects of the local business culture set the tone of competition and cooperation between firms, define the level of business ethics, the outlook on corruption, and so on. A small operator will often have to take the local culture as given. To the large international concern a major challenge in defining strategy is to decide what aspects of local business customs to emulate and in what respects to be the nonconformist (Reading 34).

Marketing infrastructure refers to the relative existence of data and facilitating agencies needed in the course of marketing management activity. Industrialized Western countries generally have a rich and reliable data base maintained by government statistical offices, but the LDCs as a rule are not equally well endowed. Corresponding conditions typically prevail with regard to market research agencies, advertising media and agencies, transportation facilities, mail and telephone systems, etc. (Reading 14).

Beyond the local marketing milieu is the *international environment*, certainly no less important than any other part of the three-tiered setting surrounding the international marketer. The significance of political arrangements and relations between nations to him are illustrated by the European Economic Community and other regional associations (Readings 2 and 3) and by the special challenges surrounding East–West trade (Readings 4 and 5). While the General Agreement on Tariffs and Trade (GATT) and later rounds of tariff reductions between the major trading nations of the world have lessened the obstructions placed on international economic intercourse by customs duties, the fact remains that tariffs still are far from eliminated and that even highly industrialized nations such as Britain and the United States will reach for import surcharges and other pseudo-tariff devices when in a balance-of-payments pinch. At this time there are many signs that the great postwar movement to reduce or eliminate tariffs is – at least temporarily – coming to a halt. Meanwhile, the role of non-tariff barriers has been rapidly increasing, both relative to tariffs and absolutely speaking (Readings 6 and 7). Not without justice these obstacles are sometimes called invisible trade barriers: their existence and/or significance often is not clear (occasionally not even *made* clear) to the international marketer until he has already made contractual commitments on the assumption that they did not exist (or would be of but little significance). Neglecting to examine the likely impact of non-tariff barriers on a proposed international marketing venture is simply indefensible. This is also true of the related area of currency controls and exchange rate fluctuations. Less likely to be forgotten in pre-transaction planning are the transportation costs and related risks (war risks, dock and maritime strikes and so on) in international commerce.

Interactive marketing strategy

Rather widely different strategies may be viable in a given market structure. The ecologic concept of marketing does imply, however, that the superior strategies are those truly interactive. These are strategies based on the fullest possible utilization of differential advantage and/or common economies of the firm in satisfying a well-defined (narrow or broad) set of consumer needs. We will conclude our somewhat abstract discussion of the ecologic approach by a few specific examples of interactive strategy.

Synergy: American railroads

Relating to the analysis of American railroads at the beginning of this essay, let us restate that one clear cut application of the ecologic concept of marketing in this case involves the diversification into community developments, recreational and industrial parks and similar large-scale projects based on strong contemporary customer needs and prevailing on the common economies (synergy) derivable from the vast land holdings of the railroads as well as their already existing cadre of real-estate oriented management.

Synergy: multi-national life cycles

A number of complex products have first been developed in highly industrialized nations and then gradually been diffused around the world, somewhat in tune with local economic development. Growth companies pursuing ecologic marketing strategies will prevail on the scale as well as common economies to be derived from hot pursuit of the international life cycles of these products (Reading 16). A typical example is Ericsson Telephone Corporation of Sweden. While that country has the second highest telephone density in the world, it is obvious that Ericsson would have to be satisfied with modest growth indeed if confined to a market of eight million people. Before the last world war, the company's major thrust of expansion was south and eastwards in Europe – in tune with the natural growth of local telephone demand. After the war the greatest rate (although not always dollar value) of expansion has been in the LDCs. Scale economies occur when export is possible from the Stockholm factories as well as some other West European plants. Common economies occur when the technical, financial and marketing skills of the company are applied in the LDCs.

Nichemanship: Volkswagen in America

Nichemanship is the successful application of a strategy of market segmentation or selectivity. Perhaps the single most outstanding example of nichemanship in history is Volkswagen's strategy in the United States in 1955–65. Instead of striving to get 10 per cent of the US car market model for model (which would be a catastrophic proposition for a European auto maker) Volkswagen said, in effect, 'let us get 100 per cent of 10 per cent of the US market.' This was the niche of the 'beetle', the standard VW economy model of which several million units were sold in the period – long before the onslaught of other European, Japanese and American economy cars. Indeed, Volkswagen even had the stamina to withhold from the American market for years its fastback and four-door models, precisely in order not to clutter its nichemanship image.

Cost and service leadership: Hong-Kong tailors

In the past two decades the tailors of Hong Kong made great inroads in the woollen clothing market among male sophisticates around the world. Their simple but effective strategy was based on two elements. Low price (based on low labor cost) without compromising quality of materials was the first element. Personal – custom-tailored is indeed the word – and speedy service was the other. The differential advantage of a rich supply of skilled labor willing to work hard at low wages was utilized to the hilt.

Massive resources and homogenization of demand: Boeing jets

The differential advantage of Boeing in the jet aircraft market was almost the opposite of the Hong-Kong tailors. What counted in the Boeing case was the ability to marshall and manage massive professional manpower, technical resources and financial strength and then to make maximum use of this type of differential advantage by a strategy of homogenization of carrier demand for jet planes.

Low profile: the differential advantage of small business

Many a small businessman is psychologically overwhelmed by the complexity and risks of international operations, and thus is confined to the domestic market. Small firms which do venture abroad soon discover that they have a natural differential advantage in their low profile. They do not invite aspersions of imperialism, exploitation or undue influence in local politics. While a large foreign concern is typically expected – or even required – to operate with considerably higher standards than those practiced by domestic enterprise, the small firm typically can avoid this kind of discrimination. The small operation also is a flexible operation. Thus, if it brings a new product, technique or strategy to the market the small international business often has an enviable package of advantages.

The multi-national corporation as a change agent:
Sears in Latin America

In contrast to the small overseas venture, the multinational corporation does not have to take all or most aspects of the local environment as given. It will be able to effectuate changes in the host culture. Indeed, only by a judicious blend of adapting to local conditions and effectuating change in them will the multi-national corporation render its most effective contribution to local development. In this manner, too, it is most likely to ensure its own long-term acceptability in that environment. An excellent example of what we are talking about is Sears, Roebuck's operations in Latin America as discussed in the introduction to this book and in the article by Peter Drucker at the end.

Summing-up

The ecologic approach to marketing views strategy as the means of satisfying specific consumer wants for which the resources, talents and differential advantages of the firm are (or can be made to be) especially suited. Harmonizing structure and strategy is difficult in domestic marketing – even though the international tier of the environment usually will not present any problem and the local marketing environment is familiar and predictable. The special challenge in international marketing is that strategy design must take into account all three layers of the environment: market structure, local marketing environment abroad and the inter-nation interface. Indeed, merely identifying all the environmental factors of relevance and their relative importance in a given business is in itself a task of entrepreneurial rank.

Complications are many and risks tend to be great in international marketing. But the compensation may be greater than average return on investment and an immeasurable sense of satisfaction from contributing to local growth and development.

References

ANSOFF, H. I. (1965), *Corporate Strategy*, McGraw-Hill.

LEVITT, T. (1965), 'Exploit the Product Life Cycle', *Harvard Business Review*, Nov.–Dec.

THORELLI, H. B. (1965), 'The Political Economy of the Firm – Basis for a New Theory of Competition', *Schweizerische Zeitschrift für Volkswirtschaft und Statistik*, Sept.

THORELLI, H. B. (1967), 'Market Strategy over the Market Life Cycle', *Bulletin of the Bureau of Market Research*, University of South Africa, Sept.

THORELLI, H. B. (1968), 'Organizational Theory: An Ecological View', *Academy of Management Proceedings* at 27th Annual Meeting, Washington, Dec. 1967.

Part Two
Inter-Nation Interface:
The Fusion of Politics and Economics

In international relations politics and economics are inextricably intertwined. It is probably still true that a majority of world trade can be explained by the operation of the classic economic principle of comparative advantage, the principle that nations as well as firms possess differential advantages (and disadvantages) being exchanged in a grand international division of labor by means of trade. But this magnificently simple view of things is vastly complicated by political factors operating on the international scene. Nationalistic, military, ideological and idealistic considerations all have played their roles in the emergence of such political measures as the Marshall Plan and aid to the LDCs, East–West trade 'freezes' and 'thaws', the General Agreement on Tariffs and Trade (GATT), and, lately, economic communities and other regional market arrangements. Part Two deals with the impact of international politics on international marketing in some areas of high interest in the seventies.

Reading 2, from a British White Paper, analyses the impact of Britain joining the EEC from the viewpoint of the entire region as well as that of some particular industries and markets. The British entry into the EEC is likely to be the single most important event in the field of international marketing in this decade. Reading 3, by Stoutjesdijk, describes several regional markets among LDCs and concludes that a modest increase in regional trade has taken place, that some industries have been established which might not have emerged without the prospect of a regional market but that overall achievements in terms of trade liberalization and industrial growth have not been overly impressive to date.

Readings 4, by Ramsey, and 5, by Duncan, deal with East–West trade. While Eastern countries have had some success in Western consumer markets, economic and political conditions in Communist countries do not yet permit much consumer goods importation. In industrial marketing the Western trader can reach the potential user by advertising in trade magazines and displays at trade fairs, but the final go or no-go decision is still being made in all Eastern countries by the mighty Foreign Trade Organizations (FTO). The Western marketer (seller or buyer) should be aware that the state trading monopolies tend to play one competing Westerner against another. Ramsey points to emerging opportunities for joint ventures and technology transfer through the marketing of know-how. Duncan's is a down to earth discussion of practical experience in marketing to Eastern Europe.

Readings 6, by Massel, and 7, from Business International, analyse non-tariff barriers to world trade – frequently more important than tariffs themselves. As competition in international marketing stiffens we would predict more frequent invocation of anti-dumping legislation. The anti-dumping rules of the EEC discussed in Reading 7 are fairly typical.

2 UK White Paper

UK in the EEC: Shot Heard Around the World of Marketing

From UK White Paper, 'Britain and the european communities – an economic assessment', HMSO, Cmnd 4289, February 1970, reprinted 1971.

The main consequence of membership for British industry is that the 'home market' will be several times larger than our existing home market, including EFTA. And the new home market will be a more rapidly growing one than the present home market. If we join the Community, companies will be able to plan their sales and investment on the basis of a prosperous home market of approaching 300 million people.

The dismantling of tariffs within the present Community and the maintenance of a moderate common tariff against the rest of the world have resulted, as might be expected, in a particularly rapid increase in intra-Community trade. This trade multiplied four times between 1958 and 1968, from £2800 million to nearly £11000 million. By comparison, UK exports to the Community over this period increased only two-and-a-half times, even though the Community was our biggest single export market during this period. This pattern is reflected in the declining share of EEC imports obtained by third countries, which fell from 70·3 per cent in 1958 to 54·2 per cent in 1968. The UK share of EEC imports of manufactures in the same period fell from 10·6 per cent to 7·1 per cent.

The market we should be joining is not only larger but growing substantially more rapidly than ours. From 1958–67 the annual rise in the gross national product (GNP) per head averaged 2½ per cent in the UK compared with 4 per cent in the Community. Although a number of EFTA countries have also enjoyed a comparatively high growth rate, the preponderance of the UK in EFTA has meant that the EFTA market as a whole has grown much more slowly than the EEC.

The more rapid growth in the EEC compared with the UK is also indicated by the fact that between 1958 and 1967 industrial production in the Six rose by 68 per cent, in the UK by 37 per cent. There were and still are a number of factors at work encouraging faster growth in the Community than in the UK. More workers now leaving agriculture for industry; the advantages of post-war rebuilding of major industries with new machinery and the latest technologies; and generally a significantly lower proportion of GNP expended on defence, though the gap has been narrowing over the last few years. Nevertheless it seems highly probable that the creation of the Community itself generated a faster rate of growth through greater specialization and greater competition than the economies of the Six member countries would have separately enjoyed and that, apart from the likely beneficial effects on growth of the enlargement of the Community, an enlarged Community would in any event continue to grow faster in future than the UK or EFTA on their own.

The creation of this very large and fast growing home market will provide greater opportunities and greater competition for British industry. The rapid development of intra-Community trade is a reflection of growing international specialization, and the need for UK industry to participate fully in this was a theme which found a considerable amount of support in recent industrial assessments. It is of course true that the widening of the field of competition will stimulate the industries of other member countries as well as those of the UK but for the EEC countries this would be a further phase in a process to which they have been subjected for a number of years, and the future rate of growth of the enlarged Community may not be exceptionally high by EEC standards. On the other hand, for the UK the new market would be a stimulus and an opportunity on a quite different scale from that provided by EFTA.

Moreover, a faster growing market will provide British industry with opportunities, which it has not shared with the rest of western Europe since the war, for a sustained high level of investment in new plant and equipment. Such investment would serve to improve our competitive position, not only in relation to the Six, but also to the rest of the world. Linked with the question of growth is the degree to which the United Kingdom will in future attract overseas investment – particularly from the United States. If the UK remained outside the Community, it is likely that American investment in the Six would be stimulated at the expense of the much smaller and less rapidly growing UK market. If on the other hand the UK entered, it is likely that we would attract substantially more American investment to this country than if the UK remained outside. The fact that net additional

American investment in this country in 1968 totalled £246 million shows that the stakes are high.

The future of the so-called high technology industries – in the rest of western Europe just as much as in the UK – depends decisively on whether or not it proves possible to create an enlarged Community. Approaching one half of manufacturing output of the United States and western Europe is in industries which rely heavily on advanced technologies – such as engineering, electrical and electronics, chemicals. These have been and still are fast growing sectors in most developed countries. Their growth depends on a number of factors – marketing and rate of innovation for example – besides research and development (R and D) which nevertheless play a most important role. In an enlarged Community there would be the opportunity, because of the larger market, for European firms, British and Continental, to grow to the point where adequate R and D expenditure became profitable and practicable in fields where today it is not.

This does not of course mean that technological cooperation in Europe as it exists is impossible. In the defence field there have been some successes. Proposals have been made for new cooperative European studies and research in the fields of computers, communications, surface transport, metallurgy, meteorology, oceanography and pollution. As a result of this initiative, leading manufacturers of computers in the UK and other European countries have already begun discussions amongst themselves about concerting their ideas for the development of advanced computers.

But such cooperation can only be fully productive within an enlarged economic union, for the goal is not cooperation for its own sake, but the opportunity over a period to build European enterprises on a continental scale and thus for Europe to hold its own in future industrial development with the United States and the Soviet Union. And in all this the record of the UK in technological development entitles us to hope and the rest of Europe to expect that our role will be a prominent one.

The benefits of membership of an enlarged Community will by no means go only to large companies of Europe. The opportunities for successful specialization by the small entrepreneur should be greater in a larger and more competitive market. Technological innovation in the United States, particularly in the new and more speculative fields, has often been supported by very small industrial enterprises. But successful competition with the United

States in the high technology industries of the future will increasingly depend on the existence of at least some west European companies of comparable size to their United States counterparts. The existence of an enlarged Community can be expected not only to provide the environment in which European companies would be able to grow in size and in command of resources, but also an environment in which companies of such size would be acceptable.

3 A. Stoutjesdijk

LDC Regional Markets: Do They Work?

'LDC regional markets: do they work?', *Columbia Journal of World Business*, Sept./Oct. 1970, pp. 53–60 based on *Economic Integration Among Developing Countries* by F. Kahnert, P. Richards, A. Stoutjesdijk, P. Thomopulos, OECD Development Centre, Paris, 1969.

During the late 1950s and early 1960s, a large number of developing countries in Asia, Africa and Latin America decided to follow the example of Western European countries which had, within the framework of economic integration schemes, recovered rapidly from the devastating effects of the Second World War. Through integration, it was hoped, higher rates of economic growth would be attainable and rapid industrialization made possible.

The attractiveness of economic cooperation to the governments of developing countries is considerable since most of these countries have small domestic markets by any economic standard. The developing world now totals about one hundred independent, non-communist countries, of which two-thirds have a population of less than ten million and an average population of only three million. More than half have a gross national product of less than one billion dollars and an average gross national product of only $400 million.

Sustained and rapid economic growth on the basis of small domestic markets alone is impossible. In these situations, the opportunity to export is crucial. Traditionally, the less developed countries (LDCs) are exporters of massive quantities of agricultural products and industrial raw materials, but for most of the agricultural commodities export prospects are far from favorable. Exports of manufactures from less developed countries to developed countries are usually small, although a few successful exceptions should be noted (Taiwan, Hong Kong, among others).

On the whole, production of goods in developing countries takes place on too small a scale, as a result of which production costs are relatively high. On top of this, producers in industrialized countries often enjoy substantial protection. It seems natural, therefore, that developing countries should look among themselves for markets, particularly markets for industrial products,

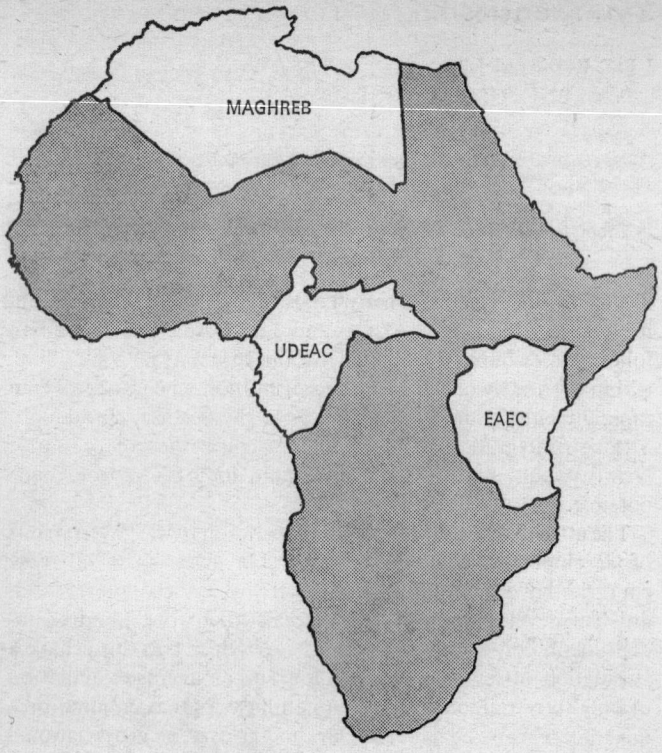

Figure 1 African regional markets

which would enable them to pursue their policy of industrialization. Partly as a result of promotional work done by the regional commissions of the United Nations (Economic Commissions for Latin America, for Africa and for Asia and the Far East), economic integration appeared to be an attractive framework for economic cooperation among developing nations. In some cases, as in East Africa and in Central Africa, the countries could confine themselves to restructuring cooperative schemes inherited from the colonial period, but in most, entirely new schemes had to be set up.

A number of these plans have now been functioning long enough to warrant an assessment of their performance. Have they brought the benefits they were supposed to bring? If they failed to do so, and there appears to be growing disenchantment among both cooperating partners and outsiders who are asked to support them financially and technically, why did they fail? Are the prospects for successful economic integration among developing countries as poor as many observers claim? If so, are alternative forms of economic cooperation more attractive?

The experience of six LDC regional markets may provide some answers to these questions. All other existing integration schemes are excluded because they are of too recent origin or because they exist in name only. The six to be discussed are:

1. East African Economic Community (EAEC) – Kenya, Uganda and Tanzania.

2. Central African Customs and Economic Union (UDEAC) – at present Congo (Brazzaville), Gabon, Cameroon and Central African Republic (Chad left the Union in 1968).

3. Maghreb Common Market (MAGHREB) – Algeria, Tunisia, Morocco and Libya.

4. Central American Common Market (CACM) – Guatemala, Nicaragua, Honduras, El Salvador and Costa Rica.

5. Latin American Free Trade Area (LAFTA) – all the South American republics plus Mexico.

6. Regional Cooperation for Development (RCD) – Turkey, Iran and Pakistan.

Regional but small

Although the six are designated regional markets, some of them are still small economic units. Table 1 gives figures on population and gross domestic product. EAEC, UDEAC and CACM are definitely small markets; only RCD and LAFTA have attained substantial size in economic terms, while the MAGHREB occupies an intermediate position. While data relate to a recent year, due to statistical problems they should not be taken to represent more than rough orders of magnitude.

Institutionally, all schemes are very similar. The policy-making authority consists of either the Heads of State or Ministers, with an executive committee preparing most of the recommendations to be approved by the authority. The committee is usually assisted by a varying number of commissions and subcommissions as well as by a secretary general with a permanent secretariat. In no case, however, have the cooperating countries been prepared to delegate any decision-making power to a supranational authority.

Table 1 **The economic size of six regional markets**

Grouping	Population (million)	Gross Domestic Product (billions of US dollars)
East African Economic Community	30·0	2·5
Central African Customs and Economic Union	8·5	1·0
Maghreb	33·0	7·5
Central American Common Market	14·0	4·0
Latin American Free Trade Area	220·0	90·0
Regional Cooperation for Development	180·0	27·0

Population data are for the year 1967; GDP relates to 1965/66.

This factor and the lack of sufficiently qualified personnel to prepare good regional studies have generally hampered progress toward a regionally integrated economy, particularly in the industrial field. However, most of the integration schemes at present in existence are well structured, at least in principle.

Since the promotion of intra-regional trade is one of the major objectives of regional integration schemes, progress on the abolition of restrictions on trade is one of the major indicators of a scheme's success. At the same time, wide divergencies can be noted in the scope of the integration agreements, and complete freedom of intra-regional trade is usually seen as a long-term objective only. The current situation can be summarized as follows: in two (RCD and MAGHREB), trade liberalization has not yet begun and is being preceded by a number of other measures; in three (LAFTA, CACM and UDEAC), trade liberalization has begun but is not yet completed; and in one case (EAEC), a virtually completed common market, the pressure of circumstances has compelled acceptance of the principle of trade discrimination vis-à-vis partner countries. In order to avoid too great imbalances in intra-regional trade and to give some protection within the regional market to the industrially less developed countries of Uganda and Tanzania, the latter two countries can, under certain circumstances, impose so-called transfer taxes on imports from within the regional market. Although such transfer taxes have a temporary character, they obviously conflict with the principle of regional free trade.

Trade liberalization itself does not necessarily lead to actual trade. Not only might trade be physically impossible because transport and communications facilities are lacking, but also countries might have a similar economic structure, producing more or less the same commodities. For this reason, some countries have preferred to build up complementary industrial sectors first – as in RCD – and free trade subsequently.

Another factor which has proved an important obstacle to the growth of intra-regional trade is the absence of a monetary agreement among partner countries, which would regulate the currency in which balances arising out of intra-regional trade would be settled. A convenient arrangement appears to be one where a clearing mechanism is set up through which balances are paid in convertible currency.

In general, both within and between regions, large variations in trade can be noted. In East Africa, Central Africa and Central America, intra-regional trade is undoubtedly important. Within each of these groupings, however, it is clearly more important to some countries than to others. For example, thirty-five per cent of Kenya's trade in recent years was directed at its common market partners, while for Tanzania this proportion reached only seven per cent. Similar variations occur in Central Africa and Central America, although they are less marked. In LAFTA, intra-regional trade has constituted a considerable proportion of total external trade in the case of Paraguay and Argentina, but for all other countries it is less than ten per cent. Most of the products traded intra-regionally are raw materials and semi-processed commodities.

Where intra-regional trade is important, it is difficult to say whether it is dependent on the integration agreement. In other words, available evidence seems to suggest that much of the trade taking place at present would have taken place anyway, even in the absence of trade liberalization. The fact that manufactures occupy a relatively minor position in total intra-regional trade, rarely exceeding 20 per cent of the total, seems to point to the conclusion that in terms of industrialization, economic integration has not yet brought many benefits.

Industrialization

Most developing countries have now achieved a modest degree of industrialization. Although generalizations in this respect are dangerous, it can be said that the pattern of industrial growth in most of these countries is often similar. This is obvious. Unless specific resources permit a different pattern, the first industrial ventures will be directed toward the domestic market, and all the countries being poor, the structure of demand will be more or less the same.

A cement factory, a brewery, some light metal working, processing of agricultural products and some textile manufacturing are among the typical components of a young industrial sector. Whenever this general picture emerges, it is clear that regional integration will pose a number of important problems. If all intra-regional trade is freed, the various small industries will become competitors, and without corrective measures, the existence of some might be threatened. Obviously, no country will be prepared to let this happen, and all would seek protective measures within the region.

Secondly, the wider market will open up possibilities for new investments in the industrial sector. Without intervention these would be located in the country which is most attractive economically – although culture, politics and climate also play important roles. In most regional markets, this tendency has led to a substantial concentration of industrial and other economic activities within the integrated area, resulting in widely varying rates of growth for the different industrial sectors. Tensions have run high on this issue, and numerous forms of compensation and correction have been introduced. On the whole, however, the impact of corrective measures has been disappointingly small, and the unequal distribution of new industrial activity and growth within an integrated area is without doubt the greatest danger threatening the viability of economic integration schemes.

A third factor of importance relates to the size of the industrial sectors of countries embarking upon a policy of economic integration. If the market is large, as in the case of LAFTA, there is a good chance that one or more countries are industrially more advanced than others in the same region. Following trade liberalization, the industrially backward countries by definition cannot protect new domestic industry from regional imports, which will in most cases harm local industrial development. There seems to be little point for a country in that situation to join an integration program, unless it receives special tariff concessions or unless certain regionally oriented industries are, by mutual agreement, located within its borders. Depending on the degree of advancement of the industrialized partners, such industries might be difficult to identify.

Problems common to all

Most of these problems have in fact occurred among the six integration programs. In UDEAC, the distribution of industries serving the whole of the customs union appears uneven. They can be easily identified because such enterprises are exempt from all import duties and internal indirect taxes and are subject to a unique regional tax. In 1965, thirty firms received such favorable treatment, of which eighteen were located in Congo (Brazzaville), six in the Central African Republic and six in Chad.

In 1968, Chad and the Central African Republic left the customs union, partly as a result of alleged unfair distribution of costs and benefits within the integration plan. The latter country has now rejoined the customs union. On the whole, there seems no doubt that location in UDEAC of those industries which serve more than one country's market has been the most frequent source of controversy in that region. Congo, Cameroon and Gabon have resisted industrial coordination strongly, preferring fiscal compensation measures, while Chad and the Central African Republic have strongly insisted on some kind of industrial allocation, given their natural disadvantages as inland states.

In East Africa, uneven growth rates of the industrial sector have been repeatedly subjected to corrective measures of all kinds. The East African experience shows clearly how difficult it is to set up an effective compensation plan if some of the preconditions to successful integration are not fulfilled. Corrective measures of a fiscal nature never fully satisfied anybody. A plan whereby various industries were allocated by country failed, partly because Kenya never ratified the agreement, and partly because investors for those industries allocated to Tanzania and Uganda were not forthcoming. At present, a highly complicated internal transfer tax system is in operation, designed to give some protection to Uganda and Tanzania, vis-à-vis Kenya, but it is too early to evaluate its success. In addition, the East African Development Bank is supposed to favor industrial investments in Uganda and Tanzania.

In the Maghreb, no progress whatever has been made in concrete terms with respect to common-market-induced industrial development. The industrial sectors of Algeria, Morocco and Tunisia are to an important extent competitive, and it has proved difficult to devise some system whereby trade is gradually freed, and future industrial growth is of a complementary rather than a competitive nature.

In LAFTA, the different degrees of industrialization among member countries have proved a major handicap to progress in the field of integration. Argentina, Brazil and Mexico are industrially much more advanced than the other LAFTA members, and it was soon clear that without protection within LAFTA, the smaller countries would not be able to benefit in terms of industrial growth. A special status was accordingly granted to them. Three categories of countries now exist in LAFTA: developed members, less developed members and members with insufficient markets, the latter two groups of countries being entitled to special treatment on the scheduled abolition of tariffs.

So far, these measures have not led to more impressive rates of industrial growth, and the establishment of the Andean Group within LAFTA, comprising Bolivia, Chile, Colombia, Ecuador and Peru, reflects to some extent the dissatisfaction felt by these countries with the present LAFTA scheme.

In Central America, the common market has probably had a positive effect on industrial growth. Several industries have been established which probably would not have been without a guaranty of regional free trade for their products. However, wide divergencies are present here in terms of industrial growth: El Salvador growing fastest (and with initially the largest industrial sector), and Honduras staying hopelessly behind. Special measures have now been taken to aid Honduran industrialization, but they have not yet had the desired effect.

In RCD, an entirely different approach to integration has been chosen, one which has avoided remarkably well most of the problems that more conventional approaches have invariably developed. It was decided that, before any trade could be freed, complementary industrial sectors had to be set up in the three countries and good transport links established. Accordingly, the countries have proceeded to select a large number of industries which would be viable on a regional basis only and determined their location. So far, each country believes that it is getting its fair share of industrial growth. UNCTAD has now completed a study on liberalization and expansion of intra-regional trade in RCD. It was discussed during a joint session of the Ministers of Planning and of Commerce in June 1970.

By and large, in all the regions achievements in the field of industrial growth have been smaller than expected and significantly higher regional trade has not been attained. Recent studies in East Africa, for example, show that few industries are dependent on the common market. What seems to have taken place in most integration programs, with the exception of RCD, is that industrial development plans have continued to be based on effective domestic demand for industrial products rather than on regional demand, intra-regional trade prospects being treated similarly to extra-regional trade prospects. Such cases reflect a lack of confidence on the part of national planners in the continuation of access to the markets of regional partners.

Achievements

Although the record of performance with respect to industrialization, one of the major objectives of economic integration, is not impressive, a number of achievements may be noted in other fields. Some of these relate to the pre-conditions of effective integration, such as good transport and communications links. Large investments have been made in these fields, and in some cases a common administration has been set up to this end. A common airline, common postal and telecommunications facilities, common customs administration and some form of integrated technical and university education system are often in operation. Where they exist, they have generally been found to be beneficial to partner countries.

However, again due to conflicts with national objectives, some of these common services have been gradually dismantled – particularly in East and Central Africa, where they were initially most important – and replaced by national institutions. In East Africa, for example, the East African Currency Board was replaced by three national Central Banks, and the University of East Africa is gradually being divided into three national universities. In Central Africa, the common postal and telecommunications agency was discontinued, as was the central administration of customs revenue. The University of Brazzaville, initially a regional institution, is gradually becoming a national university. In all other regions, including Central America, common infrastructural projects and the operation of common services began much later and are in the process of being built up.

The question thus arises whether regional integration is, for developing countries, a convenient policy to accelerate economic growth. A major problem in answering this question is the difficulty of ascertaining with any degree of accuracy what would have happened to the economic development of the countries concerned had they not joined an integration plan. Trends in rates of growth of total production and trade are usually too erratic and too dependent on factors having little to do with economic integration itself to serve as a guideline. The identification of all effects related to economic integration is usually impossible due to data limitations. Moreover, some might argue that it is too early to judge.

In some of the smaller developing countries, the possibility of efficient production on the basis of the domestic market alone still exists, or in economic jargon, the import-substitution potential is not yet exhausted. Capital (foreign and domestic), technical skills and managerial ability are much more important constraints on economic growth than is the limited domestic market. As the effect of economic integration on the supply of these factors of production is uncertain, the benefits of the policy of economic integration may be very small. They will arise only when efficient import-substitution is no longer possible.

Although this argument certainly reflects the planning philosophy in many developing countries, there is an important counter-argument. The possibility of efficient import substitution on a regional basis is bound to be larger because the advantages of economies of scale can often be secured through specialization and because industries might be viable on a regional basis but would not be so in separate domestic markets. In the RCD, viability forms the group's basis of existence.

Mechanism lacking

What seems to be lacking in the other regions is not so much the awareness of these potential benefits, but the lack of a well-designed mechanism which would guarantee that each country gets its fair share of regionally based activities. Ambitious time-tables, initially agreed-upon to free intra-regional trade, subsequently conflict with national economic planning objectives. The obvious step to take, therefore, seems to be the adoption of a regional investment policy in which the major goal is harmonization of national objectives and regional investment possibilities.

At present, regionally based projects are considered mostly on an individual basis, and this practice must necessarily lead to controversies regarding project location. Rarely is a package of different industries considered so that each partner can have its fair share of regional activity. A regional investment policy would be an effective means to achieve the benefits of regional specialization. To a large extent, it would render unnecessary the complicated compensation agreements which now appear to be required.

The form which such a policy would take varies from case to case. Most countries would be reluctant to delegate supranational powers to a regional planning office, which would have to remain a coordinating agency. It would study industrial and other opportunities on the basis of the regional market and determine the location of projects, keeping in mind the requirements of regional balance. A strict adherence of partner countries to an approved regional investment plan would be required, and cooperation from outside would be highly desirable.

The success of regional investment planning depends very much on the implementation of the plan, and it is likely that a regional investment bank would have to be established to channel investment funds. It is crucial that each country receive what it considers its fair share of new investment, and if private investment does not come forward, the financing may have to come from the regional investment bank. Foreign aid donor countries could play an important role, but foreign private investors should also be encouraged to cooperate. With respect to the latter, it might be necessary for the regional planning agency to have authority to grant industrial licenses, so that foreign private investment will also take place in accordance with the regional investment plan.

4 J. A. Ramsey

East–West Business Cooperation: The Twain Meet

J. A. Ramsey, 'East-west business cooperation: the twain meet',
Columbia Journal of World Business, July-August 1970, pp. 17–20.

One of the novel experiences of the 1960s was the emergence of a new type of economic relationship in the East–West trade pattern, one based on what have come to be known as cooperative agreements. Essentially, such agreements reflect an enhanced need in Eastern Europe for assistance in economic development, whether in the form of capital infusions, management skills or transfers of technology. They are in many respects a substitute for an equity participation which is not allowed under the laws of these states, Yugoslavia excepted.

Originally, the agreements seem to have grown out of the practice of repaying Western credits for purchase of plant and equipment from the production itself, once the installation was in operation. From these beginnings there has been a steady evolution into various forms of economic, commercial and technical collaboration between Western firms and Eastern enterprises.

Although the agreements are basically of an ad hoc nature, being tailored to fit the circumstances of each individual case, several different types have emerged. Perhaps the most common is a joint manufacturing operation under which each side supplies components for assembly into the finished product by one or the other party. Technical assistance, training of personnel and possibly a license may also be included. The project usually culminates in a joint marketing effort. Arrangements of this type have been concluded for tractor manufacture by the Hungarians and Rumanians with Steyr-Daimler-Puch of Austria and Fiat of Italy respectively.

A variant of a joint manufacturing operation is one in which the Western side supplies designs and specifications rather than components. Agreements along these lines have been developed by the Simmons Machine Tool Corporation of the United States with Škoda of Czechoslovakia and by Krupp of Germany with the Csepel Machine Tool Factory in Hungary. Here too a joint marketing effort is involved, with the products in the former case bearing the names of both partners: Simmons–Škoda.

A form of cooperation that is increasing in significance is one where the Western partner supplies the necessary wherewithal, including credits, for expansion of a plant's capacity or construction of new facilities to produce according to his specifications. An example is the agreement between the German firm Rheinstahl and the Hungarian Danube Iron Works. Rheinstahl contracted to plan a new radiator factory in Hungary, deliver over half the necessary machines on credit, make available technical know-how and train Hungarian personnel in its own installations. The Hungarians in return guaranteed Rheinstahl over a five-year period returns either from a fixed percentage of the production at world market prices or industrial goods of equivalent value.

Tourism agreements

Cooperative arrangements in the service industries are of special and growing importance. These usually relate in some way to the expansion of tourism, a major hard-currency earner for most of the Eastern European countries. Prominent among them have been agreements for the construction of Inter-Continental Hotels in Prague, Budapest, Bucharest and Zagreb. The US side makes available a credit for technical and management assistance, training of personnel and delivery of fittings and other equipment. The Eastern partner provides the land, construction materials, labor, engineering and technical services, and various items of equipment. Repayment of the credit is guaranteed by setting aside a fixed percentage of room rentals over a specified time period.

A further form of cooperative agreement consists of an arrangement under which Western and Eastern enterprises in the same field divide the markets for different products between them in order to enable each to concentrate on certain items with a potential for expanded output. Such agreements generally envisage continuing technical consultation and coordination.

Although not much has been done so far, a fruitful area of collaboration lies in the research and development field. Most of the Eastern European states now have pools of engineering and other professional talent which are in many cases underutilized. The costs of engaging the services of these groups can be substantially lower than in the West. Furthermore, as a result of joint R and D efforts it has been noted that not all advanced technology flows from West to East. There is a growing reservoir of technological achievements in Eastern Europe, some of them stemming from the introduction of new methods and processes by a Western partner, which can be of advantage to both sides. Hungarian progress in water purification and flotation processes, for example, is being exploited through a joint production and marketing agreement with the Austrian firm of Simmering-Graz-Pauker.

Cooperation in the third world

East–West cooperation in developing countries is another field of expanding activity. Sometimes participation is on a subcontracting basis, as in the case of agreements that the Austrian steel firm Vöest has with factories in adjacent parts of Czechoslovakia and Hungary for projects in the LDCs. In other cases, a package approach is used, with each participant, including the one in the developing nation, providing components according to his capabilities. For exploitation of agricultural resources in an African country, for example, the African partner will supply the raw material, labor and construction materials; the Eastern partner certain items of equipment, engineering and technical expertise; and the Western partner other items of equipment, marketing know-how and assistance. Sometimes the Western firm can in this way take advantage of the bilateral commercial relations an Eastern European state maintains with a developing one. Simmering-Graz-Pauker again has an agreement with the Hungarian organization Komplex to build power plants in India with financing arranged through the Hungarian–Indian clearing agreement.

Marketing agreements

Of considerable importance in the formulation and implementation of most of these agreements is the marketing arrangement. Whenever possible, the Eastern side seeks to have the Western partner accept a fixed marketing responsibility. Under this arrangement the Westerner contracts to guarantee a market for an agreed percentage of the goods or services produced as a result of the joint undertaking. In the case of hotel agreements, for example, the Western side is guaranteed returns from rentals of a percentage of the rooms only if it in turn guarantees their occupancy. In practice, this usually takes the form of a tie-in with a travel agency, airline or other groups that promote international travel. In the cases of cooperation in product manufacturing, the marketing effort is organized either through the existing facilities of both sides or by means of a dually owned corporation established specifically for the purpose. Thus, jointly produced Italian–Bulgarian grinding machines are sold through a jointly owned (50 per cent each) trading company in Switzerland, and Polish–German cranes through a similar organization in West Germany.

The marketing feature of cooperative agreements is naturally one that can impose a serious obstacle to their conclusion, since not every Western firm is willing to accept responsibility for selling and distributing something produced by a factory it does not own. From the Western point of view, such an arrangement is feasible only if the agreement provides adequate safeguards on quality control and delivery dates. It would appear to be largely for this reason that the agreements are basically of an ad hoc nature.

The advantages to Western firms of cooperative agreements with Eastern enterprises have been recognized for some time. They include access to a new market area, the ready availability of labor reserves as well as professional and technical expertise at lower costs than in the West and the general absence of labor disturbances. To these can be added the fact that a large part of the Eastern European region, which until the Second World War was essentially agrarian in nature, is now in various stages of industrialization and increasingly needs the advanced technology that the West offers. It is also worth keeping in mind that, considered from the standpoint of international investment opportunities, the countries of the area have a relatively high degree of stability and generally excellent commercial reputations.

The economic and commercial advantages to the Eastern enterprises are no less significant. The agreements extend their area of market operations in directions that would be much more difficult for them to reach by themselves. In this respect, the marketing responsibility of the Western partner is of considerable importance. The knowledge that he has this role to play makes it imperative for him to provide the necessary resources, expertise and personnel to do the job right. He thereby contributes to the modernization of the enterprise and enhances its competitive position.

Planning incentive

A corollary benefit of a Western presence is that it assists the Eastern planners in overcoming the managerial lethargy which is inherent in their system. In other words, the enterprise director and his staff too often tend to be satisfied if they meet their planned production and profit goals and have little interest in anything which could disturb the routine they have worked out to achieve them. The result, of course, is that the enterprise, while producing satisfactorily from the viewpoint of adding to total national product, in time becomes commercially less competitive. A market-oriented Western partner is sure to insist on the correction of such conditions.

The fact that the production of Eastern European enterprises has been too little attuned to market conditions did not matter so long as the autarchic trends of the earlier postwar period prevailed. The picture changed, however, with the arrival of these enterprises on the international scene, a development inspired largely by the need for hard-currency earnings in order to acquire the necessary Western plant and technology for continued economic growth. They have since been discovering that it is difficult to sell successfully in the sophisticated markets of the West with products that are obsolete, out of style or inferior in quality. Hence, there is strong emphasis on the marketing responsibility of the Western partner. In effect, they are saying to him: 'If you wish to continue to sell to us, you must help us market what we produce. It is no longer enough for us to buy your expensive modern installations. We also need your market-oriented production technology and access to the markets themselves.'

The development of cooperative agreements ranges from a low in the Soviet Union to a high in Yugoslavia, which now permits an equity participation in most of its enterprises with a repatriation right of 80 per cent of net profits. Of the other countries, Hungary appears to be the most advanced, with a highly diversified program to attract foreign partners. Rumania is following closely in the Hungarian footsteps. Poland has also been active, especially with West German and Scandinavian firms. The Soviet Union, although offering the greatest opportunities for such arrangements, has for politico-economic reasons restrained their development, limiting itself largely to technical cooperation agreements with internationally known firms like Krupp, Montecatini, Olivetti, Mitsui, Fiat and Imperial Chemical Industries.

One result of the elaboration of cooperative agreements is that they are slowly bringing the multinational corporation to the Eastern European scene. So far the agreements have been characterized by a collaboration without formal organizational ties except for such links as a Simmons–Škoda nameplate. Nevertheless, there is a certain interchange of personnel through training programs, hiring of agents and technical arrangements. Similarly, the joint marketing arrangements can provide for a product mix and greater diversification on both sides.

What will the future bring? While no one knows for sure, it can be noted that ten years ago this form of doing business hardly existed. As the Yugoslavs discovered, the imperatives of economic development force many a compromise with ideological and political concepts. Insofar as the other Eastern European countries are concerned, the major question mark would seem to be the attitude of the Soviet Union as a world power with strong interests throughout the area.

As the Czechoslovak experience has shown, the Soviet Union continues to insist that these countries look to it and not to Yugoslavia as a model for the basic structure of their societies. Two things could change this picture – a decrease in world tensions, especially a settlement of the German problem, and, as in the case of Yugoslavia, economic necessity. The Soviet Union, which has many of the same problems, is hardly in a position, economically or financially, to meet the expanding needs of all these states. It is therefore possible that with the continued evolution of cooperative agreements, a formula will eventually be found to permit the equivalent of an equity participation, a de facto rather than a de jure share in ownership.

5 M. W. Duncan

Union Carbide: A Case Study in Sales to Eastern Europe

Adapted from M. W. Duncan, 'Union carbide: a case study in sales to eastern europe', *The American Review of East–West Trade*, vol. 3, no. 314, 1970, pp. 23–29.

Union Carbide's efforts to heat up some portion of the East European market have been in two areas. The first is product sales where we have been quite successful. These activities date back more than ten years, and in recent years we have achieved an average 15 per cent annual compound growth rate. Today our sales are running from ten to fifteen million per year – approximately half of these to the USSR and half to the rest of Eastern Europe. The second area is technology sales where we launched a serious effort four years ago and so far have been singularly unsuccessful in consummating our first sale. I propose to relate to you some of the problems we have encountered in product and technology sales and some of the techniques we have used to overcome them.

Product sales

1. *Export controls:* We learned early in the game that the red tape, delays, uncertainty, and inconvenience to our customers related to US export control procedures represented almost as much of a competitive disadvantage vis-à-vis European and Japanese competitors as did the actual prohibition of exports of many products on a unilateral basis. In view of the new Export Administration Act, it remains to be seen how many, if any, products previously prohibited for export to Eastern Europe will now be freed. This will depend upon the interpretation and implementation of the law by the President and the Commerce Department. At the very least, however, hundreds and perhaps thousands of products for which validated licenses have been required but routinely granted will be removed from the control list, and this will go a long way towards making us competitive in service with Western Europe and Japan.

2. *Most favored nation (MFN):* One of the biggest obstacles to growth in our sales to Eastern Europe is the United States denial

of MFN tariff treatment on imports from them (with the exceptions of Poland and Yugoslavia). This results in highly discriminatory tariffs which impede socialist exports to this country, and since they pretty much balance their trade on a country-by-country basis, a negative effect on our sales to them is inevitable. But with the problem of export controls now pretty much alleviated, influential legislators are turning their attention to MFN and I think we can expect action in the foreseeable future.

3. *Credit:* US companies and financial institutions are prohibited by law from granting credit other than short-term commercial credit to the socialist countries of Eastern Europe. Foreign competitors are able to arrange much more attractive credit terms and this, of course, gives them a competitive advantage.

4. *Foreign exchange shortage:* All of these countries seem to have a perpetual foreign exchange shortage. This encourages them into bilateral country-to-country trade pacts wherein they agree to a fixed and usually large trade volume between the two nations. Since such agreements do not exist with the United States, we find ourselves excluded as potential suppliers for large segments of their imports.

5. *Limited accessibility to the public:* We are largely stuck with supplying established needs and cannot through advertising and promotion create consumer demand which is the basis of many successful marketing programs in our economic structure.

6. *Socialist country business organization:* The business organization of East European countries consists of companies called Foreign Trade Organizations (FTOs) which are monopolies in every sense of the word, and the same problems exist as would be encountered in dealing with a monopoly in any part of the world. These companies have responsibility for buying the country's total requirements of certain products, and the resulting volume of their purchases gives them tremendous leverage on price which they use to good advantage in world markets. These organizations also largely insulate us as vendors from the business and technical organizations which are the ultimate customers for our products. It is like never being able to get past the purchasing agent of a domestic customer. Admittedly, the purchasing agent may be the single most important party to your negotiation, but still it can be helpful to get to a plant or lab to demonstrate, promote, or assist in the use of your product. This cannot be done except by very

difficult and somewhat cumbersome prearrangements in most Eastern European countries.

To be fair, though, it should be pointed out that there are also advantages to us in the FTO system. For one thing, these companies are staffed with very capable businessmen of high integrity and generally of a linguistic ability which facilitates our doing business with them. It is also convenient to be able to solicit and possibly negotiate a country's total requirements of a product by calling at a single office.

7. *Short-term purchase practices:* Because of their budgeting and financial procedures, it is difficult and rare to get a commitment on product sales covering a period longer than a year. This makes it impossible to plan production capacity to provide for their needs on any kind of an orderly basis and tends to reduce the business to an on again-off again opportunistic basis.

8. *Pressure for reciprocity:* Since the same FTOs that have responsibility for purchasing total requirements of some products also have responsibility for exporting the country's total surplus of other products, they are under considerable pressure to look to their suppliers for trade reciprocity and to buy preferentially from companies that will in turn buy from them. Unfortunately, they seldom have products for sale that match the needs of a specific US manufacturer who has product for sale to them.

UCC's approach to the market

But we don't want to overemphasize the problems, so let's turn now to some of the things we have done to develop business in the face of these difficulties.

1. *Continuity in personnel involved:* We have attempted to establish continuity and as much longevity as possible in relationships between individuals in our organization and our business contacts in Eastern Europe. Most authorities on this subject would cite this as the most important single factor, and I am inclined to agree with them. Once plans are formalized in these socialist economies, the individuals involved are held rigidly accountable for successfully implementing them, so they are under strong compulsion to deal with individuals as well as companies that they know and trust from previous experience. For this reason, you may find your initial efforts slow and frustrating and you may well be tested with small orders over an extended period of time before you really crack the big business. But once you have

established your identity and created a high confidence level you will find your Eastern friends cooperative and eager to do business with you. We maintain an office in Vienna from which we serve Eastern Europe. Our sales manager for the USSR has been responsible for that business for the past seven years.

2. *High-level management exchange visits:* A number of delegations of high ranking UCC officers have visited Eastern Europe. We have hosted a number of delegations of high ranking officials from Eastern Europe, particularly the USSR, with visits to plants, laboratories, and our headquarter's offices in this country. These are extremely useful for furthering the understanding of each other's objectives and capabilities, for opening the door to decision-making offices in our customers' organizations, and knowing that a good relationship exists at these high levels definitely has a salutary effect on the response and cooperation we get at lower levels.

3. *Reciprocal purchases:* We make a genuine effort to find things we can buy from the socialist countries. We know the business will go better if we can make it a two-way street. In our case, we included a ranking representative of our Purchasing Department, in one of our high level delegations to the area. Our Purchasing Department, both headquarters in New York and the Geneva office, are constantly on the alert for such opportunities. Admittedly, our success thus far in this activity has been quite limited but we will continue trying.

4. *Use of trading companies:* In spite of our significant direct sales effort, we continue to use trading companies. There are many of these in both the US and Europe, specializing in East–West trade. They are professionals at barter, three-way transactions, exploitation of clearing accounts, etc. They are frequently the best possible solution to foreign exchange and reciprocity problems. When possible, however, the East Europeans actually prefer to deal directly with a supplier rather than through an intermediary.

5. *Demonstrations and seminars:* As mentioned earlier, routine 'selling in depth' is virtually unknown in Eastern European countries as it is practiced in the West where a businessman automatically calls on the plants and laboratories of his customers as well as on the Purchasing Office. It is, however, possible in some situations to arrange formal demonstrations, seminars, or private exhibits to which appropriate representatives of the FTOs

ultimate customers will be invited. We have utilized this technique a number of times. Once we staged a two-day full dress technical seminar in which a number of our AgChem specialists made presentations to an assembly of fifty representatives from various Soviet technical and agricultural organizations. On other occasions we have managed to arrange plant demonstrations of the processing characteristics of some of our chemical intermediates.

6. *Trade shows and exhibits:* These are far more important in the East than in the West. They represent one's best, and in some cases only, opportunity to get product and company exposure to the public and to both business and technical management beyond the FTOs. They also offer an opportunity to enhance one's image with the all important FTOs and the Ministries which attach great importance to these affairs. We had a major exhibit at the International Chemical Exposition in Moscow in 1965 and will be back with a major exhibit again in September of 1970 [note date of article]. Just to give you an example of the importance attached to these exhibits, I might mention that Premier Kosygin came to visit our pavilion twice in 1965. Also five years later, top officials of the Ministries and FTOs still give verbal acknowledgement to our participation in their trade fairs as evidence of our sincere desire to do business with them.

Technology sales

So much for product sales. You will recognize that some of UCC's product sales efforts also have a contributory effect in our attempts at technology sales. Technology sales however, represent some special problems. What have we learned in this area?

First of all, we have found that in some instances we are miles apart in evaluation of the true worth of our technology. In our first major attempt at a technology sale to the USSR, we valued our know-how and engineering services at $20 million and they valued them at $2 million. In spite of much negotiation in good faith on both sides, this proved to be too big a gap to close and negotiations collapsed. During the course of this negotiation, we introduced the possibility of their contracting for substantial product purchases during the four years prior to the time that their own facilities would come onstream. The profits on these sales would have permitted us to reduce considerably our asking price for the technology. We thought it made sense from their point of view. They could use these imports on an increasing scale to develop their internal use for the product in preparation for their own facility coming onstream. They declared it impossible to negotiate on this basis, though, on the grounds that their allocation of funds for capital projects and product purchases are handled by two different foreign trade organizations and covered by separate budgets.

Another area where we have failed is in offering technology with a definite termination date on the offer in an attempt to force costly and frustratingly drawn out negotiations to a decision. (One negotiation for polyvinyl chloride involving another company dragged on for eight years before consummation!) We found that their system is not flexible enough however, to enable them to react to such deadlines no matter how much the individuals involved might like to. Price, of course, must have a time limit and it is possible to make an offer with price subject to escalation after a period of time.

We have found that the Soviets in particular have one unique criterion in evaluating an offer for a chemical plant. They tend to evaluate a plant purchase like Americans value pork chops – by the pound. They have established average cost/weight relationships for typical classes of equipment and use this cost/weight relationship as well for comparing competitive bids on whole plants. For this purpose, they require all bids to contain data on weight, materials of construction, and cost broken down by equipment categories.

In a more general vein, UCC has found that the USSR is getting more selective all the time in purchasing plants and technology. Soviet officials have told us quite frankly that a few years ago they were so desperately in need of plants and technology that they would buy most anything offered. But now that they have their petrochemical industry well established, the pressure is off and they can afford to be more choosey. They are now insisting on the largest and most modern facilities and are particularly impressed by large single train units. Their aspirations in this regard are modified, however, by their insistence that anything they buy must be proven at the scale of operation being proposed. They prefer to buy turn-key plants with themselves providing all the civil works, including site preparation, etc., and the contractor providing the rest. If your company – like UCC – has engineering resources that are only adequate for internal requirements, this necessitates a marriage with an engineering contractor which will translate your technology to required scale and local conditions and assume responsibility for construction and start-up. Your

Eastern European customers will generally require a performance guarantee and if you have a cooperative project with an engineering company, you as a licensor will be responsible for process and product quality and the engineering company for the mechanical aspects of the project.

Mode of payment is another problem. Just as with product purchases, East European countries all have foreign exchange problems with plant purchases. A more or less conventional deal would provide for 15 to 20 per cent case payment with the balance financed over five to seven years and five to ten per cent held back subject to the performance guarantee being met. More recently they are emphasizing interest in arrangements which are tantamount to sort of a quasi-joint venture. These are arrangements where the seller would accept payment for plant and technology in product from the plant's production over a period as long as ten years after plant start-up. Such arrangements have many obvious complications but could be attractive under certain circumstances.

6 M. S. Massel

Non-Tariff Barriers as an Obstacle to World Trade

Slightly abbreviated from M. S. Massel, 'Non-tariff barriers as an obstacle to world trade', in D. Thompson (ed.), *The Expansion of World Trade: Legal Problems and Techniques*, The British Institute of International and Comparative Law, 1965.

My thesis is that agreements to reduce import duties constitute only the first step of an effective programme to free world trade. If tariffs are reduced to a minor role in international trade, the non-tariff barriers will take on major importance. As a consequence, even an effective programme to lower tariffs, standing alone, may not achieve a major improvement in the flow of international trade. Indeed, the complete elimination of tariffs would encourage the proliferation of a wide variety of the more subtle import barriers which bear the tag 'non-tariff'.

The non-tariff barriers elude any general, fixed definition which can be covered by a few international agreements. Many of them cannot be controlled through precise contractual arrangements entered into by overt formal action of governments. Rather they require continuing examination and analysis because so much of their influence is indirect and their variety is limited only by man's ingenuity. Since many of them derive from day-to-day practices engaged in by lower administrative echelons, they cannot be eliminated by pen-strokes at an international meeting.

A potent programme for dealing with non-tariff barriers would require continuing, positive international co-operation. Mere prohibition is not enough. The effective elimination of many of these obstructions will require affirmative joint programmes undertaken by the nations concerned, programmes which deal with some of the underlying conditions which have led to these barriers as protective devices.

I propose here to outline the scope of these non-tariff barriers and the sophisticated problems involved in analysing them. Against this setting we can consider the methods which might be employed to cope with them. Because of the unlimited variety of these bulwarks against imports, no general definition covers them except for the colourless appellation they carry. They include all barriers other than tariffs. Accordingly, we can only describe, in rather general terms, a moderate number of types of such barriers in order to demonstrate their wide scope and to serve as the basis for a discussion of how they can be treated.

Types of non-tariff barriers

Before discussing the types of non-tariff barriers, an explanation of the illustrations used might be in order. Almost all of the examples given are taken from the experience of the United States. This procedure is followed because of my greater familiarity with American barriers, not because the policies found in the United States are unique.[1]

Quotas and embargoes

Some non-tariff barriers are clear and specific. For example, quotas on imports, embargoes, currency controls and import equalization taxes are overt and can be dealt with by procedures which are similar to tariff negotiations. In fact, tariff discussions frequently deal with them.

Recent years have witnessed a considerable number of such bars to imports. For example, the US Agricultural Adjustment Act authorized the restriction of imports if they interfered with domestic price supports for agricultural goods. At various times quotas have been imposed on such products as sugar, flaxseed, peanuts, butter, fats, oils and rice. Outright embargoes have been applied as health measures. Countervailing duties have been levied to counteract subsidy programmes of other governments.

At various times, many countries have employed currency restrictions to block imports or to regulate their flow. Unless an import transaction is approved, an importer cannot secure international funds to pay for the goods even when his supply of domestic funds is ample.

1. During the discussion a speaker from the EEC said that he was struck by the similarity of the United States practices and those found within the European Economic Community. He listed specific illustrations for each type of barrier which was discussed. He stated that within the European Commission there was complete agreement with the thesis that the non-tariff barriers constitute a basic element in the establishment of free trade. As tariff barriers were dismantled within the Community, there was a growing awareness of the impact of the non-tariff barriers and of their subtle forms. Hence, the attention given to non-tariff barriers in the Rome Treaty was well founded [Ed.].

Customs administration

Even though a country may maintain a schedule of low tariffs, its customs administration may provide barriers that are more difficult to surmount than the formal tariffs may indicate. For example, some American *ad valorem* tariffs are based on the United States selling prices rather than the prices paid by the importer. As a result, the duties paid may be considerably higher than the formal tariff schedule. While this practice has aroused considerable criticism, it is confined to a relatively small group of items. Other obstacles may be found in the procedure for setting customs classifications. An importer may find, months after he has completed a sale, that the customs classification of the goods has been changed and that he must pay a higher duty. Since he cannot recoup the additional payment, he will probably be wary about future imports of the same item. Indeed, the new duty may be so high that he would not have undertaken the first transaction if the effective classification had been set before he undertook to import the goods.

Administration of anti-dumping laws

While it would be difficult to justify dumping goods at discriminatory prices in other countries, the administration of anti-dumping statutes may make importation unattractive and even impractical. If a complaint has been issued charging that an import was made at unfair low prices, the resulting administrative procedures may, in themselves, set obstacles in the way of international commerce. Even when the allegation is rejected, the procedures may be prohibitively expensive for the exporter. If many months pass before the final decision is handed down, the interference with normal commercial practice may discourage further transactions. The prospects of future uncertainty faced by exporters and domestic customers may cancel interest in further imports of the same type.

Protection of industrial property

Many domestic regulations may, as a practical matter, create barriers which are more effective than tariffs. Prominent among them are laws to protect industrial property. National patent and trade-mark systems are employed by domestic sellers to bar goods which originate in other countries. The validity of the patent in the originating country is unimportant. If it is enforceable in the importing country, it stops imports effectively. In addition to the conventional operation of patent and trade-mark laws, such countries as the United States permit the domestic producer to institute a procedure in 'unfair competition' in order to obtain a decree denying entry of patented products or goods made by patented processes. This procedure can avoid expensive patent litigation. Some observers feel that this course might enable a producer to use his patent as an import barrier, even though it might not be upheld in the direct test of domestic litigation.

Health and safety rules

Domestic rules to protect the health and safety of a country's population may block imports or force considerable additions to the cost of importing. Great variety in the minimum standards employed in different countries may compel a producer to comply with so many diverse regulations that it curtails his export opportunities. Administrative requirements may make it tedious and expensive to export to a country. For example, a United States rule requires that samples of the colouring materials used in food products must be approved by the Food and Drug Administration before the colorants are employed in processing the final product. This procedure is not too difficult for domestic producers. However, for processors in other countries this is a fairly cumbersome proceeding and may add greatly to the burden of exporting to the United States.

Health and safety rules allow wide administrative discretion which can be used to protect domestic producers. For example, because of outbreaks of hoof and mouth disease in a few sections of Argentina, the United States set up an embargo against all meat from that country. This blockade has been applied to mutton, even though the disease has not been found in the regions in which sheep are raised in Argentina.

Many health regulations set limits by requiring inspection at the point of origin. The operation of local 'milk sheds' within the United States demonstrates this barrier. Every major municipality requires that fresh fluid milk sold within its limits must come from inspected dairies. Since the inspectors travel limited distances, the rule creates effective territorial demarcations of the sources of supply. Incidentally, some appended regulations demonstrate the significance of these inspections. For example, until recently, Washington, the nation's capital, required that to pass inspection a farmer must milk his cows sitting on a three-legged stool in a stable that has a smooth ceiling, using hemstitched linen towels of specific dimensions to wipe off the cows' teats.

Labelling requirements

Labelling requirements can affect the flow of international trade in the same way as health regulations. A requirement may be so detailed that it provides a practical impediment for imports. For example, in the course of an international negotiation, one country agreed to the importation of certain food products if they met some unspecified labelling conditions. Further discussion disclosed that the labels on canned goods would have to show the origin – by country and state – of each ingredient. Since food canners, of soup for example, follow seasonal supplies of raw foods, they would not find it possible to satisfy this labelling requirement.

In the United States we have had extensive experience with differences in the labels required by the several states. For certain products, such as margarine, there exists a wide variety of state regulations concerning packages and labels. Some states require that eggs which are laid in other jurisdictions must be stamped before they can be sold in commerce. Others set up rules which make it impossible to refer to another state's product as 'fresh eggs'.

The labelling requirements of many nations interfere with large-scale distribution because of variations in the units of weights, measures and sizes which are employed. Even shoe sizes and food measures are not standardized. Nor are there standards for the electric power used in various types of appliances. While these differences may not be calculated to impede imports, as a practical matter they provide substantial hurdles.

Government purchases

Government purchases can have a substantial influence on the flow of international trade – a force of growing importance because of increasing public activity. When a government purchases from its own nationals exclusively, it clearly restrains the free movement of goods across its borders. Similarly, if it awards research and development contracts to its own citizens exclusively, it gives those nationals strong, often unassailable, positions as future suppliers.

Obviously, a government may feel compelled to purchase some

military items from its own nationals for security reasons. On occasion, a government agency places such dependence on a supplier's skill and reliability that there is a clear operating advantage in dealing with domestic companies. However, major segments of government purchasing can be purchased abroad.

Subsidies

Government subsidies, either for domestic sales or for exports, clearly affect international competition. When subsidy is paid to domestic suppliers, it may block imports as effectively as a tariff. Conversely, when a subsidy is paid on exported goods, the exporter has a competitive advantage, and the subsidy may invite other countries to retaliate with new trade bars.

Compulsory preferences

A number of methods are employed to compel the use of domestic products in addition to outright quotas and embargoes. For example, some mixing regulations provide that a minimum percentage of homegrown wheat must be used in grinding flour. These rules clearly reduce the imports of foreign products even though consumers may prefer them.

Taxes

Many domestic taxes give rise to impediments to international trade. Turnover taxes may take a larger toll from imported goods than those produced by integrated domestic manufacturers. Tax rebates on exports may induce other countries to take countervailing measures, such as off-setting levies on imports. Graduated taxes on products may penalize goods of foreign origin. For example, the French road tax on automobiles takes a sharp rise at certain horsepower points. Since the power ratings of most French-made cars are below these points, while the ratings of most American cars are higher, many of the home products enjoy a competitive advantage.

Some countries levy differential tariffs, charging the higher rate on goods which the domestic industry can produce. If an industry inquiry shows that a domestic plant can fill an order in the time specified, the import tariff on that order is raised.

Import permits

Import permits can be used as a flexible valve to control the flow of competing foreign goods. In some countries import permits are issued on the recommendation of committees of domestic companies in the related industry. Hence, those companies can keep out foreign products whenever they choose to manufacture the items.

Export controls

Some non-tariff barriers are administered by the exporting country. A nation may have grounds for believing that new barriers will be erected against its goods if its exports to another country are too high. In that case, it may control the volume of its exports voluntarily. For example, there is evidence that Japan limited its foreign shipments of some items in order to avoid new import restrictions in the United States and in some countries in Western Europe. There seems to be a basis for believing that some 'voluntary' export restrictions are responsive to informal international pressures. In those instances, only the form of the restriction seems to differ from the more common import barriers. Similar practices are developed through international commodity agreements.

Restrictive business practices

When all else fails to blunt the edge of international competition, a number of techniques may be applied by private industry. Transnational agreements may assign the markets of certain countries to specific manufacturers exclusively. Similar results can be obtained through domestic trade boycotts. Under such arrangements domestic distributors may agree to sell domestic products only, or the country's producers may cut off any distributor who handles imported items. Variations on these techniques can be found in agreements to set up private import quotas or to sell the imported products at higher prices.

The sharing of international markets does not always depend on overt agreements. By parcelling out exclusive patent rights in various countries, producers can effectively divide up market territories. This practice avoids any market allocation contracts. Similarly, if two or more manufacturers use the same trade-mark in several countries, each can protect his domestic market effectively.

It is noteworthy that some restrictive business practices are encouraged or supported by government regulation. National patent and trade-mark laws support market allocations. Embargoes, import permits, and differential tariffs can be used to implement domestic cartels. National anti-cartel laws provide exemptions for export agreements.

It should be noted that this thumbnail sketch of types of non-tariff barriers is not intended to be encyclopaedic. It is presented merely to demonstrate the wide variety of techniques which are available and their scope.

Institutional factors

Effective analysis of non-tariff barriers must encompass a consideration of the institutional factors within the pertinent countries. Unless such institutions are taken into account, one country may be singled out for a practice which is engaged in by many. On the other hand, in the absence of such consideration many effective barriers will be overlooked because of their subtle workings.

Comparisons

The importance of institutional factors in making international comparisons is illustrated by the concern about the 'Buy American' policy of the United States. On the surface, the United States is the only country which favours domestic suppliers to the government. However, a closer analysis indicates that this American policy is paralleled in many jurisdictions despite the absence of such statutes as 'Buy British', 'Buy French', or 'Buy German'.

The 'Buy American' policy was established because of the institutional framework of the open-bid procedure in the United States. Several statutes require that American Government buyers accept the lowest bid which is tendered unless they can demonstrate the inadequacy of the lowest bidder or of the goods he offers. Therefore, when the United States decided to counter the policies of other governments which favoured their own nationals, its only recourse was to legislate a preference for domestic producers. This legislation provided that purchases would be made from domestic suppliers unless their prices exceeded foreign sources by a specified percentage. With time, the size of this margin has been reduced. Indeed, the 'Buy American' policy is subject to domestic criticism by many who are interested in the cost of government or in free trade.

On the other hand, many other countries do not require open-bid procedures. Procurement officers use their own discretion in making awards. It is reported that some American companies complain that they are frequently refused permission to enter bids in some countries. Further, even when they do submit bids, they cannot obtain information about either the contract price or the successful bidder. This closed-door procedure and the related procurement discretion permit some countries to follow the same policy as 'Buy American' with even more effective protection for domestic producers.

Now, the point is that such policies must be considered in their institutional setting. This discussion does not justify the 'Buy American' policy. It does, however, imply that an agreement to cancel the preference should take account of the policies of other countries.

Administrative subtleties

The treatment of many non-tariff barriers differs from tariff reduction because of distinctions in the levels of government which are pertinent. Tariff enactment and reduction require overt action by the top levels of government. In contrast, many types of non-tariff interferences depend upon the administrative practices of the lower echelons. For example, tariff classification, anti-dumping procedures, health inspection, individual government purchases, and the issuance of import permits must depend upon day-to-day operations, activities which do not ordinarily come under the surveillance of the top levels in the absence of a specific drive to lower such import bars.

On the administrative levels there are many pressures to restrict. Inspectors are not prone to take many chances. Bureaucratic self-protection frequently supports strict interpretation. Fear of industrial criticism of a classification of foreign goods or a health inspection, may create a restrictive atmosphere for the application of many import regulations.

Therefore, analysis of the non-tariff barriers must encompass the subtleties of many administrative practices. Short of a detailed examination, it would be impossible to grasp the significance of many existing barriers or the emergence of new ones. The effectiveness of the concealed impediments to international commerce rests on administrative nuances rather than formal rules. The level of a tariff may not be as important as the procedures of customs classification. The cumbersome administration of an anti-dumping regulation may convert a reasonable regulation of commerce into an effective bar.

The influence of a formal tariff schedule may depend on its administration. How are the import valuations set? How are the customs classifications determined? No system of classification which eliminates personal judgement has been designed. Rapid technological changes and new products seem to defy the possibility of devising a stable, objective structure of classes. Further, even if customs classifications were stable, the efficiency of the customs procedure may have a profound influence on international trade.

Uncertainty about import regulation may, of itself, discourage the flow of imports. The effective distribution of many types of imports requires considerable expenditures for sales promotion programmes and distributive organizations. If tariff classifications, import permits, and anti-dumping administration do not produce clear, consistent rules, potential importers are discouraged from expending the money and effort required for effective sales promotion and distribution. Therefore, these obscure frictions may create stronger bulwarks against imports than tariffs themselves.

Similar analytical problems affect the evaluation of many other non-tariff barriers. For example, the effect of health and safety regulations cannot be understood without a detailed review, nor can label requirements, government purchases, domestic taxes and business restrictions.

Problems of elimination

The elimination of non-tariff barriers would be a more complex undertaking than tariff reduction. While such barriers as patent systems could be dealt with through overt agreements, many others cannot be abolished without a continuing review of administrative operations and related institutions.

The cancellation of these impediments to imports requires positive international cooperation as well as a programme of continuing analysis and investigation. An effective assault on these barriers must include serious consideration of their underlying causes. Many interferences with international trade are but symptomatic of basic national problems. Repetition of *laissez-faire* theology will not overcome an argument for a health measure which stops imports because of a nation's need to protect its population. Many such barriers cannot be abolished unless satisfactory solutions are found for the underlying cause. For example, an international safety standard may be needed to eliminate national barriers.

Need for review

It is readily apparent that an effective programme to remove non-tariff barriers will require a continuing review of many aspects of government and private activity. Many, if not most, of these impediments to the flow of international trade cannot be eliminated by the mere stroke of a pen. They require continuing international cooperation and detailed analysis.

Some progress might be derived from public exposure of the barriers, even in the absence of agreement. A public understanding of the 'tricks of the trade' may compel some governments to abandon restrictive administrative practices. Consumers who become aware of the effect of such barriers may speak out forcefully. Those who are concerned about economy in government may bring effective pressures to bear against some practices. The growing numbers of citizens and legislators who are aware of the advantages of encouraging international trade may exert a telling influence. Hence, public exposure of many practices may produce significant therapeutic counterforces by itself.

Affirmative action

Some non-tariff barriers may reflect necessary safeguards of the health and safety of a country's citizens as well as its balance of payments. Such barriers probably cannot be eliminated without positive international programmes to provide such protection. Separate national standards for the protection of health may, despite non-restrictive intentions, impede imports. Differences in the standards used for weights and measures, for clothing sizes, and for rating electrical power can serve to reduce the importation and sale of foreign products. These limits on trade cannot be avoided without effective international standards, which might require uniform systems of inspection and certification for some products.

The need for such cooperation can be demonstrated by the example of the United States with its fifty separate state jurisdictions. When the Federal Government does not provide adequate protective standards, many states and cities feel compelled to do so. On the other hand, when the Federal Government began to control the labelling of hazardous substances, the need for uncoordinated local action disappeared. Hence, the labelling requirement provided more adequate health protection and eliminated some impediments to inter-state commerce.

Similarly, when a country curtails imports in order to protect its balance of payments, it would be difficult to deny the move unless there is an affirmative cure for the underlying cause. Hence, the elimination of such barriers will, in the final analysis, depend on international programmes to avoid the recurring balance of payments crises. Unless such underlying needs are met by positive international cooperation, it would seem to be impossible to expect the several nations to forego their basic power to protect themselves.

Private barriers

Practical alleviation of non-tariff barriers requires considerable attention to the private impediments which are attained through international cartels and similar restrictive devices. In the absence of improved international cooperation, private business organizations can continue to erect many barriers to replace government impediments which are removed.

Effective international action to regulate private barriers will depend upon general agreement on the pertinent goals. National attitudes regarding restrictive business practices cover a broad spectrum. At one end is the policy, typified by American anti-trust law, of enforcing and encouraging domestic competition. At the other end is the policy of permitting and even encouraging cartels. In between are varying degrees of tolerance, including the policy of allowing monopoly as long as it does not abuse its power. However, because of a growing concern about private business restrictions, it seems possible that even countries which encourage domestic monopolistic practices might agree on a programme to deal with international cartels.

7 Business International

Antidumping Rules in the European Community

Business International, 'Antidumping rules in the european community', in *The European Communities Today and Tomorrow: New Rules for the Seventies*, Business International, 1969, pp. 75-78.

An essential instrument of the Six's foreign trade policy is their common antidumping code, which went into effect in July 1968. Third-country firms exporting to the EC need not fear that this legislation will be used for protectionist purposes. Occasionally, it is possible that EC customs authorities will question the adequacy of transfer prices in the case of intercorporate sales between a third-country manufacturer and its EC subsidiaries. Generally, however, the EC's antidumping policy will be applied on the basis of a 'confrontation of views' allowing the EC authorities – who have been vested with discretionary bargaining powers – to work out a compromise acceptable to the exporter and to the EC when there is supporting evidence of dumping.

It is expected that the authorities will model their attitude in enforcing antidumping rules on the flexible West German practices. In that country, instances of dumping are frequently reported to, and verified by, the authorities. But the foreign exporters found guilty of dumping have always consented – after negotiations with the authorities – to revise their prices upward rather than face antidumping duties.

The EC code also authorizes the Council to refrain from applying antidumping taxes (even in a clear cut instance of dumping) when such a move would be 'politically untimely', and to make exceptions for imports from the less developed countries.

Code features

The common EC antidumping code, patterned on the GATT rules, concerns only imports from third countries and is applicable to both industrial and agricultural products. Its three major features are:

Antidumping duties may be applied in cases of 'hidden dumping', i.e. where the foreign supplier's export price cannot be determined reliably. This provision may be applied to sales to EC companies by related firms based outside the Common Market.

The code contains precise criteria for defining 'injury' to EC production of a given product (see EC criteria for defining antidumping injury, below). An antidumping duty may be levied when the dumping of a product on the EC market causes or threatens to cause material injury to an established industry, or materially retards the establishment of an EC industry.

Investigations of both import prices and alleged injury are conducted simultaneously by the Commission when a case of dumping is reported. If no injury is apparent, no further action will be taken to determine whether dumping actually occurred.

Dumping will be deemed to exist when the price of a third-country product imported into the EC is:

1. less than the price practiced in the exporting country, or, in the absence of such a price,
2. less than the (higher) price practiced on exports to a third country, or
3. less than the production cost in the country of origin, plus a reasonable amount for administrative, sales or any other costs, and for profits.

Under the common antidumping code, any EC physical or legal person, and even an association that has no legal personality, may file a formal complaint. In the absence of a complaint, member states may lay an antidumping case before the Commission. The proceedings are carried out by the Commission, assisted by an Advisory Committee composed of representatives of each member state and presided over by a representative of the Commission. When preliminary examination of the facts shows that dumping exists, that there is sufficient evidence of injury, and that the interests of the EC call for immediate action, the Commission may, at the request of a member state or upon its own initiative, levy a provisional antidumping duty. To levy provisional or final antidumping duties, the Commission submits a proposal to the Council, which decides by qualified majority. Duties may not be applied, or increased, retroactively.

It does not necessarily follow from the adoption of a common EC code that the member countries' respective national antidumping legislation is no longer valid. However, if national legislation is in conformity with the common EC code, there should in fact be no reason for the member country not to apply the EC regulation directly.

Intra-EC 'dumping'

It is clear that after the end of the EC's transition period, i.e. after 1 January 1970, EC companies no longer enjoy protection from 'dumping' practiced within the Common Market, as this injury is incompatible with the idea of a customs union. Where such dumping practice continues, the Commission authorizes the injured member state to take protective measures determined by the Commission itself. After 1 January 1970, products originating from or having been allowed entry for consumption in, one member state, and which have been exported to another member state, have to be admitted free of duties and/or any other restrictions when they are reimported into the territory of the first country.

The EC antidumping provisions are applicable, by analogy, to products benefiting from a bounty or subsidy (including subsidies for their transportation) in the country of origin or export.

Beside antidumping duties, the Six and the EC authorities may adopt 'special measures' against unfair export practices. These measures would be mainly applicable to non-GATT countries. For example, the Commission is presently studying various methods of preventing East-bloc countries from exporting to the EC at abnormally low prices. Undoubtedly, the Commission would be quick to establish import quotas if the low-price products came from a non-GATT country. If the East-bloc country were a GATT member (e.g. Czechoslovakia) the Commission would probably curb abuses by causing import licenses to be denied for products with 'impossibly low' prices.

EC criteria for defining antidumping injury

The criteria contained in the EC's common antidumping code for defining 'injury' to EC production of a given product are:

The evaluation of injury is to be based on an examination of all factors having a bearing on the state of the EC industry concerned, such as: development and prospects with regard to turnover market share; profits; prices (including the extent to which the delivery price of the third-country product, including customs duties, is lower or higher than the most representative comparable price for a like product in an arm's-length transaction within the Community); export performance; employment; volume of dumped and other imports; utilization of capacity of the Community industry; productivity and restrictive trade practices. Not one or several of these factors can necessarily give decisive guidance.

In order to establish whether dumped imports are causing injury, all other factors which, individually or in combination, may adversely affect the Community industry concerned, will be examined. The factors to be considered are, *inter alia*, the: volume and prices of non-dumped imports of the product; competition in the specific EC industry; contraction in EC demand due to substitution of other products or to changes in consumer tastes.

The determination of the injury will be made only when the dumped imports are unequivocally the principal cause of the damage. The actual effects of dumping will be weighed against all other factors that may adversely affect the EC industry concerned. To determine a threat of injury, the Commission must examine facts, not merely allegations or conjectures.

Within the context of the EC antidumping legislation, the term 'EC industry' covers EC producers (of the product under investigation) as a whole, or those whose aggregate output represents a major share of total EC production. Producers that are also importers of the allegedly dumped product may, however, be excluded.

Part Three
Local Environment: Public Policy Sets the Scene

Public policy is as important at the national level as at the international. Part Three deals with government influence on the local marketing environment. The nuclear role in all cultures is played by the rules of the game in the marketplace as defined by public policy on competitive practices. Between cultures, these rules range all the way from the strongly pro-competitive antitrust laws of the United States via *laissez-faire* all the way to compulsory cartelization. Closely related are regulations concerning misleading advertising, trading stamps, door-to-door selling, informative labeling and other measures to protect consumers. Intertwined with public policy are the rules of behavior of the local business culture, such as views of competition and cooperation, business ethics and outlook on corruption, nepotism, and reciprocal dealings, respect for commercial obligations, and so on.

Reading 8, by Edwards, surveys the laws governing competition and monopoly around the world. One important dimension of this discussion is the conflict of national laws and the extraterritorial application of antitrust laws in international marketing. In this area it is wise not to tread far without the benefit of expert advice. Reading 9, by Sassen, gives a bird's eye view of the competition policy of the EEC. While clearly inspired by the antitrust laws of the United States the EEC approach differs considerably from the American.

Reading 10, by Preston, deals with governmental controls on marketing in the LDCs. Such controls are analysed in the context of local economic development policies. While indirect regulation of markets tends to be the rule in industrial countries, the regulatory arsenal in the LDCs characteristically also includes more direct and detailed intervention – such as price and quality controls – and participation in some markets by public enterprises. The contribution of many conventional LDC marketing regulations to economic development is quite doubtful; it would clearly be foolhardy to ignore their existence. At the same time, the framework of regulation in the LDCs is generally more flexible than in industrialized nations. The larger the firm and the more desirable its activities in the local scale of priorities, the greater the probability that it may strike a bargain with local authorities exempting the company from certain restrictions or introducing special regulations in its favor.

Reading 11, by Thorelli, is a brief case study of public policies in a country which contains within itself a highly industrialized and a highly underdeveloped subculture. This so-called dual economy problem South Africa has in common with Latin America and most LDCs around the world. Paradoxically, South Africa wants to keep these subcultures apart but finds it difficult to do so, while most LDCs at least pay lip-service to the ideal of economic integration without being successful at achieving it.

8 C. D. Edwards
The World of Antitrust

Adapted from C. D. Edwards, 'The world of antitrust', *Columbia Journal of World Business*, vol. 4, 1969, pp. 11–25.

Doing business in more than one country, a multinational enterprise is exposed to more than one system of national law. Although this fact is not new, it currently receives increased attention in the United States because more firms are multinational and have exposed themselves to a greater variety of national laws by widening the territorial scope of their operations.

Before the First World War there was substantially no antitrust legislation except in the United States and Canada. Elsewhere US firms could disregard legal problems that might be raised by their own restrictive conduct abroad and had no possibility of legal protection from restrictive conduct by others. Though there were beginnings of antitrust legislation in some other countries in the period between the two World Wars, they were overshadowed by government-supported cartelization in Italy, Germany, Japan, the Netherlands, Belgium, and in important industries in England and France. Until the Second World War, however, it continued to be roughly true that US antitrust laws forbade business firms to engage in restrictions that were either permitted or positively required in most countries outside North America.

Although the foreign legal situation has changed, business appreciation of its problems has lagged behind the facts.

When US law applies

Applicability of US law can be analysed in two ways, either by inference from the few proceedings pertaining to conduct in foreign countries or from the far more numerous proceedings pertaining to conduct in domestic markets. Either way, the inferences are of uncertain value. Most of the few proceedings that covered conduct abroad have pertained to collusive activities, carried on partly in the United States and designed to restrict flagrantly either trade within the United States or imports into it.[1] These cases throw little light upon the problems that confront a firm when, in a less lurid setting, it considers the bearing of US antitrust upon such activities abroad as exclusive dealing, joint sale, patent licensing, or participation in mergers or joint ventures.

The numerous proceedings that have involved similar activities in domestic markets are unreliable precedents for conduct in foreign markets. A practice that is clearly unlawful in the United States may not be clearly so in a foreign country because US commerce is not significantly affected by it or because it is required by a foreign government or for some other reason. What is unlawful *per se* in domestic markets may be decided under the rule of reason in foreign markets. The principle that the law permits restrictions ancillary to nonrestrictive purpose may have a broader application in foreign trade than in domestic trade.

With standards of legality thus uncertain, much of the conduct that is described as unlawful abroad appears to be not clearly illegal but of uncertain legality and hence hazardous. Criticism by careful lawyers tends to make the point that antitrust hazards are often great enough to inhibit desirable action. Criticism by laymen, usually less precise, often brings together and describes as illegal conduct that bears different degrees of legal risk.

To understand the nature and the limits of the antitrust risks that may arise for a firm in its activities outside the United States, one must bear in mind the broad characteristics of US antitrust laws. Resting on the constitutional power to regulate commerce, these laws apply to activities that affect the interstate or foreign commerce of the United States. They forbid unauthorized private concerted restraint of that commerce, private monopolization of any part of it (or attempt at such monopolization) and various acts or practices that create a reasonable probability that competition in that commerce will be substantially reduced. Except for certain particular acts and practices, the applicability of the laws depends not on the question whether or not what is forbidden took place in that commerce, nor on the question whether

1. See decisions reproduced in *International Aspects of Antitrust*, hearings before the Antitrust Subcommittee of the Senate Judiciary Committee, Part 2, Appendix, 1967. Restraints that took effect within the United States or allocations of territory designed to keep foreign competitors out of the United States were central in all of these cases in which violations were found except the case involving coated abrasives. In the abrasives case, firms dominant in the US market had undertaken joint production in other countries, with consequent reduction of exports from the United States by themselves and their US competitors.

or not the persons involved were engaged in that commerce, but on the question whether the relevant commerce was (or was likely to be) adversely affected in the specified way. Thus, the laws apply widely to intrastate enterprises and activities if interstate commerce is restricted by them. They may also be and have been applied to activities outside the United States by US or foreign firms that have the forbidden effects upon the domestic market or the country's imports or exports. Conversely, activities devoid of restrictive effects upon US commerce are beyond the reach of the antitrust laws even if they severely restrict the trade of a foreign country or US intrastate trade.

Broadly speaking, then, activities and agreements outside the United States by firms operating there are subject to US antitrust laws if they affect US commerce in the prohibited ways.

Areas of restriction

The areas of US antitrust restrictions may be illustrated by referring to seven cases. The first of these cases had to do with the inability of a US firm to condition the sale of its product to a French firm upon agreement by the latter that when the purchased article became a component of the French firm's products, these should not be shipped to the United States in competition. The second involved inability by US chemical firms in Belgium to join a cartel that controlled exports from Belgium (presumably including exports to the United States). The third pertained to the need for a US firm to refrain from becoming party to one or more cartels that restrained US trade by acquiring an interest in an Italian firm that was party to the agreements. The fourth was concerned with the jeopardy that a US firm would incur if, for a type of mineral that it produced from a concession in a foreign country, it were to take part in a scheme to raise profits on such minerals by means that included material restrictions on US commerce. Though the restrictions were not specified, the statement about them implied that they might include such schemes as price fixing on an international scale or allocation of world markets. The fifth and sixth examples had to do with risks that a US firm might incur if, in a particular foreign country in which it did business, it joined a cartel that applied such restrictions as price fixing or joint use of facilities to forestall construction of additional facilities. The seventh example involved the inability of several US firms to agree that their subsidiaries in the European Economic Community should limit their product lines.

The types of restriction on free markets involved in this sample of cartel agreements are those characteristic of the hard core of US antitrust cases – price fixing, allocation of territories or of types of goods and limitation of future supply. They are like those in the cartel cases that evoked, during and immediately after the Second World War, a popular outcry against international cartels and a series of Congressional anticartel riders to foreign aid agreements and bilateral treaties of commerce.

The argument for modifying US law and policy to tolerate such restrictions rests initially on the point that the alternative to restriction is loss of a business opportunity that might otherwise be available. It is important, therefore, to note the nature of the foregone opportunities in the different examples.

These differ greatly in magnitude. In the fourth and fifth cases cited, the argument for permitting cartelization rested on a foreign government's desire that the US firm join the cartel, expressed by pressure falling short of legal compulsion. One of these cases involved the possibility that refusal might result in loss of a mineral concession; the other appears to have involved only the subtle effects of being considered uncooperative. In the sixth case, the difficulty for the US firm was that of entering a tightly controlled market without coming to terms with the business group that controlled it; in the third case, that of losing the advantage of an ownership interest in the Italian firm as a means of promoting exports to Italy; in the second case, that of competing alone in export markets against the group efforts of cartel members; in the seventh case, that of not attaining the economies which might have been achieved if each producer had made a shorter line of goods; and in the first case, merely the inconvenience of having to choose between loss of a good foreign customer and the risk that this customer might be strengthened as a potential competitor.

Four types of restriction relating to patents or unpatented know-how are also involved in the examples: (a) exclusion of the foreign licensee from the US market; (b) exclusion of the US licensor from export markets that are reserved for the foreign licensee; (c) use of the combined power of cross-licenses to exclude third parties (as well as each participating party) from markets assigned to a particular participant; (d) requirement that the licensee obtain from the licensor such accessory equipment and materials as he needs in using the licensed product or process.

When what is licensed is unpatented technology, the antitrust laws are fully applicable to whatever restraints of US commerce take place in these ways. When patents are licensed, the applicability of antitrust law must be considered in the light of the monopoly right conveyed by a patent. But this right does not include the right to restrain trade beyond the territory covered by the patent grant, to restrain products that are not patented nor to impose restrictions based upon the combined power of two or more patentees. Where a patentee possesses a US patent and counterpart foreign patents, he can keep the products of his foreign licensees out of the United States by retaining and using his monopoly right under his US patent. Similarly, he can use his ownership of a foreign counterpart patent to keep both US exporters and licensees under other foreign counterpart patents out of the country in which he retains exclusive patent rights. Such action needs no exclusionary contract. The use of one is likely to raise a question whether more restriction is not being obtained than is obtainable by enforcing the patent.

The arguments offered in these statements for greater leniency toward international licensing than would be applied to domestic licenses are two: First, a US firm that cannot agree to grant a foreign licensee exclusive rights to a certain export territory may find that the prospective licensee chooses alternative technology available to it from a foreign firm that is not precluded from granting such rights. Second, the profitability of foreign licensing is reduced. The US licensor loses the benefit of potentially profitable trade restrictions: (1) markets protected by allocative cross-licensing; (2) monopoly in selling unpatented accessories to licensees; (3) ability to get license fees from unpatented technology without incurring the risk of competition from licensees in markets where they have no license. The prospective US licensor of unpatented technology may face an inconvenient choice between acceptance of the risk of competition by foreign licensees and relinquishment of the benefits from foreign license fees.

Joint venture problems

The most numerous examples presented in these papers pertain to joint ventures among firms. Though some examples are presented as if mere participation by a US company in a foreign joint venture is legally vulnerable, other examples make no such presumption, nor is the presumption persuasive. Even in the United States, no legal challenge has been offered to joint ventures as such, and in foreign countries joint ventures presumably operate in many instances without restrictive effects on US trade. A joint venture is capable of restraining US commerce, however. This possibility may arise in two forms. First, the joint venture itself may undertake restriction. For example, it may use discriminatory dumping to drive competing US exporters from certain export markets. When restriction is thus overt, a question may arise whether the US firm that participates in the joint venture is thereby part of a combination in restraint of trade. The same question may be raised about more subtle restrictions. The joint venture may refrain from exporting to the United States, preferring not to compete with one of its owners. If so, the capital that is withheld from such competition is not only that of the US owner but also that of the foreign participant, and a question may arise whether the joint venture does not inherently include an implied undertaking by the foreign firm to stay out of the US market.

Second, supplementing the joint venture, the US firm and the foreign firm in which it has participating ownership may agree upon restrictions that would be, if there were no joint venture, clearly a cartel agreement. The agreement may provide that the foreign joint venture will not ship to the United States, or that the US part-owner will not ship to the territory of the joint venture, or that both will maintain the same prices, sell through the same distributors, buy from the same sources or take similar restrictive action. If the substance of such an agreement restricts US commerce and thus is vulnerable under the antitrust laws, the question posed by the existence of a joint venture is whether the ties of ownership between the parties remove this vulnerability by converting the agreement into mere managerial decision by a single firm.

The problems involved in joint ventures are among the most difficult that arise in applications of the antitrust laws, whether to domestic or to foreign commerce. Involved are the circumstances under which restrictive agreements are implied by conduct that might have nonrestrictive explanations, as well as the boundary beyond which a corporate complex should be regarded as a single enterprise rather than two or more. The difficulties that arise for US firms abroad are similar to those at home – the ambiguity of laws that are still evolving. The relevant question raised by the examples is whether joint ventures in foreign countries are so desirable that such ventures should be treated more favorably than other joint ventures, either by more cursory examination of the inherently difficult issues or by more permissive rules of substantive law.

In the aggregate, these examples indicate that wherever operations abroad can have significant effects upon US commerce, US firms need to consider the effect of their action upon such commerce and that, in operations abroad as well as at home, they may find that antitrust considerations make it wise to avoid conduct that, in other respects, would be profitable. However, the sacrifices involved seem to be neither so frequent nor so severe as to be of major importance for the success of US trade in foreign countries. They consist in avoiding participation in international cartels that include restrictions upon imports into the United States, limiting the trade restrictions that accompany licenses of technology to those that are authorized by patent laws, and eliminating restraints of US commerce from business practices associated with joint ventures.

Some relief

Although these limitations may be inconvenient, there are mitigations and offsetting advantages. Two of these are worth noting.

First, foreign as well as US firms are subject to the US antitrust laws when they deliberately restrain US trade; and, like US firms, they enjoy no immunity because their restrictive conduct took place outside the United States. The British Imperial Chemical Industries as well as the US du Pont were subjected to orders by a US court in a case involving a world-wide allocation of chemical markets; the Dutch Philips as well as the US General Electric were subjected to orders in the case involving international cartelization of incandescent lamps. In neither case was the liability of the foreign defendant limited to what it had done within the United States.

The effect of application of US law to foreign firms is to mitigate whatever disadvantage US firms may incur but not to eliminate it. In several respects the impact of the law upon foreign firms is less severe than upon US firms. Unless a foreign firm does some business within the United States, proceedings in US courts cannot take place for lack of jurisdiction. When US trade is restricted by a foreign firm's conduct outside the United States, the proof needed for application of the laws is more difficult than in the case of US firms. Either type of firm is vulnerable if what was done abroad was part of a pattern that included action in the United States. In the National Lead case, the decision acknowledged that 'conduct abroad, on the part of foreign nations, relating to the commerce of foreign nations' would not be subject to US action, but pointed out that 'a conspiracy was entered into, in the United States, to restrain and control the commerce of the world, including the foreign commerce of the United States. The several agreements relating to manufacture and trade within the European markets are but some of the links in the chain which was designed to enthrall the entire commerce in titanium.'

Foreign action is also vulnerable if its effect on US trade was intended and clear. In the aluminium case, the test applied in determining whether cartel agreements made abroad by foreign firms violated US law was that 'both were unlawful, though made abroad, if they were intended to affect imports and did affect them.' The court held that proof of intent to restrict imports was sufficient to place upon the defendants the burden of proving that the purpose was not accomplished. But, provided the foreign firm is not party to a cartel agreement with US firms, the fact that its interests and operations lie chiefly abroad means that foreign restrictions by it are more likely to lack demonstrable purpose to influence US trade than are comparable restrictions by US firms.

When a foreign firm violates US law, corrective orders against it are likely to be more limited and less effective than orders against comparable conduct by domestic firms. In the incandescent lamp decree, the general injunction against agreements that restricted US exports or imports was applied to the Dutch defendant Philips only with respect to agreements with US manufacturers, whereas the US defendants were enjoined from restrictive agreements (more inclusively defined) with anyone. Moreover, Philips was exempted from the decree for any action abroad that was unlawful under the applicable foreign law. The Netherlands thereupon enacted a law that forbade compliance with decisions by a foreign state about restrictive conduct except after permission by the Dutch government.

In the case involving Imperial Chemical Industries, the US court's efforts to subject British patents on nylon to the decree's provisions for nonexclusive licenses were defeated by a suit filed in Britain by the exclusive licensee, a firm in which Imperial Chemical Industries had a 50 per cent stock interest. From the limits imposed by US jurisdiction, limits of proof as to purpose and effect and limits of effective corrective action, foreign firms may derive considerable opportunity to do what US firms cannot do.

Second, the duty for US firms to comply with the antitrust laws can be a source of advantage for them in cartel situations. When the law keeps them out of cartels, one possibility is that abstention makes establishment of a cartel impossible. US firms, like others, may dislike the resulting competition, but in being exposed to it they suffer no handicap, since their foreign competitors must compete also.

The other possibility is that foreign firms can and do establish the cartel without US participation. When foreign firms agree to fix prices, limit output or sales, allocate markets, or limit new capacity, US firms that do not join the agreement find advantage in their independence. So far as the agreed restrictions improve their prices and profits and reduce the intensity of the competition to which they are exposed, these benefits are theirs without action by them. While their foreign rivals are bound, they are free. They can 'woo the customers that the cartel will not make, or engage in the price competition from which the cartel abstains' (Edwards, 1964)[1]. Unless a cartel can effectively use exclusionary restrictions to keep independent firms out of cartelized markets, US firms are helped when they remain independent.

US and foreign curbs

Nearly all of the major industrialized countries and a few others now apply antitrust legislation. The members of the European Communities also apply the antitrust provisions of the Community treaties. When doing business in these countries, US firms find themselves subject to at least two systems of antitrust law and their foreign competitors subject to at least one. The foreign laws, however, differ substantially from the law of the United States, as well as from other foreign laws.

In some of the foreign countries, antitrust legislation covers only restrictive activities that are carried out within the particular country, as in the case of New Zealand. For a US firm and for its local competitors, liability for acts in such a country might also exist under US law if the activities there had direct effects upon US trade. Where legal relationships between foreign and US laws have this character, the foreign laws are likely to be more permissive in some respects, less so in others. Where they are more permissive, they may permit, for example, concerted agreements for exchange of technology that include prohibition of exports. Where they are less permissive, they may make it necessary for a

1. The ensuing passage describes a case in which a US firm that refused to join a price and quota cartel was sheltered by the cartel arrangement while it modernized its plant in preparation for an aggressive sales campaign.

US firm to abstain locally from practices that are permissible in the United States. Thus, in particular countries, resale price maintenance by an individual supplier, which is permissible in the United States where authorized by state law, may be forbidden unless it receives special exemption.

In other foreign countries, national laws are so broadly applicable that a US firm may face two-sided extraterritorial liability. Like US law, these other laws endeavor, in varying degrees, to curb restraints that affect domestic trade, no matter where these restraints are imposed. The German cartel law is applicable 'to all restraints of competition effective in the area of applicability of this law, even if they result from acts done outside such area.'[1] The Austrian cartel law covers 'cartel agreements made abroad, insofar as they are to be implemented in the territory of the Austrian Federal Republic.' Under the British Monopolies Act, orders 'may be so made as to extend to acts or omissions outside the United Kingdom', but only if those subjected to such orders are British subjects, British corporations or persons doing business in the United Kingdom. Though the Swiss Act on Cartels and Similar Organizations does not explicitly convey jurisdiction over what is done outside the country, a Swiss federal court decided in 1967 that the law 'also applies to actions in restraint of competition which take place abroad and have effects in Switzerland.' The laws of Spain and Denmark cover restrictions that have effects in domestic markets and hence may be reasonably interpreted as applicable where domestic effects spring from acts that occur in foreign countries, though neither statute makes this application explicit. Even under Dutch law, though the agreements covered are only those applicable to domestic trade that include at least one enterprise established in the Netherlands, nonresident participants have a duty to register the agreement. Since registration by one participant terminates the duty of the others to register, the obligation on the nonresident is significant only if resident participants fail to comply. In such a case, however, theoretically the nonresident could be prosecuted for non-compliance and convicted *in absentia*.

Application of the provisions of the Treaty of Rome that forbid restrictive agreements affecting trade between members of the European Economic Community is not limited either by the nationality of the enterprises involved or the place in which the

1. The laws mentioned in this section appear in English translation in OECD's *Guide to Legislation on Restrictive Business Practices*.

restriction takes place. In applying this treaty, the Community's Council has made registration of agreements a prerequisite for grant of the exemptions that the treaty authorizes; and the agreements registered have included agreements made outside the Community by firms in other countries. Thus important jurisdictions have adopted for trade regulation the principle that their laws apply where their trade is affected.

The spread of this so-called 'extraterritorial' principle of jurisdiction is not surprising. Incentives to adopt it are provided by contemporary business structure. Firms that operate internationally through establishments located in different countries can make individual or collective decisions in any country in which they choose to place their executives or hold their business meetings. They can restrain the trade of any country in which they have substantial operations or into which they make substantial shipments, by agreements made elsewhere: (1) to curtail the flow of their shipments to the country, (2) to raise the prices of what they send there, (3) to limit what they export from the country, or (4) to limit what they invest in it or the use that they make of facilities they already possess within it. The vulnerability of a country to restraints of trade that are executed beyond its borders differs only in degree, not in kind, from the vulnerability of a state in the United States to trade restraints that are executed in other states. As international trade has increased in volume and importance and as international firms have become more important in that trade, this vulnerability has increased.

The impact of reciprocal extraterritorial claims of jurisdiction has been minimal thus far. There are two reasons for this: the recency of the foreign laws in which such jurisdiction is asserted and the tendency for the foreign governments that assert such jurisdiction to concentrate their attention initially upon their own domestic restraints. In the United States, proceedings that involved international cartels and overseas activities were negligible for decades after the Sherman Act became law. But the potential of the reciprocal concepts is there and even today has some slight operative significance for US firms that operate in the Common Market. Since US firms are prominent and feared in international trade, this potential is likely sooner or later to express itself in foreign countries in action as vigorous as in the United States.

Where this happens, US firms that do business internationally are likely to find that in so doing they incur significant dual liability. So far as the substance of control over restrictive activities differs in the United States and in another country, acts that are permissible in one country may be unlawful in the other if they have a restrictive impact there. More importantly, restrictive agreements and actions in export trade from either country, though exempt in the exporting country for lack of domestic effect, may be unlawful in the importing country as restrictions related to that country's imports and sales. Moreover, in each country firms with dual liability are likely to encounter competitors that have liability only under one country's laws, because they do business only in that country or do business abroad only in countries without antitrust laws. Since these competitors enjoy greater freedom of action than the firms with dual liability, problems of competition with uncurbed competitors are likely to appear.

It is conceivable that in a particular instance the problems thus created for US business might be eliminated by unilateral change in the antitrust laws of the United States. To abandon US principles of control merely on the ground that they conflict with the principles applied by another country is not inviting. But this is not the only difficulty. There are two others. The first is that, since most countries with antitrust laws are indifferent to restrictions that take effect abroad, there is no way for the United States, without gross discrimination against its own citizens, to relax its control of restrictions on its imports in toleration of reductions that are permissible in other countries and, at the same time, tighten its control of restrictions on its exports to prevent effects that are unlawful in the countries to which the goods are sent. The second difficulty is that US law would have to be changed to conform to the laws of several countries whose laws do not conform to one another.

Foreign curbs

US firms that operate in several foreign countries, including one or more that assert jurisdiction where domestic effects are due to action abroad, potentially encounter problems from the differences among foreign laws. The effects of their action, lawful in one foreign country, may produce antitrust risks in another country that asserts extraterritorial control. If they operate in two or more foreign countries that assert extraterritorial control, they may encounter dual liability. The extent of these possibilities increases with growth in the number of the countries that have antitrust laws.

Like the problems of dual liability that involve US law, the problems of dual liability under laws that are wholly foreign have not yet appeared in specific proceedings. Since the reasons are the same as for the other kind of dual liability – the recency of the foreign laws and the initial preoccupation of officials with domestic issues – this is not surprising. But the chances are that those who assert extraterritorial jurisdiction will eventually exert it. When they do, both kinds of dual liability are likely to create problems.

Such dual liabilities may become, in fact, considerably more than dual. With several foreign jurisdictions asserting extraterritorial authority, US firms that do business in most of these countries probably will encounter, in time, several instances of dual liability, differing from country to country in the limits imposed by foreign law and hence in the points of differences between foreign and US law, and between one foreign law and another.

The more numerous the dualities, the harder to cope with them. Yet the more numerous they are, the clearer it must become that the difficulties they create cannot be met by unilateral relaxation of the US antitrust laws.

Multiplicity of curbs

The problems of differences in policy toward trade restrictions between US law and some foreign law, or between two (or more) foreign laws, are likely to be enhanced as the number and diversity of laws increases. At some point in this growing complexity the problem changes character, at least for firms that do a far-flung international business. Such firms are no longer primarily concerned with particular differences in business opportunity traceable to the different application of antitrust laws. Instead, they are likely to find that antitrust legislation is so diverse that in the aggregate it creates obstacles to coherent management of international enterprises. Where activities involve possibilities of trade restriction, they may find that each of the more attractive lines of action is questioned by one or more countries, that no test of the legitimacy of action is valid in all countries and that efforts to make action acceptable under the different antitrust laws of the various countries entail truly impressive burdens of legal analysis, negotiation and delay.

Whether or not diversity has yet reached these forbidding dimensions is uncertain. It is clear that diversity is already formidable and that its effects upon international business are likely to increase as administration of the newer laws and the ones more laxly applied becomes more thorough.

Only by examples can one make vivid the extent to which the diverse provisions of the national laws and the international treaties are sources of multiple and partly inconsistent substantive requirements applied in a vexing variety of ways.

A firm that does business in each country in Europe, North America and Japan is obligated to report its restrictive agreements in seven different countries and, if it wishes to qualify them for exemption from the prohibitions of the EEC Treaty, also to the EEC Commission. The reporting requirements differ as to the meaning of 'agreement' and of 'restriction', the extent of the information that must be supplied, the kinds of agreements that are exempt from reporting, and the legal effect of failure to report. In five of these countries the obligation to report extends beyond restrictive agreements if the firm has a dominant position or individually engages in restriction, but the definition of those who must report and the scope of what must be reported differ from country to country. Mergers and similar acquisitions must be reported in three countries – in one country in advance and regardless of size, in the others subsequently and only if the acquirer is large (by a definition that is different in each country). In two countries a firm is subject to special reporting requirements if it is foreign, and in one country, if it is large, it must report its stockholdings.

Substantive control over restrictive activities is equally dissimilar, with a different pattern of diversity for each kind of restriction. The status of exclusive dealing will serve as an example. A US firm that desired to use exclusive distributors in selling its products in the United States, Canada, Japan and Western Europe (except Finland) would need to consider the bearing of the restrictive practice legislation of fifteen countries and of the EEC upon its proposed program. In one country, Canada, the law would seem to contain no relevant provisions. Conspiracies to restrain trade and monopolies, against which the most nearly relevant parts of the Canadian law are directed, are so defined that there is little likelihood of the law's use against exclusive dealing. In four countries, the United Kingdom, the Netherlands, Belgium and Switzerland, any curbs that might be relevant would be found only among provisions applicable to powerful business enterprises. In the other ten countries and in the EEC, controls applicable to agreement or to restriction by single firms would be such that they might apply to exclusive dealing even by a relatively small firm.

If the firm considering the program were sufficiently large that it needed to consider the laws of fourteen countries, it would find that in five of these countries the statutes and related official documents would make the legal status of exclusive dealing reasonably clear. In the other nine countries, the legality of its proposed program would depend upon the interpretation that might be given to diverse legal standards by the various official bodies charged with decision. These standards are concerned with the effect of the program upon the interests of firms excluded from the arrangement, upon competition or upon the public interest. To assume that even similar and relatively specific statutory language might be differently interpreted by different official bodies would be reasonable, but in most of the nine countries the applicable legal standards are of a kind deliberately designed to convey considerable discretion to those who apply them, and the leeway for divergent interpretation is correspondingly wide.

Reference

EDWARDS, C. D. (1964), *Cartelization in Western Europe*, US Department of State.

9 E. M. J. A. Sassen

Ensuring Fair Competition in the European Community

Slightly abbreviated from E. M. J. A. Sassen, 'Ensuring fair competition in the european community', *Community Topics*, no. 35, European Communities Press and Information Service, Washington, DC, 1970, pp. 3–8.

On 1 July 1968, the last tariff barriers between the six member states of the European Economic Community were removed. Tariffs and quotas, the traditional instruments of mercantilism, trade wars and the quest for national self-sufficiency, disappeared. Labour and capital can now move freely within the Community. National markets which for decades were self-contained are becoming increasingly exposed to competition, as new competitors emerge in the member states and as competitors from outside the Community seek to profit from the opportunities offered by the large European market.

An additional factor has been the speeding up of technical progress, reflected in a shortening of the time-span between the moment of innovation and that of industrial application. In the nineteenth century it took about 100 years from the discovery of the principle of the steam engine to its commercial application. For the telephone and photography it took about fifty years. The time-lag in our era has shortened to five years for the splitting of the atom and for cybernetics and to three years for semi-conductors.

The Community's competition policy should take account of modern technical developments and their impact on the Common Market's economy. Its competition policy must be more than a mere 'anti-trust' policy, whether directed against restrictive agreements or monopolies. True, bans on restrictive agreements and on abuses of dominant market positions provided for by the Common Market rules of competition are important and permanent components of competition policy. Care must be taken that the actions of firms or governments do not undo the Commission's aims and achievements in freeing trade from the artificial barriers and distortions set up by restraints of competition. Consumers and businessmen alike expect the Common Market to improve living standards. This expectation, in addition to the political desire for European unification, was one of the main motivations for concluding the Community Treaties.

But our hopes will not be fulfilled unless firms in the Common Market really compete with each other as tariff, tax and legal barriers to the formation of a single home market are gradually removed. Only competition can ensure optimum use of the factors of production, maintenance and strengthening of European firms' competitiveness on world markets and – beyond the purely economic objectives – the safeguarding of freedom in a way consistent with the Community's social objectives.

The Commission's record

The Commission is determined to apply the bans on restraints of competition whenever the need arises. It made this clear in July 1969 when in two cases it imposed heavy fines under Article 85 of the Rome Treaty, which deals with infringement of the rules of competition. One decision related to the international quinine agreement, the other to concerted price-fixing for aniline dyestuffs by manufacturers from the Community and two non-member countries.

The instruments of Community competition policy – the ban on restrictive agreements and prohibition of abuse – correspond to those provided by American anti-trust law. The mere pursuit of a 'prohibition policy' would, however, not enable the Commission to cope adequately with the actual situation of firms in the Common Market. The integration process and technological progress require firms to make far-reaching adjustments almost daily. Even the reorganization of entire industries may be needed.

The second important task of those in charge of Community competition policy is therefore to help firms to adapt themselves. It is not the Commission's task to force a company's management to take measures of adaptation. Nor is it our task to arrange cooperation between firms or to help finance adaptation investment. We must use other means of helping firms to bring about the necessary adaptation.

Policy on restrictive agreements

One of the ways in which a firm can adapt itself to new market conditions is by cooperating with other firms. Cooperation may, to quote a few examples only, take the form of specialization agreements, joint purchasing or selling arrangements, joint research and development, and licensing or exclusive-dealing agreements (see Annex).

The European Treaties' rules of competition apply to all these forms of cooperation. The rules forbid as a matter of principle all restraints of competition which impair trade between member states; but they exempt forms of cooperation whose overall economic effects are likely to be beneficial. Obviously the opportunities for adaptation made available to firms through cooperation depend on how these rules are interpreted and applied. Here competition policy must provide assistance wherever it is required and justified.

The Community's competition policy should be based on an approach consistent with economic reality. It would be inconsistent with current economic conditions in Europe if we held that every reduction in the number of independently operating firms necessarily entailed less competition. From the angle of pure logic, this theory looks convincing, but it is not compatible with the current structure of many economic sectors in the Community. Agriculture is an obvious example, but so are retail trade or those markets where many small firms vie with a few giants. In such a situation small firms, if operating independently, may be too small to matter to the big companies; but cooperation may enable them to challenge their powerful rivals.

Here is a practical example from the Commission's experience. Europe's marine-paint market is shared by the big international groups and a large number of small manufacturers. The big groups operate sales agencies in all major ports, so that the purchaser can be offered the same product everywhere. This selling point, of great importance for paint repair work for instance, is not available to the small manufacturers and so their ability to compete is restricted. As a result, a number of small firms from several countries thought of offsetting this disadvantage by jointly developing paints, laying down quality standards and selling under the same trade mark. This project should transform small firms of merely local importance into serious competitors for the international groups; the Commission accordingly authorized it because it expects that it will bring keener competition.

Effect on market

This example shows how our assessment of various forms of cooperation depends on the effect the agreements are likely to have on actual market trends. An agreement's effects on the market may vary fundamentally according to the market context. For this reason we feel that mere knowledge of the terms of an agreement is not a sufficient basis for a decision on the application of the Community's rules of competition. Market analysis is essential to a Community competition policy.

A predominantly economic approach such as this must influence the definition of 'restraint of competition' and consequently the scope of Community law on restrictive agreements. If the effect of an agreement on the market is what matters, it stands to reason that the rules of competition should apply only to agreements that appreciably influence market conditions. Accordingly, the Commission concentrates on the really important cases. This approach is also in the interest of firms in the Common Market, and particularly for the large number of small firms. But it also benefits the economy as a whole, since concentration of the Community's work on a smaller number of cases facilitates the development of case-law.

At present firms are entitled to know as soon as possible what Community competition law prohibits and permits – what is clearly forbidden, and what may conceivably be authorized.

We are trying to clarify our competition policy in two ways. We devoted the first few years after Community competition law came into force mainly to laying the foundations by passing implementing provisions. We are now trying to increase each year the number of decisions on different kinds of restrictive agreements; more decisions were issued in 1968 than in any previous year since the start of European integration. We choose particular cases so that a decision on them clarifies the situation for the greatest possible number of similar cases. An example of this working method is the recent Commission decision on exclusive dealing agreements. This has made it possible to settle by a simplified procedure another 1100 agreements which have been notified to the Commission. The decision also clarifies how exclusive-dealing agreements for sales in non-member countries are to be legally assessed in the future.

Bloc exemptions

The second way the Commission is trying to clarify its competition policy is based on the possibility, provided by the EEC Treaty, of granting bloc exemptions from the ban on restrictive agreements. The Commission has already granted a bloc exemption for certain exclusive-dealing agreements, and we shall try to do the same for other forms of cooperation. We are now considering the possibility of granting bloc exemptions for agreements on

1. Uniform use of standards or types.
2. Research and development.
3. Specialization.
4. Joint buying or selling.
5. Certain licensing agreements.

We are considering whether the Commission could facilitate the conclusion of such agreements by withdrawing the notification requirement. We are also trying to find out if general criteria can be established to determine whether a restraint is 'appreciable'; this would enable the Commission to adopt regulations that would exclude cases of negligible restraint from the scope of the rules of competition.

This work is running into great difficulties. No experience is yet available on the effects of such general measures on agreements of the kinds just described. It is proving extremely difficult to formulate general rules exempting certain forms of cooperation that are comprehensive enough to make exemption a meaningful proposition and yet not so comprehensive as to include agreements which do not justify exemption.

This is a new area of the law on restrictive agreements. We have moved into it because traditional policy cannot adequately handle today's situation in the Common Market. Pressures of technological and other developments compel European business to seek out new methods of research, production and marketing and Community competition policy to break new ground.

Policy on mergers

Our policy on industrial mergers is determined by our concept of the future structure of European business. It also depends, of course, on the legal opportunities provided for the Commission under the European Treaties.

The structures of European markets must satisfy two conditions. There should be enough independent firms to ensure effective competition. At the same time, however, these firms should be large enough to solve problems of research, production and marketing. Each firm must decide for itself whether to seek the right scale of operations through internal growth or through amalgamations. In any event, since the beginning of European integration a steadily increasing number of firms seem to have been choosing the merger method. At present hardly a day passes without the press reporting new mergers or merger negotiations. Most of these companies seem to be responding to the growing pressure of competition on the European and world markets. Generally these firms do not want to restrict competition, but to improve their competitiveness and to adapt themselves to the new scale of the market. In these cases, a reduction in the number of independent firms can intensify competition. Such mergers are in harmony with the objective of Community competition policy for, to use a quotation from the United States Supreme Court which aptly describes the Commission's policy, 'It is competition, not competitors, which the Act protects.'

Cross-frontier mergers

At present there are few mergers between firms from different member countries. Most mergers take place between companies of the same nationality, or between a firm from a member state and a firm outside the Community. The Commission is working hard to eliminate the obstacles – especially in the area of tax and company law – to cross-frontier mergers. Unfortunately, some recent cases show that the governments of some member countries prefer to restructure industries in a national framework and therefore use pressure to prevent multinational arrangements.

This trend is a matter of concern. Mergers between firms from different member states could speed up the integration of markets. In addition, the Common Market, not national frontiers, should be the framework for the development of new market structures. If a firm wants to combine with another firm to boost its productivity, it should in general be able to choose the partner whose production range or marketing system makes the best match. The economic success of the Community depends on optimum allocation of the factors of production.

In a few industries, however, additional mergers between certain firms would endanger workable competition. The European Treaties bind the Community to act if competition is distorted. We construe Article 86 of the EEC Treaty which prohibits 'the abuse of a dominant position', to mean that a merger which eliminates effective competition constitutes a case of abuse and is consequently prohibited.

At present, as national markets are more and more exposed to competition, including competition from firms outside the Community, workable competition is threatened on only a few markets. Thus the Commission has so far had no occasion to apply Article 86 to a merger.

The Commission is in a stronger position over mergers in the coal and steel industry, because the European Coal and Steel Community Treaty allows them only if they are authorized by the Commission.

As these industries are passing through a period of structural reform, we have in the past endorsed most plans for cooperation and concentration. But we realize that the maintenance of effective competition between a small number of competitors in the coal and steel industries – particularly the latter – will pose an increasingly difficult problem.

Conclusion

Our aim is to make the Community's economy strong and efficient. The European Economic Community has provided us with a great opportunity to achieve this objective. As integration spreads to an ever larger number of markets, it releases stimuli which can have a creative effect, provided the free play of market forces is safeguarded. This is why the task of ensuring free and undistorted competition has a key position in the European Treaties. Those in charge of the Community's competition policy bear the great responsibility for accomplishing this task.

Annex: Commission's criteria for permissible business agreements

In a statement defining its policy on trading and research agreements between firms in the Six, the Commission announced in July 1968 that it welcomed cooperation among small and medium-sized companies if this enabled them to work more rationally and increase their productivity and competitiveness on a larger market. It considered the encouragement of cooperation of this kind as part of its task. Cooperation among large firms could also, in the Commission's view, be economically justifiable and compatible with the Community's competition policy.

The Commission authorizes agreements if the total market share of the participating companies is too small to cause an appreciable restraint of competition in the Common Market or to hamper trade between the member states. The Commission does not specify the permissible share of the market which may be involved; this depends on a number of factors, including the nature of the industry and products involved, and the availability of substitutes for the products concerned.

Although the Treaties' rules on preventing distortion of competition are becoming more important as economic integration of member states advances, it is also becoming crucial for firms to adapt themselves to the Common Market and to keener competition on world markets. One major way in which adaptation can be facilitated is by cooperation between firms. To encourage this, and to dispel uncertainty about its positive attitude, the Commission statement set out the forms of cooperation between firms which in its opinion do not contravene Article 85(1) of the EEC Treaty and Article 65(1) of the ECSC Treaty. The statement was intended to make it easier for businessmen to know which agreements do not need to be notified to the Commission for 'negative clearance'.

Eight types

In interpreting and applying the provisions of the Paris and Rome Treaties on competition, the Commission regards the following eight categories of agreement as permissible:

1. Agreements whose sole object is an exchange of opinion or experience; joint market research; joint preparation of statistics and calculation models. There may, however, be a restraint of competition where concrete recommendations are made, or where conclusions induce at least some of the firms to behave identically on the market. Where there are special intermediary bodies to register orders, turnover, investment and prices, it would be wrong to assume automatically that the rules of the Treaties are waived, particularly on an oligopolistic market for similar products.

2. Agreements whose sole object is cooperation in accounting; joint provision of credit guarantees; joint debt-collecting associations; joint business or tax-consultancy agencies. The Commission stated that debt-collecting associations which also fix or influence prices may, however, restrict competition. Application of uniform conditions by all participating firms and joint comparison of prices could constitute cases of concerted practices. The use of standardized printed forms must not be combined with an understanding or tacit agreement on uniform prices, rebates or conditions of sale.

3. Agreements whose sole object is the joint implementation,

placing and sharing out of research and development projects among the participating firms. The mere exchange of research experience and results, the Commission stated, serves for information only and does not restrict competition. It therefore need not be mentioned expressly. If, however, firms restrict their own research and development (R and D) activity or the use of the results of joint work so that they do not have a free hand for R and D outside the joint projects, this can constitute an infringement of the rules of competition.

Where firms do not carry out joint research work, contractual obligations or concerted practices binding them to refrain from research work of their own, either completely or in certain sectors, may result in a restraint of competition. The sharing out of sectors of research without an understanding providing for mutual access to the results is regarded as a case of specialization that may restrict competition. So too are undertakings to manufacture only products developed jointly.

There may also be a restraint of competition if certain participating firms are excluded from the exploitation of the results, either entirely or to an extent not commensurate with their participation, or if the granting of licences to nonparticipants is expressly or tacitly excluded.

4. Agreements whose only object is the joint use of production facilities, of storage facilities and of transport equipment. There may be a restraint of competition if the firms go beyond organizational and technical arrangements and agree on joint production.

5. Agreements whose sole object is the setting up of working partnerships for the common execution of orders, where the participating firms do not compete with each other over the work to be done, or where each of them by itself is unable to execute the orders. If, however, the absence of competition is based on concerted practices, there may be a restraint of competition. Where the firms participating in an association do normally compete with each other, there is no restraint of competition if the firms cannot execute the specific order by themselves because they lack experience, specialized knowledge, adequate capacity or financial resources. Nor is there a restraint of competition if it is only by setting up an association that the firms can make a promising offer. There may, how-

ever, be a restraint of competition if the firms undertake to work solely in the framework of an association.
6. Agreements whose sole object is joint selling arrangements or joint after-sales and repair service, provided the participating firms are not competitors over the products or services covered by the agreement. The Commission pointed out that often small or medium-sized firms competing with each other sell jointly, but that this does not entail an appreciable restraint of competition.
7. Agreements whose sole object is joint advertising. If the agreement prevents the participants from themselves advertising, there may be a restraint of competition.
8. Agreements whose sole object is the use of a common label to designate a certain quality, where the label is available to all competitors on the same conditions. There may be restraint of competition if the right to use the label is linked to obligations regarding production, marketing or price formation, for instance when the participants are obliged to manufacture or sell only products of guaranteed quality.

Dominant positions

The statement added that the Commission intended to establish, by means of suitable decisions in individual cases or by general notices, the status of the various forms of cooperation in relation to the provisions of the Rome Treaty. But it could not at that time make a general statement on the application of the Rome and Paris Treaties to the abuse of dominant positions within the Common Market or within a part of it.

As a general rule, firms need no longer apply to the Commission for negative clearance for the eight types of agreements listed. Nor should it be necessary for the legal situation to be clarified through a Commission decision on an individual case. This means that notification will no longer be necessary for agreements of this type. In cases of doubt firms are free to apply for negative clearance.

Specific cases

The Commission statement cited three recent cases in which it approved the agreements involved, and which illustrate the principles underlying its attitude to cooperation between firms.

1. Alliance de Constructeurs français de Machines-outils. The aim of this agreement is to create a joint exporting service for the company's nine members, and the Alliance's sole activity is business negotiation. The members of the Alliance are small and medium-sized firms. Their total turnover accounts for a little more than 10 per cent of total French output.

   The Commission stated that a joint export service does not conflict with the objects of the EEC Treaty, if the service acts merely as a joint market prospection agency for non-competing products and does not constitute an intermediate stage in distribution. It also took the view that the commitment by each Alliance member neither to manufacture nor to sell machines liable to compete with those manufactured by other members did not constitute a restraint of competition because this was the formal expression of a *de facto* situation which already existed before the Alliance was set up, and because the market for machine-tools is tending to encourage specialization. Furthermore, the members represented only an insignificant part of the EEC market for machine-tools. These three factors combined caused the Commission to issue a negative clearance in this case.

2. Socemas. The Société commerciale et d'Études des Maisons d'Alimentation et d'Approvisionnement à Succursales (Socemas) is a French trading and research company set up to facilitate cooperation between about sixty food-retailing chain stores. One of its aims is to prospect foreign markets in order to purchase on favourable terms on behalf of member firms.

   The Commission's approval shows that it regards Article 85 of the Treaty as applicable to agreements between purchasers in the same way as the Article is to those between sellers. Negative clearance was granted because the activity of Socemas in EEC countries other than France was not on a sufficiently large scale to entail appreciable restraints of competition. An additional factor was that its activity has not increased in recent years.

   This decision represented a first step towards solving problems of competition related to cooperation between firms engaged in trading.

3. ACEC-Berliet. The aim of this joint research and development agreement between S.A. Ateliers de Constructions Electriques de Charleroi (ACEC), of Brussels, and the Société Automobile

Berliet, of Lyons, is the design and marketing of a new type of bus with an electrical transmission system.

When a marketable prototype has been designed under the cooperation arrangements, it is agreed that ACEC will supply the electrical transmission system and Berliet the mechanical parts of the vehicles. In the Common Market, however, ACEC will be free to deliver its transmission systems to only one manufacturer in each of the four other member countries, in addition to Berliet in France and to Belgian users.

The Commission accepted this agreement, although it contains certain restraints of competition, because it considered the restraints indispensable to obtain economically desirable results from the agreement – in particular, improved production and technical progress. The exemption from the Rome Treaty ban was for five years.

10 L. E. Preston

Market Control in Developing Economies

L. E. Preston, 'Market control in developing economies',
Journal of Development Studies, vol. 4, no. 4, 1968, pp. 481–496
(some footnotes deleted).

In most of the developing countries, and in such countries scattered throughout the political spectrum from capitalism to communism, internal trade is primarily conducted through controlled markets. The specific character and function of controls vary widely, but the line between market socialism and controlled capitalism is thin; whereas the difference between both of these and, on the one hand, unrestricted markets and, on the other, purely administrative coordination systems, is evident to even the casual observer. In controlled markets, whether embedded in a capitalist or socialist economic structure, public authorities operate continuously not only to establish specific limits on market outcomes, but also to influence the direction and purposes of market activity. However, in contrast to administrative co-ordination systems, controlled markets leave a significant scope for independent action and individual flexibility.

Examples of market control activities may be gleaned from almost any study of a developing economy. However, in such examples, the unique circumstances of the individual case tend to dominate, and the common elements and alternatives among control activities are obscured. This tendency to see market control in terms of unique cases is also characteristic of control administrations. The division of control authority over different industries and market levels among different, and often rivalrous, ministries and agencies serves to hide, rather than reveal, the basic similarities and inherent inter-relationships of many control activities; and thereby stimulates the development and persistence of inconsistent and even mutually offsetting policies.

The purpose of this paper is to identify domestic market control as a significant aspect of development planning and administration, quite apart from the particular ideological context or product/industry setting in which the controls may operate. To this end, we characterize the principal objectives of market control and the methods used to achieve them: we then touch on the problem of evaluating control effectiveness. Throughout the paper, examples are cited in order to draw attention to both the contextual diversity and the underlying similarity of control activities.

Market control: what and why

For purposes of this discussion, a *market* may be defined as any exchange relationship in which the trading parties exercise a range of choice with respect to their selection of trading partners, products, prices, or quantity purchased or sold. The range of choice may include, of course, the alternative of abstaining from trade entirely. The general term *market* is intended to include such disparate phenomena as the assembly of agricultural products from primary producers and the distribution of manufactured goods to consumers, as well as the purchase and sale of materials and products within the industrial sector. Market control is not simply *demand* control; supply management activities may be of equal or greater concern.

Market control may be aimed at any or all of the results of market activity – the character and quality of merchandise and services exchanged, their volume and prices, and the distribution of sales and purchases among potential sellers and buyers. An essential aspect of control administration is the inter-relation among the several results, and the appraisal of control effectiveness rests on the comparison of results achieved with those that might have occurred under unrestricted market activity or administrative direction.

A preliminary question arises: Why have so many developing countries, capitalist as well as socialist, chosen market control over either free markets or comprehensive administration as a principal form of domestic supply and demand coordination? The answer appears to lie in both ideological and practical considerations. A preference for markets reflects, in part, the sheer difficulty and cost of providing a satisfactory administrative substitute. Although the relatively small size and industrial simplicity of many developing countries would appear to facilitate the use of administrative mechanisms, these advantages are as a rule offset by the absence of essential information and of the skills and social habits necessary for administrative efficiency. As a result, small and simple developing countries are as difficult to coordinate administratively, for economic as well as political purposes, as large and complex developed ones. Further, the task of economic coordination without markets becomes more rather than less difficult as the development process proceeds, because of the increasing variety of products and services available and the widening range of choice among economic and non-economic activities. On the ideological side, political recognition of the value and strength of individual preferences provides an additional rationale for the use of markets. This recognition is particularly important in countries where a large traditional sector continues to exist alongside a developing core of urban industry. If the fruits of development are to be made available to village populations, then products, services and distribution arrangements must be adapted not only to traditional requirements but also to the opportunities for experimentation and gradual change that arise as development continues.

These practical and ideological considerations account for the use of controlled markets in circumstances that might otherwise favour more centralized planning and administration. In private ownership economies, adoption of controls over markets otherwise free is primarily intended to bring the activities of private owners and purchasers into conformity with basic development goals and to achieve specific welfare objectives. The need to maintain low food prices for an industrial labour force or to prevent profiteering from temporary shortages are obvious examples. In addition, market controls are intended to curb the mercantile psychology prevalent in many developing societies, in which the maximum gain on the immediate transaction is preferred to long-term market expansion. In these circumstances, one feature of market control is to substitute the long-term production and sales goals of the western capitalist for the short-term view of the traditional merchant. In addition, of course, rapid development of poor countries typically requires some centralized administration of primary investment decisions, foreign exchange, and basic subsistence supplies, no matter what the form of government or pattern of property ownership. And such administrative activity frequently generates a network of supplementary controls with varying impact on domestic markets.

Market control objectives

Market controls are not ends in themselves but are intended to facilitate the accomplishment of basic development goals – stimulating domestic production and consumption, conserving foreign exchange, and improving human welfare. Specific market control activities can rarely be conducted or appraised by direct reference to these goals, however, because of the many factors involved in achieving any major goal and because of the multi-dimensional character of the goals themselves. Thus, specific market control activities must be aimed at more specific objectives, which in turn contribute to the long-run development strategy. Unfortunately, failure to specify these objectives and to observe the inter-relations among them has been characteristic of both the analysis and the practice of market control in the developing countries.

Marketization

A major characteristic of traditional economies is the relative weakness or absence of markets. Not only are subsistence households and communities commonplace, but – much more important – sizeable production and demand potentials exist side by side but separated by ignorance, institutional barriers, or high marketing costs. A substantial increase in output, and the well-being of both producers and users, may be achieved if all the potential trading parties can be made aware of the exchange possibilities and drawn into a market relationship.

Marketization typically involves both organizational change and educational or promotional activity; it may require facilities for investment as well. Constructing public market places, establishing buying or selling agencies to act as market intermediaries, and introducing regular storage and communication-transportation facilities are typical activities aimed at this objective. The primary purpose of these innovations is to make the exchange possibilities apparent, and to lower the cost of contact among market participants. At the same time, however, marketization monetizes both costs and revenues that were previously accounted, if at all, only in real terms. Great inconvenience and ignorance may be overcome by means of relatively small money expenditures – as in the payment of market participation fees or taxes – or by the adoption of fairly simple standard operating procedures or standards. But these expenditure and operating changes are readily observable, whereas the unmonetized real costs, which perhaps prohibited exchange altogether, and traditional operating procedures are accepted as normal. Marketization therefore frequently appears to involve increases in costs and inconvenience for potential market participants, rather than the reduced costs or improved cost/return ratios which are its goal. To overcome these difficulties – often summarized as 'these people don't know what's good for them' – an element of compulsion may be required, in addition to systematic educational and promotional effort. It may also be necessary to introduce a variety of auxiliary control elements aimed at assuring the trading parties specific benefits from market participation, and – perhaps of equal importance – of demonstrating that the benefits promised are actually received.

Marketization may also be an essential preliminary to other more specific types of control activity. For example, the formal market reorganization associated with the establishment of marketing boards in the agricultural countries of the Sterling Area has been primarily justified as creating conditions for market stabilization. The idea is that the institutional and regulatory system of the boards would make possible the conduct of stabilization policies. Critics, such as Bauer and Yamey (1954), have charged that this power to stabilize involved too great an interference with other aspects of market activity. More recently, one careful analysis has raised considerable questions about the ability of the boards to achieve any significant stabilization results (Helleiner, 1966). Another example is the susceptibility of markets to redistributional techniques such as price manipulations and rationing; in the absence of markets, redistribution of goods – as, for example, of food supplies – may be attainable only through confiscation or forced collectivization.

Increased volume

Marketization implies an increase in the volume of goods flowing into trade channels. It is therefore quite compatible with the broader control objective of increasing the volume of goods produced and consumed. Increased output may come from both previously operating and new sources, and increased consumption may be aimed at welfare goals (increased *total* consumption) or at the diversion of demand from imports (increased consumption of domestic products). Whatever the detailed problem, the obvious strategies are to stimulate output by price increases, and to stimulate use by price reductions. Evidently, when the intent is to increase both domestic production and use of the same product – the typical case – these two strategies are in direct conflict.

The simultaneous increase of buying and decrease of selling prices requires either that intermediate trading margins be narrowed, or that subsidies be provided from the general treasury. Intermediate trading margins may fall for two reasons: (1) the cost of intermediate activities, such as central market trading, financing, transport and storage, is reduced; or (2) intermediate monopoly positions exist and can be eliminated. Both of these may be real possibilities, but both are apt to require considerable expenditure of funds and considerable managerial skill on the part of control authorities. By contrast, increasing production and use through price manipulations appears relatively easy, and subsidies thus become common features of volume expansion programmes. As a result, one evidence of the success of such programmes, at least in the short-run, in accomplishing their output and use objectives is their increasing money cost; the greater the increase in volume, the greater the subsidy required.

Subsidy costs can be reduced, and the impact of price manipulations sharpened, when specific price incentives are linked to specific producer or user characteristics or behaviour. For example, advantageous selling prices may be established only for over-fulfilment of marketing or production quotas, and low buying prices made available only to specific industries or to households in accordance with employment status or family needs. These selective techniques make it possible to apportion the total increase in volume among specific sources and uses, and may also reduce subsidy costs substantially as compared to a general subsidy programme. However, selective programmes also require a much more detailed administration and present innumerable opportunities for abuse, both by control authorities and by subsidy receivers.

Inflation control

Increased investment and rapid urbanization in the course of economic development, as well as specific subsidies for output and consumption referred to above, commonly tend to generate inflationary pressures, particularly in consumer goods lines. Although fundamental adjustment to these pressures must lie in some combination of taxation and increased output, a certain amount of direct control over the price level is characteristic of almost all developing economies. If effective, such control may avoid the spread of an inflation psychosis throughout the economy, and thus facilitate the accomplishment of fundamental development goals. Stringent short-run price controls may also avoid the necessity of downward price adjustments when a more nearly balanced market situation is attained. However, the simple control of explicit prices, whether or not accompanied by systematic rationing, familiar in the developed countries as a wartime emergency measure does not provide a model for inflation control in economies experiencing a substantial amount of 'permanent' inflationary pressure in the course of development. Three essential differences stand out:

1. Control environment and administration: Inflation control in the advanced countries is generally a temporary, and fairly simple, addition to an already well-articulated public and private market information system. In the developing countries, no such system exists. Little reliance can therefore be placed on established reporting practices or routine self-policing devices. Nor can appeals to patriotism or emergency requirements be expected to have effect over the long term. On the contrary, where basic supply and demand imbalances remain uncorrected, exceptions to the basic control pattern tend to multiply, leakages expand, and the need for compulsion increases. Crucial to the success of any control system is that the policies announced be, in fact, carried out, and that control administration be honest and open, in appearance as well as in practice. The personnel, procedures and knowledge required for efficient price control are rare enough in advanced countries, and inevitably lacking in less-developed ones.

2. Diverting inflationary pressures: As important as the selection of items and prices to be controlled is the availability of activities into which inflationary purchasing power can be diverted. The alternative of accumulating liquid savings or securities is seldom viable, because savings and investment institutions themselves are not generally available or accepted as reliable, because liquid savings are peculiarly susceptible to taxation or confiscation, and because of the inflation psychosis. Traditional means of hoarding, such as the purchase of jewels and precious metals, usually provide a sufficient outlet only for small savers. A major outlet for savings in the non-communist countries in recent years has been urban real estate, particularly housing. Although speculative booms in construction have been frequently criticized as diverting resources from primary development tasks, they are probably preferable to black market financing or simple capital flight. The high labour content of construction results in the diffusion of purchasing

power among lower income groups, and construction typically uses large proportions of domestic rather than imported materials. For these reasons, the maintenance of an outlet, such as private building, for inflationary pressures may be a significant element of inflation control in other sectors of the economy.

3. Decontrol: The idea that inflation control contributes importantly to the development process implies that controls can be relaxed as development proceeds. Again, unlike wartime control systems, this relaxation is not likely to occur all at once, or as a result of changes in external or economy-wide factors, but rather gradually and selectively as particular development goals are attained. It is a particular danger of price control systems that they will not be abandoned when their immediate purpose is served, but will rather live on to serve other purposes. In many countries – not all of them particularly underdeveloped – vestiges of post-World War II price control systems may be observed still in operation, but with their purposes changed to maintaining high and stable prices for some particular industry or trade rather than holding prices down and rationing short supplies.

Product quality

The most numerous type of market controls in the advanced countries are those concerned with merchandise quality. Standardized grades and labels, minimum health and safety standards, regulation sizes and packages are pervasive throughout both industry and agriculture, and provide a basis in law and language for long-term market development among diverse suppliers and users separated by great distances. The developing countries, by contrast, have been slow to perceive the value of standardized quality for its own sake, and quick to note the high, but frequently once-for-all, costs associated with standardization. Such controls as do exist in the developing countries arise primarily from the demand of foreign buyers. For example, developing countries coming into association with the European Common Market are compelled to grade and standardize their raw material and agricultural exports in order to obtain favourable market access conditions. The success of Israel and Lebanon in the export of fresh produce, chiefly to western Europe, has been based very firmly on high and uniform product standards, established and enforced by joint government and private controls. By contrast, a substantial element in the deteriorating world market position of Egyptian cotton has been the virtual collapse of the classification and grading system within the country.

With rare exceptions, the potential contribution of quality standardization to domestic market expansion in developing countries has not as yet been perceived. When such controls are found, they are frequently directed at maintaining *low* rather than high quality items in domestic consumption, either as a protection device for specific industries or as an element of price control. For example, in many countries controls over commercial baking that were originally established, at least in part, as a consumer protection device have been gradually transformed into a system of varying the quality of bread so that the price can be maintained constant in money terms. Another feature of the general neglect of quality maintenance within market control systems is that imbalances among prescribed market results – e.g. volume, prices, etc. – may work themselves out in the form of quality changes, typically unfavourable and, in the end, expensive.

Redistribution

Quite apart from increasing the extent of market utilization, changing the volume of goods, prices or quality levels, market controls may aim at the redistribution of goods and income among various classes of market participants. Redistribution is usually thought of in terms of the availability of consumption goods and services to particular economic or social groups, especially those that have been historically disadvantaged or for whom a particularly strong economic stimulus is desired. However, redistribution applies equally well to the supply side of the market, where it involves changes in the opportunity to make sales, particularly under favourable selling conditions. In addition, altering marketing arrangements so as to remove the monopoly position of middlemen or credit sources is also a redistributional policy.

The standard means of changing the distribution of a flow of goods among potential suppliers and users is to impose a licensing or rationing system which limits, or even eliminates, the participation of individual sellers and buyers in the market. Rationing, in effect, adds a second medium of exchange – the ration card – to the primary medium of money. Either both may be required to effect a transaction, or the card may substitute for money in making limited quantities of merchandise available at special prices. Redistribution may also be accomplished by the compulsory channelling of particular supplies of (or demands for) merchandise into new directions, or by prohibiting certain classes of traders from buying, selling, or otherwise participating in the market.

Miscellaneous welfare goals

A large number of specific market control activities have as their objective the protection of individual groups of consumers, producers, traders or professionals from the rigours of competition or the pressures of economic and social change. Controls of this type seem to be more prevalent in the upper range of developing countries, where certain minimum standards of life have been achieved by particular groups in the population and where the rate and direction of development has not been such as to assure these groups of their continued good fortune. As a result, protective restrictions designed to freeze patterns of doing business or trade conditions in the interest of specific groups are enacted. Although numerous in detail and annoying in operation, controls of this type are probably of limited long-run effect. Their principal impact may be in the rate of adaptation of the economy and its socio-political character. For example, the political power of small shop-keepers and their landlords has had obvious effects on the speed and pattern of introduction of mass retailing in most countries, but does not seem to have prevented it in any instance. Indeed, in spite of opposition, mass retailing in many countries appears to have been introduced more rapidly than demand conditions warranted.

Market control methods

Three principal methods are used, either separately or in combination, in the developing countries in order to attain these control objectives. They are: (1) centralizing some key marketing function or activity in a state agency for control purposes; (2) establishing state enterprises to compete with private firms, or among themselves; and (3) supervising and regulating private marketing activities directly.

Key-function centralization is characteristic, for example, of foreign trade, and of domestic trade in raw materials and fresh produce in many countries. The function itself may be an essential element of the marketing process – as in the case of state-monopoly export trading companies, publicly administered central markets, or credit and storage facilities – or may be an additional function created purely for control purposes – as in the case of licences, permits and taxes. In any event, key-function centralization provides a device for monitoring the entire flow of market activity, and influencing the broad pattern of market results, without regulating them in detail. The most obvious variable subject to control is the total volume passing through trade channels; however, auxiliary regulations may easily alter merchandise quality and allocation among sources and uses as well. A particular strength of this control method is that prices and procedures at any centralized market level tend to become reference points for prices and procedures at other levels. Thus, by exerting control over the reference price, quality or volume, authorities can influence the entire marketing structure without concerning themselves in detail with its individual elements.

Like key-function centralization, market control through the competition of state and private enterprises also relies considerably on unrestricted market activity to work out results in specific detail. The role of the state enterprise is to provide a competitive alternative to the offerings of private traders; the latter are then brought into conformity by the forces of competition. This conformity may not, of course, involve identical behaviour by private and public enterprises. Rather, the public enterprises offer a norm against which the different quality, service, location and other features of the private firms can be evaluated. This type of market control is attractive because it avoids both compulsion and inspection. Its effective operation requires, however, that the market alternatives of the public enterprises be readily accessible throughout the market, and that customers be skilled in discovering and evaluating alternatives. The effectiveness of this type of control is limited by (1) the ability of the state enterprises to manage their own operations successfully in open competition, which is no mean task; and (2) the ability and willingness of private firms to conform to the control system rather than leave the market entirely. Evidently, the latter implies that controlled market results will not generally deviate very far from those that would otherwise occur. However, one of the special strengths of the state enterprise is that it can vary its activities from time to time and market to market in such a way as to offset particular adverse developments in the short-run. The massing of available supplies in order to maintain price stability in areas temporarily subject to shortage or excess demand is a particular example.

Direct regulation of market results through supervision and enforcement by government agencies, who in fact perform no essential marketing function themselves, is undoubtedly the most common market control method. Even in developing countries where most production activity is concentrated in state-owned enterprises, a formal structure of price and related controls over some substantial part of domestic trade is usually found. In addition, elaborate systems of permits and licences, and other *ad hoc* regulations, are characteristic. Many of these control activities are directly related to foreign trade, either preventing high prices for scarce imports or maintaining low prices for import substitutes. Also, these regulatory systems constitute a kind of reserve force; they may be without appreciable effect on market activity at any moment of time, but they can be invoked on short notice if the need should arise. An important feature of such regulations is that they are subject to a considerable amount of administrative variability, which allows their effects to be somewhat more selective than their formal structure might indicate. For example, although formal two-price systems, whereby particular classes of buyers or sellers enjoy a favourable (unfavourable) position relative to others, are difficult to justify and maintain, *de facto* two-price systems can be easily operated by uneven enforcement of price controls.

The formal and administrative selectivity of direct controls are, however, the source of their greatest disadvantages as principal means of economic coordination. Detailed regulation requires close supervision and elaborate record-keeping, and thus control administration becomes expensive and onerous, even if desirable results are obtained. Further, the multiplication of exceptions and instances of uneven administration may eventually neutralize the effects of the system entirely. Finally, the very specificity of direct controls requires the fragmentation of control authority, with increasing possibilities of conflict and inconsistency among objectives and results.

Appraising control effectiveness

Given the multiplicity of control objectives and the complexity of techniques, it is little wonder that the effectiveness of market control activities is seldom carefully appraised. Operating authorities are generally satisfied with an 'it works' kind of evaluation, and – when control is obviously not working – to recommend the revision of objectives rather than of control methods. Although this approach can be easily criticized, it is difficult to specify criteria for appraising the effectiveness of controls in a development context, even at the conceptual level. If the combination of development effort and control is successful in changing underlying economic conditions, then a comparison of pre- and post-control market results does not provide an appropriate basis for judgement: the two situations will be different in too many important respects. A similar problem arises in the comparison of contemporaneous transactions taking place within and without the control system, since the results outside the system are likely to be influenced by it nonetheless. For example, uncontrolled prices may follow controlled prices because of the pressures of market competition, or, as in the case of black markets, may differ from them in direct proportion to the effectiveness of control. (That is, black market volume is small and price high *because* controlled market volume is large and price low.)

It is, in addition, misleading to think that market control systems can be evaluated entirely within a simple supply-and-demand context. Marketing activities are heavily institutional, and thus strongly condition the way in which basic supply and demand forces come into being and interact. Market controls therefore change not only the specific results of market activity but also the way in which these results are obtained. Market operations also involve a dynamic mechanism, so that a unique and non-reversible sequence of results is generated over time. As a consequence, even short-lived controls may produce long-term effects, both desired and otherwise.

A final problem in appraising control effectiveness is that market controls comprise a part of the total political and social policy structure, and generate overtones and reactions within that structure. In a society politically committed to the principle of strong central administration, even relatively ineffective market controls may perform some function as elements of a comprehensive scheme of economic planning. By contrast, in less centralized societies, even fairly effective market controls may prove to be social and political liabilities.

References

BAUER, P. T., and YAMEY, B. S. (1954); 'The economics of marketing reform', *J. Pol. Econ.*, vol. 62, pp. 210–35.

HELLEINER, G. K. (1966), 'Marketing boards and domestic stabilization in Nigeria', *Rev. of Econ. and Stat.*, vol. 48, pp. 69–78.

11 H. B. Thorelli

The Guarded Capitalism of South Africa

Adapted from H. B. Thorelli, 'South Africa: its multi-cultural marketing system', *Journal of Marketing*, vol. 32, no. 2, 1968, pp. 40–47.

It is tempting to liken South Africa to Italy as regards the extent of government ownership, direct regulation, and general economic planning. In both countries, too, one finds sprawling, government-operated industrial development corporations. Although the parallel could easily be taken too far, one might say that the special set of policies for regional economic development of Southern Italy have their South African correspondence in the set of regulations enforcing the policy of economic apartheid. The key difference, of course, is that while the special policies in the former nation focus on economic integration, their aim in the latter is to promote separate development of the different races.

Separate development

Some measures of importance to South African long-term economic, political and social development should be mentioned. Foremost – and perhaps most objectionable in the minds of foreign critics – are the restrictions on geographical and occupational mobility. In principle the native population in the Bantu homelands is expected to remain there, while at the same time barriers have been raised against the influx of additional white traders and white capital. The Bantu Investment Corporation and several other government funds have been established to promote the development of Bantu trade and industry in the homelands. It is, however, fair to say that this process – as well as the takeover of existing white establishments in these areas by Bantu businessmen – is a very slow one.

To provide employment opportunities for homeland Bantu outside agriculture and to provide a means for white capital to assist in rural Bantu economic development, the government has encouraged the establishment of so-called border industries on the outside fringes of the Bantustans, to which Bantu employees may commute. In 1967, the government was given the power – if it wishes to use it – to force new firms, or extensions of old ones, in several industries to locate in the border areas. While in the short term the border industries contribute to higher standards of living among the rural Bantu, it is still an open question whether in the long run they will promote or retard indigenous economic development in the homelands.

The urban economy has reached a level of development which simply could not be sustained without the large-scale engagement of Bantu employees. The policy of separate development in this case requires the Bantu to live in special locations on the fringes of existing cities. Regardless of his views of apartheid in general, a fair observer would have to admit that the physical appearance of many of these townships is a good deal more pleasant than that of the ghettoes of the large cities in the United States. Whites are not freely allowed in these towns. Indigenous development of the Bantu towns is hampered by regulations and by the habit of the Bantu to make most nonfood purchases in the downtown areas, where most of the urban Bantu spend their working day anyway. In effect, the Bantu towns presently represent a sort of 'slumber suburbs'. In the cities, occupational mobility has been limited by the traditional policy of job reservation, by which certain skilled trades have been reserved for the white man, and, conversely, certain manual jobs for non-whites.

Most insightful observers seem to agree that continued rapid economic development in South Africa will call for more congregation rather than for rigid separation of the racial groups. While especially in the area of job reservation economic forces have broken down many of the old barriers, the Nationalist Party majority is unequivocally committed to a policy of apartheid; from time to time new measures have been enacted to enforce this policy. The long-term dynamics of the tensions between economic development and political philosophy is the basic element of uncertainty on the South African scene.

The government of markets

As in other countries, several aspects of government regulations immediately affect marketing men in South Africa. By and large, these measures seem to have been inspired by three major objectives of public policy:

1. The stimulation of industrial development.
2. The achievement of dynamic economic equilibrium.
3. The control of monopoly and the protection of consumers.

Actually, most regulations have been intended to promote several objectives at once. Regulations of special relevance to marketing include tariffs and direct import controls. While until well into this decade international trade policy was dictated mostly by the urge to promote local industry of the 'import replacement' type, the government in recent years has found it natural to reduce trade barriers as a means of combating inflation. Again, maladjustment in the balance of payments has prompted reversals in liberalization from time to time. Generally, South Africa has felt freer to use foreign trade regulation as a flexible tool of economic policy than most developed nations. There is, however, wide agreement that these control powers have been equitably administered.

Exports of most farm products are controlled by an array of agricultural marketing boards. Many of the most essential foods involved in these schemes (such as corn and wheat flour, sugar, milk and other dairy products) are subject to price control in the domestic market. Under the Price Control Act the government enjoys considerable discretion in specifying items to be controlled at any given time. Ever since World War II the overall trend, subject to much temporary fluctuation, has been one of gradual relaxation. The current list of products under control is well-nigh exhausted if to the products just mentioned we add bread, coal, fertilizers, certain iron and steel manufacturers, petroleum and rubber products, and rents. Controlled goods must be price-marked.

Monopoly control in South Africa is directed toward the abuse of the economic power of monopolies and cartels rather than toward the existence of such power. The spirit of enforcement has not been remarkably vigorous, but the existence of the legislation is well known to most businessmen. By the end of 1967, the government was expected to publish a report on resale price maintenance. In the meantime, the liquor industry has agreed to refrain from boycotting a dealer who would not adhere to a resale price agreement.

The prime concern of the excellent South African Bureau of Standards is the promotion and administration of industrial standardization. However, it has also launched a seal of quality for locally manufactured goods guaranteed to possess certain minimal properties or to have been made by certain specified processes. The Hire-Purchase Act of 1965 is strongly consumer-oriented. Trading stamps are illegal as are certain types of promotional lotteries. As yet, organized consumer protection by public and private means has not progressed as far in South Africa as in most of Western Europe and the United States, although a government-sponsored Consumer Council was set up in 1970.

Part Four
Market Structure: Demand Analysis and Market Resource Base

The attention in Part Four is still on structural factors. The thrust is demand analysis – the most critical aspect of market intelligence. A subsidiary focus is the market resource base, comprising the availability of transportation and warehousing, marketing research and advertising agencies, sales promotion media and other facilitating aspects of the local marketing environment.

It being out of the question to deal with individual product markets in any detail here, we have chosen to treat markets in industrialized countries in terms of a generalized discussion of consumer styles of life. Intercultural differences are a great deal more significant in terms of consumer than industrial goods markets. Reading 12, by Katona, Strumpel and Zahn, analyses individual and social structures in various European countries and contrasts them to the United States, all the while tracing implications to local consumption patterns. Katona and co-authors infer that consumption habits in the EEC are still far from homogeneous. This is further documented in the Readers Digest Association Survey of Europe Today (1970), a useful compendium of data. Reading 13 by Anderson and Sharpe examines the current differentiation and individualization of life styles in the United States. It is also of interest as possibly portending developments in Western Europe and other affluent cultures.

The first part of Reading 14, by Lipson and Lamont, discusses marketing opportunities in the LDCs in broad-gauge terms, while the second section points up the importance of a thorough examination of the local marketing infrastructure before entering such markets. These authors include the availability of foreign exchange, local sources of supply and distribution systems in the local marketing resource base. The final section of this article is a prelude to Part Five on marketing strategy. Reading 15, by

Moyer, introduces some quantitative stringency in the analysis of markets in the LDCs. While no doubt a mind-stretching experience for non-quantitatively oriented readers, the article is included as a sophisticated example from a large body of writings on the use of quantitative methods in marketing research and analysis. As Moyer indicates, one of the limitations on the use of such techniques is the limited availability and reliability of data in many countries. In the LDCs especially *caveat emptor* is the rule of prudence in the use of the local data base.

Reading 16, by Wells, analyses the international 'migrations' of industrial products. The thesis is that a new industrial product typically emerges in the US or some other advanced country. As the product reaches the rapid growth phase of its life cycle in the country of origin, exports begin to build up to country B. After a while demand abroad is sufficient to call for local production in B. In a third phase facilities in the country of origin and in country B compete in export marketing in country C. In a final phase, plant facilities in country B or C – prevailing on lower labor costs – are ready to export back to the country of origin, that is, the international product life cycle is complete. The theme is familiar – as are several variations on it. The strategic implication is that it behooves marketers to plan with the international product life cycle in mind. This is desirable both to capitalize on natural opportunities and to predict and forestall competitive inroads.

12 G. Katona, B. Strumpel and E. Zahn

The Sociocultural Environment

Adapted from G. Katona, B. Strumpel and E. Zahn (eds.), *Aspirations and Affluence*, McGraw-Hill, 1971, pp. 27–38.

The economic environment of the Western consumer is fairly similar in all highly developed countries. To be sure, there are differences in the economic position of the different countries as well as in their rate of progress. Yet they all participate in the trend toward improved well-being and increased opportunities for educational and occupational advancement.

Nevertheless, studies have revealed substantial differences in the economic behavior of the people in different nations and have found those differences to be related to differences in their attitudes and expectations. These attitudes and expectations, in turn, may be traced to differences in the cultural and social structure of the different countries.

Whether or not individuals tend to take advantage of economic opportunities and participate in the modern affluent society may depend to a large extent on the traditions and behavioral patterns of the groups to which they belong. This article reviews some of the cross-national differences in social behavior the origin of which may be found in historical experiences and traditions and, most of all, in different roles imposed by society on the individual. The attempt to explain differences in people's responses to economic and social opportunities in various countries also requires an analysis of social stratification. Modern societies used to be divided into various classes based upon such considerations as wealth or income, education, religion, and occupation, particularly with regard to whether one's occupation involved manual or nonmanual work. Recent observers of the social scene have noted a tendency away from the conventional stratification into upper and lower classes and toward a more uniform society characterized by such middle-class values as making provisions and plans for the future, achievement in one's occupation and advancement in one's career, and education for one's children. Without attempting to deny that there is a certain degree – in the United States even a great degree – of this process of the 'embourgeoisement' of manual workers taking place in all affluent countries, it should be pointed out that it is far from universal. Indeed, the data presented in this article offer striking evidence of a rather surprising degree of rigidity among certain groups in certain countries in remaining within the life styles of their parents.

Nevertheless, modern society is no longer a class society with fixed categories of a social hierarchy. There is considerable social mobility. In feudal or early industrial societies, tradition-oriented patterns of behavior were transmitted from the older to the younger generation, and upward mobility was restricted to a small number of people. Today standards of behavior are often challenged by the young, and the authority of tradition is increasingly being replaced by the influence of the mass media and of reference groups – peer groups or groups to which an individual wants to belong. The latter are coming to function as initiators and transmitters of new ways of behavior in the complicated processes of social interaction. The extent to which traditions are transmitted from one generation to the next varies from country to country, as do degrees of class consciousness with its concomitant attitudes and expectations.

Trust in people and self-reliance

Participative behavior and adaptation to change are facilitated if the social environment is perceived as friendly and if there is trust in people and confidence in the institutions. Adaptive behavior in modern society means investing time, money, and energy in human interaction. Experience in human interaction therefore is becoming increasingly important. Success depends on the approval of other people. Those who endeavor to succeed in a large organization, who build up a business, or who run for public office can prevail only if they can get along with people and if people respond favorably to them. The ability and willingness of people to establish rapport with others, often with remote and anonymous others, is a prerequisite in the network of social roles in modern society. This is in contrast to traditional societies where interaction among people has been more limited to enduring and intimate personal relationships.

Belief in a benign human environment appears to be more widespread in the United States than in Germany or Italy. Civic competence and pride in the political system characterize the political culture of the United States. In contrast, a lack of general attachment to the political system and an orientation as a subject rather than a participant are common in Germany.

Evidence for these statements has been provided by a cross-cultural study of political attitudes conducted by Almond and Verba (1963). The authors used questions developed by Morris Rosenberg to measure 'faith in people' (Rosenberg, 1956). The American and British respondents are at the low end of the continuum on measures of social distrust and at the high end on the measures of trust (Table 1). In all four countries confidence in the human environment tends to increase among the better educated and the economically more privileged sectors of the population.

A variety of additional findings by Almond and Verba is relevant in our context. In the Anglo-Saxon countries, young people more frequently behave as members of a cooperative unit than in Germany and Italy. The proportion of respondents who recall

Table 1 **Social trust and distrust** percentage of respondents who expressed agreement with five statements in four countries

Statements	United States	United Kingdom	Germany	Italy
Statements of distrust:				
'No one is going to care much what happens to you, when you get right down to it'	38	45	72	61
'If you don't watch yourself, people will take advantage of you'	68	75	81	73
Statements of trust:				
'Most people can be trusted'	55	49	19	7
'Most people are more inclined to help others than to think of themselves first'	31	28	15	5
'Human nature is fundamentally cooperative'	80	84	58	55
Number of respondents	970	963	955	995

Source: Almond and Verba, 1963, p. 213.

having influenced family decisions when they were about sixteen years old differs: 73 per cent of Americans, 69 per cent of British, 54 per cent of Germans, and only 48 per cent of Italians remember having had some influence. When asked whether they had felt free to complain of unfair treatment in school, or whether they had ever actually complained, American respondents answered in the affirmative far more often than any other nationality.

In the United States and Britain, the more cooperative attitudes of small groups and the prevailing belief that people are generally cooperative, trustworthy, and helpful have consequences for political behavior. Respondents who trust others are more wont to believe in their ability to do something about unjust local or even national regulations and feel inclined to form groups with others to join in political activity. 'General social trust is translated into politically relevant trust,' conclude Almond and Verba. Thus the proportion of people who feel they have some say is considerably higher in the Anglo-Saxon than in other countries. Only 28 per cent of all Italians and 38 per cent of Germans, but 62 per cent of the British and 75 per cent of Americans feel they personally can do something about national politics. About 13 per cent of Italians, 22 per cent of Germans, 43 per cent of the British, but 74 per cent of Americans say they would enlist the aid of an informal group to influence an unjust local regulation.

A greater sense of participation and involvement, of responsibility and self-reliance manifests itself also in people's behavior in their work. Thus attitudes of British as compared to American and Canadian workers have often been criticized. When workers finish a job in Great Britain, 'they wait for the foreman to tell them what to do next. It is his responsibility; they do not worry about output at all. They work the slow steady gait they have been taught to maintain by their unions and fellow workers. In the United States and Canada they would not wait until they ran out of work to ask the foreman what to do next' (Ord, 1963).

Related evidence has been produced by an investigation carried out by Britain's Imperial Chemical Industries Ltd, the purpose of which was to discover why productivity was so much higher in the United States than in Britain. It is not because Americans work harder, the study concluded. It is because American hourly workers desire and expect to be personally responsible for much of their work. There are fewer managers and supervisors. A sense of involvement with the fortunes and prospects of the company and the units where they work is reflected in the workers' awareness of the need for efficiency and profitability. Flexibility in the allocation of work results in more interesting jobs. 'American individual employees are self-reliant. They are frequently motivated by a desire for self-improvement, to seek training and education which increase their skill and knowledge, and the chances of advancement to better jobs' (*Financial Times*, 1966).

Lack of self-confidence and of aspirations, it should be noted, is found not only among blue-collar workers but also among certain groups of white-collar employees in Europe, as demonstrated by a survey of Dutch administrative employees carried out by J. Berting in nine big companies in Amsterdam. Many feel locked in the organization, and there is little attachment to the job. By and large they rate the opportunities for occupational advancement high, agreeing that 'hardworking people with ability can get ahead.' Despite this overall opinion they perceive a definite barrier separating them from the upper-middle class of department heads and managers and view their own specific chances for advancement as confined to the level of their present administrative duties.

Two other extensive studies on the attitudes and behavior of Dutch blue-collar workers and white-collar employees, respectively, carried out recently by P. J. A. Ter Hoeven and J. H. Buiter have supplied further data on the lack of occupational and educational aspirations in Holland. Ter Hoeven concludes that the Dutch workers have become affluent consumers but that the higher level of consumption has hardly changed their mentality. Social subordination in the work organization continues to be prevalent. Both Ter Hoeven and Buiter found that people are by and large satisfied with their income and that they do not indulge in invidious comparisons with the income of other groups of people. Much of what has been called the managerial gap between the United States and Western Europe appears to consist not of a difference in know-how and organization but of a difference in occupational aspirations and in the employees' sense of self-reliance.

Interestingly enough, the persistence in Europe of traditional values of different social classes has not impeded occupational mobility. The process of industrialization, the movement from farms to cities, indeed the overall pattern of occupational mobility appear to be much the same in all industrial countries. This is an important finding as it permits the conclusion that it is not impossible for traditional ways of behavior and patterns of authority to survive even in the midst of changes in the structure of the labor force. The move from manual to nonmanual jobs does not automatically result in the emergence of more dynamic forms of economic behavior.

Some indication of the extent to which patterns of obedience, self-confinement, and authority are being preserved in spite of economic progress and increasing social opportunities can be found in cross-national comparisons of educational standards and of patterns of childrearing. Recent studies, for instance, have shown that in many ways American children are treated differently from English children, just as middle-class children are treated differently from working-class children in both cultures. In the working classes, discipline tends to be inconsistent and sporadic, penalties and controls being imposed more for the convenience of the parents than for the welfare of the child. The American family is more egalitarian than the English family. The difference in the strength of parental authority might be even greater if Americans were to be compared with German and Italian families.

Working-class patterns and middle-class values

International differences in cultural patterns are most pronounced among blue-collar workers. Among white-collar employees and especially among people in professional or managerial positions living in different countries, differences in attitudes and in behavior are much less noticeable. The higher the education the less likely it is that people will be affected by the particular history and culture of their country. There are striking differences in the amount of higher education prevalent in different nations, and they in turn can be traced at least in part to the lag in the educational attainment and aspirations of the blue-collar segments of the population.

Differences in the economic behavior of blue-collar and white-collar workers in Europe are worth studying. Do lower-class patterns of living resist modernization to a greater extent in Europe than in the United States? Have prosperous manual workers in Europe – unlike their American counterparts – failed to acquire new social perspectives and modes of behavior which reflect middle-class rather than working-class values? There is no doubt that in terms of income the relative position of manual workers in all affluent countries has improved in the last few decades. Many blue-collar families have acquired incomes comparable to or even larger than those of many members of the lower white-collar middle class – the families of clerks, small shopkeepers, or teachers. There do, of course, exist differences in security and in income expectations. The white-collar worker is more likely to be promoted and less liable to be laid off in times of recession.

Several European studies have provided evidence for persistent differences in the patterns of living of manual and nonmanual workers even when their economic situation is rather similar. The British sociologists Goldthorpe and Lockwood speak of 'a far-reaching adaptation of the old working class subculture to a considerably changed physical and social context, rather than of any significant move towards a middle class mode of existence' (Goldthorpe and Lockwood, 1962). These authors disagree with others who have somewhat hastily assumed that with the coming of the affluent society the working class is being outmoded, that is, that manual workers are becoming indistinguishable from other groups in society. Goldthorpe and Lockwood find that although, with higher incomes and less threat of being unemployed, the workers have become more acquisitive and more concerned with maximizing their income, they have nonetheless not adopted middle-class attitudes, values, and modes of behavior. In Britain even affluent blue-collar workers, living in new communities, seem to have become more concerned with the style of their domestic living and with status distinctions between 'rough' and 'respectable' families than in moving across class lines. Segregation from the middle class still persists in neighborhood relations and in leisure activities. At the end of the 1950s in Britain only the TV set was equally represented among working-class and middle-class families. The washing machine was owned by 40 per cent of middle-class but only 24 per cent of working-class families; the respective figures for cars were 45 to 15 per cent, and for refrigerators 28 to 6 per cent.

Similar findings have been made in Germany. The proportion of middle-class families who own four standard items of durables (automobiles, refrigerators, cameras, and telephones) increased by twenty percentage points from 1953 to 1958, whereas ownership of the same package among working-class families increased by only seven points. In the highest income class within the manual group only 18 per cent owned all four items, while the proportion was somewhat higher among white-collar families in the next lower income category. Where the middle class had an automobile, the working class tended to have a motorcycle, a motorbike, or a motorscooter. When blue-collar families did buy automobiles, they tended to buy less expensive ones. These differences persisted even when differences in income level were controlled in the statistical analysis.

Homes and home entertainment devices like television sets and electric record players, in Germany as in England, rank relatively high on the scale of lower-class values. Whereas entertainment of middle-class families more frequently takes place outside the home, the radius of social contacts of workers is more limited. German blue-collar workers even after achieving a relatively high income level, spend less money on family outings, on cars, entertainment outside the home, and on vacations than do white-collar workers. Television viewing all but monopolized the entertainment of the former. Food plays a very great role in working-class families, where common meals reflect family cohesion.

According to data collected by the authors in 1968 there were hardly any differences in ownership rates of TV sets in England and Holland, either among income groups or among blue- and white-collar people. In Germany low-income blue-collar workers had an even higher ownership rate of TV sets than low-income white-collar workers. Car ownership rises greatly with income in all three countries both among blue- and white-collar families. Nevertheless, sizable class differences also prevail in the rate of car ownership in Germany and England (see Table 2).

The slow pace of higher income European manual workers in acquiring middle-class symbols of consumption suggests a lack of incentives to advance in status. It testifies to the persistence of a ceiling to their goals and horizons. As Papitz and his collaborators observed in an investigation of the workers in a German steel plant, they ignore changed reality and their opportunities in it. There is a peculiar mistrust of 'those on the top', a feeling of being passive objects of decisions made in the upper-class power structure, and a retreat to the realm of leisure and television (Papitz, et al., 1961).

In the United States less rigid class differences and the tradition of social mobility have joined forces with the rapid economic growth to make for faster adjustment and lesser survival of class- or occupation-specific economic behavior. It should be said that the differences in this respect between America and Europe, though important, are differences in degree. In the first instance it must be acknowledged that in the United States too there prevails a fairly strong influence of the fathers' occupation and the fathers' education on their children's education and on at least

Table 2 **Relation of occupation and income to ownership of durables*** (percentages of families)

Country and Occupation	Own a car		Own a TV set	
	Low income	High income	Low income	High income
Germany:				
Blue collar	27	45	82	84
White collar	33	56	65	85
All respondents	25	50	77	84
England:				
Lower class	24	59	89	98
Middle class	44	71	95	96
All respondents	34	73	92	95
Holland:				
Blue collar	31	51	87	86
White collar	31	59	87	85
All respondents	26	56	84	85

* The income groups were selected according to the following annual disposable incomes:

Country	Low income	High income
Germany	7,200–9,599 DM	9,600–17,999 DM
England	Less than £1,200	£1,200–2,499
Holland	Less than 10,000 hfl.	10,000–21,000 hfl.

Source: surveys conducted by the authors in 1968.

their first jobs as well. The American business elite is disproportionately derived from Protestant, Anglo-Saxon, native-born, well-to-do families, although an increasing, if continuously small, proportion of business leaders do come from families other than this privileged group. Furthermore, according to studies by Richard F. Hamilton (1964), many American skilled workers are opposed to social mobility. Hamilton speaks of a 'stable working class commitment' among workers and of values partly independent of the dominant values of the larger society.

All this is not to deny that there is a trend in blue-collar modes of living toward middle-class patterns in all industrial societies. The spread of the automobile among manual workers during the 1960s is eloquent warning against a wholesale rejection of the convergence hypothesis. Yet middle-class living patterns spread slowly, and their diffusion appears to be much slower in some countries than in others.

Contributing to a change in orientation away from the confined standards and values of blue-collar living are increased leisure time and the movement of many workers to new housing developments remote from the old working-class districts. In new communities, working-class life is no longer characterized by intimacy and gregariousness. The home in which one was once allowed a limited amount of rest and recreation in reward for working hard has increasingly often become the focus of life. The job and the degree of involvement it requires is valued to the extent that it contributes to satisfying the desired goals, including consumption and leisure.

The increasing home commitment of the worker, the changing orientation from the sociability of the pub, club, backyard, and corner shop toward his home and family life is, as we have seen, closely connected with a strong concern with home comfort and entertainment, in particular to massive exposure to nonlocal, nonclass-bound mass media. TV, radio, and stereo set provide nonparochial, national, or regional information and entertainment contributing to quite a radical change in sources of influence, communication, and frames of reference.

It would be wrong to attribute the apparent lower level of aspirations in Europe exclusively to conservatism inherent in the traditional pattern of lower-class culture. It is necessary to consider as well the expectations with which Europeans are confronted today. Members of lower-income groups and of occupational groups with lower status are still expected by many people to behave in a manner appropriate to what was thought to be 'their place' in society.

There exists a variety of European behavior patterns in which differences among occupational groups are conspicuous. Important examples are habits of saving, especially in financial institutions, credit buying, and leisure-time pursuits on the one hand, and educational attainment and educational aspirations on the other hand. It may suffice here to call attention to some manifestations of role expectations in Europe, which sometimes conflict with the values and goals of individuals.

A survey conducted in Holland found many married women with attitudes favorable to taking a job outside the home. However, they refrained from doing so because of their belief that their husbands would be opposed. They also knew that holding an outside job was not in harmony with the traditional role of a married woman in the middle classes. Female employment is not valued as a positive achievement but is seen as a deviation from the common pattern; moreover, it is associated with a bad state of financial affairs at home. Although many women express dissatisfaction with these norms, only a few decide to ignore them. A similar role conflict has been observed in France by Chombart de Lauwe. In Germany social values define the role of the wife as a perfect housekeeper whose services cannot and should not be replaced by commercial products or services.

A further example are cultural taboos against credit buying. In Germany and Holland credit buying is widely perceived as living beyond one's means. The largest Dutch mail order company specializing in sales on credit uses unmarked packaging and unidentifiable trucks to make its deliveries!

Needless to say, in all Western societies strongly motivated individuals do go beyond the confines of traditional roles and norms. Cultural norms and values cannot be ignored in seeking an explanation of behavior and of cross-societal differences, but of course do not tell the whole story. Part of the story was found to reside in the attitudes, expectations, and aspirations of some individuals which appeared crucial in impelling them to cross lines and take themselves outside the social and economic patterns into which they had been born.

References

ALMOND, G. and VERBA, S. (1963), *Civic Culture: Political Attitudes and Democracy in Five Nations*, Princeton University Press.

The *Financial Times* (1966), 'What ICI discovered about productivity', 18 November.

GOLDTHORPE, J. H. and LOCKWOOD, D. (1962), 'Not so bourgeois after all', *New Society*, October–December, p. 181.

HAMILTON, R. F. (1964), 'The behavior and values of skilled workers' in A. B. Shostak and W. Gomberg (eds.), *Blue Collar World*, Prentice-Hall, p. 42.

ORD, L. C. (1963), *Industrial Frustration: Commonsense for Trade Unionists*, Mayflower, p. 54.

PAPITZ, H., BAHRDT, H. P., JÜRES, E. A. and KESTING, H. (1961), *Das Gesellschaftsbild des Arbeiters*, Mohr.

ROSENBERG, M. (1956), 'Misanthropy and political ideology', *Am, Soc. Rev.*, vol. 21, pp. 690 ff.

13 W. T. Anderson, Jr and L. K. Sharpe

The New American Marketplace: Life Style in Revolution

Adapted from W. T. Anderson, Jr and L. K. Sharpe, 'The new marketplace: life style in revolution', *Business Horizons*, vol. 14, 1971, pp. 43–50.

Product proliferation in the quarter-century since World War II has resulted in and from increasing materialism, but has also initiated and responded to other more basic reorientations in consumer priorities and values. The five typologies that will be proffered are overgeneralizations, yet suggest the diversity of motivations, methods, and objectives emerging on the American scene.

These differences are expressed in increasingly divergent patterns of consumption behavior. Kelley puts it this way: 'People are not as likely to see themselves as consumers in the future, but as something else – perhaps as individuals creating their own style of living by using the services of business.' Accordingly, he says, '... marketers are not selling isolated products which can be viewed as symbols; they are selling, or consumers are buying, a style of life or pieces of a larger symbol' (1963).

First, a segment of society has remained true to the traditional production orientation and techniques. The Traditionalists are essential because of the necessity of preserving and maintaining the productive mechanism. Alternatively, the Anarchists have been quick to point out the inadequacies, inequities, and inefficiencies of traditional institutions, but seem to offer no viable alternatives.

A third segment, the Liberated, seems involved in a frenetic search for freedom from perceived constraints of the existing social order. By contrast, the Reformers seem bent on perfecting the productive mechanism, providing the same goods but with lower social costs. A final segment may be termed the Counterculture. 'Counter' is perhaps too strong; this segment depends upon the existence of the mass production culture to satisfy basic economic wants, yet seems interested in producing individualized output without reference to traditional notions of economic efficiency. Its aim seems to be personalization and humanization.

What does all this mean for marketing in the decade ahead? In the sections which follow we shall examine some of the varied motives, methods, and changing life style requirements emerging within the American culture and speculate upon their implications for marketing in the 1970s.

The Traditionalists

The Traditionalists occupy most positions of authority, responsibility, and power within social institutions, including the government, the church, the legal structure, and the business community. They are definers and defenders of the conventional wisdom, and are widely distributed across the socioeconomic spectrum:

> ... the conventional wisdom is ... articulated on all levels of sophistication. At the highest levels of ... scholarship some novelty of formulation or statement is not resisted. On the contrary, considerable store is set by the device of putting an old truth in a new form, and minor heresies are much cherished. And the very vigor of minor debate makes it possible to exclude as irrelevant, and without seeming to be unscientific or parochial, any challenge to the framework itself. ... The defenders are able to say that the challengers of the conventional wisdom have not mastered [its] intricacies. Indeed these ideas can be appreciated only by a stable, orthodox, and patient man. ... The skeptic is disqualified by his very tendency to go brashly from the old to the new (Galbraith, 1964).

Ultimately, changing circumstances and events pose the greatest threat to conventional wisdom and, hence, to the Traditionalists. But, because of their myopic adherence to the conventions of the past, the Traditionalists are immune to much of it. Galbraith notes that, for them, the conventional ideas have great stability, even a mystique.

The Traditionalists fall into two segments, distinguishable not by the strength of their conviction in the conventional wisdom, but by their ability to articulate it. The Technocrats populate the upper occupational and socioeconomic strata and the suburbs of our major metropolitan areas. William H. Whyte, Jr, observed them behind a desk, behind a drink in 'classless' suburbia, and behind the great productive machinery of American industry. Anchored to the material artifacts and status of a production-oriented society, their stake in its orderly functioning is great.

The Technocrat is a true professional. His job tempers every facet of his life and synchronizes it to the automated sphere which he inhabits. Time is a constant denominator of work and leisure, increasing in importance as he rises through the organizational hierarchy. Social space becomes condensed as interactional politics figures heavily in occupational and status mobility.

In contrast, the Reactionaries, the second type of Traditionalists, are hard-working, hard-headed, red, white, and blue hardline advocates of the Protestant ethic and the American 'Way'. Their skills lie in their direct control of the machinery of industrial progress, and they are loyal to the factory, the union, their families, and the local pro teams. They fill the intermediate and lower occupational and socioeconomic strata, and the bars, bowling alleys, and stadiums on week ends.

Because of automation, this group is threatened with extinction and is becoming increasingly reactionary. This tendency may be seen in the feather-bedded railroad unions, the prohibitive admission requirements of craft unions, and in their paranoid view of change.

The marketing implications of the Traditionalists, like the group itself, are essentially divergent. The Technocrats are likely to reflect their occupation-status orientation in virtually all aspects of consumption behavior. Technology will be an overriding appeal. If a product is faster, newer, more luxurious, or offers greater convenience than existing products, it will likely be attractive to the Technocrats. Immersed in technology, they will consume technology for its own sake. Conspicuous examples of this orientation are found among the proliferating electronic and automatic gadgetry which clutters the kitchens, family rooms, dens, garages, and patios of suburban America.

The extended time-consciousness of the Technocrats has prompted significant product and institutional innovations for preserving or releasing time for alternative uses, for example, one-stop shopping centers, quick-service restaurants, automatic automobile washing installations, along with the multiplying array of convenience food products, appliances, and accessories. These trends will likely continue.

Reactionaries comprise what is basically the blue-collar socioeconomic strata. Under heavy pressure from automation and the fragmentation of traditional social goals, they exhibit considerable paranoia which extends into consumption behavior. Threatened, they have withdrawn into the past, a happier time when social position and status were relatively more secure, or at least less complicated. The Reactionaries represent, more than any other segment, an extension of the acquisitive trend. They are home-centered collectors, devoting considerable time, effort, and money to acquiring home appliances and home furnishings to rivet themselves in place.

A second implication for marketing stems from the frustration of this group. Any outlet for aggression – hopefully vicarious, as in spectator sports – is likely to find a ready market among the Reactionaries. Similarly, traditional appeals, such as masculinity and patriotism, are likely to be well-received.

The Anarchists

The Anarchists are volatile, vocal, rebellious, and sometimes revolutionary products of affluent middle America. A generation separates them from the Depression psychology of their parents.

Theirs is an experimental world of ideas, contrasting markedly with the cluttered, regimented, thing- and time-oriented world they grew up in. The generation gap is drawn and dramatized in them, and they evidence the deterioration of the nuclear family structure.

Apparently rootless, yet anchored to the symbols of change, contemporary causes find ready exponents among the Anarchists. They are characterized by a kind of seat-of-the-pants logic and a street-corner philosophy, with contemporary causes and the flag frequently visible. Their threat to the stability of existing social institutions is real, but they offer no real alternative to the present system, or even meaningful alterations of it. They are con – but not pro. The depth of their commitment against the existing order is somewhat suspect, yet their rejection of it seems to be their unifying concept.

Three points summarize the marketing implications of the existence of the Anarchists: they are anti-Establishment; they have no particular ideology of their own; and they possess considerable purchasing power, since their membership draws support from the Technocrats, primarily their parents, who are typically deeply embedded in the technocracy.

Although numerically small, the Anarchists offer an attractive market because of their purchasing power. Their attractiveness dims considerably, however, when one realizes that the lack of a unifying ideology makes the Anarchists subject to waves of fad and fashion. These fads are, as a practical matter, unpredictable, though contemporary entertainers frequently lead. The only sure thing is that they will occur frequently and will not support the technocratic establishment.

The Liberated

The Liberated represent a strange amalgam of frustrations and fantasies crystallizing into varied, frequently conflicting movements. They are essentially a bifurcated group, however, one petulant, one pathetic.

The do-your-own-thing contingent is the more visible of the two. Bra-burning women and male peacocks are their more spontaneous and colorful spokesmen. Equally significant are those advocating freer sexual expression and variations on monogyny. The Seekers, by contrast, are those excluded or displaced from the productive mechanism who seek fertile ground for new roots. They are displaced persons unwillingly swept up into a world in motion.

To the Traditionalists, the Do-your-own-thingers are bizarre, *avant-garde*, and 'far out'. They are viewed with some skepticism and even amusement, but are considered essentially harmless. In fact, because they do not activate the Traditionalists to antagonism, they exercise a subtle influence upon their backward counterparts.

The Do-your-own-thingers consider themselves very much 'in'. Yet, to some extent, this means being viewed as 'out' by the rustic majority. 'In' is generally interpreted as 'now' in liberated behavior and, hence, time is a significant dimension of their order of priorities and purposes. But their time-consciousness is different from that of the Technocrats. Apt to be innovators in dress and topical in conversation, they are less incendiary and more prudent than the Anarchists they observe with some fascination, if not downright admiration.

The Seekers are animated remnants of their past. Still anchored to the ruins of the mechanized technocracy that expelled them as unessential or obsolescent, they have been mobilized by the hope of finding stability and security somewhere else. Their mobility is different from that of the Technocrats, whose rootlessness stems from their professional orientation. Mobility for the Seekers is half escapism, half escapadism.

The Liberated are characterized by rootlessness. The essential difference between the Do-your-own-thing contingent and the Seekers is their reaction to it. The former, a small but affluent, cosmopolitan, and highly visible group, have become the arbiters of what is 'in'. Like the Anarchists, they are racked by fads – but the fads are seldom openly anti-Establishment. They seem to be highly independent innovators, as *Women's Wear Daily* discovered in the 'midi' debacle. For marketers, the group is an especially interesting testing ground for innovations, particularly in fashion, art, and entertainment.

The Seekers are quite different. Essentially lower socioeconomic status workers displaced by technology, they seek stability and security, but at lower cost. The Seekers have provided much of the impetus for apartment growth, mobile homes, and 'sun cities'. This group is sizable, if not affluent, and offers perhaps the greatest growth potential of any segment.

The Reformers

The Reformers embrace chameleons of varying hue, but most are recruited from among the well-educated status-occupational strata. In many ways indistinguishable from the Traditionalists, they share a common awareness of a harsh fact of life: 'Nothing in life is free.' Technological progress has a social cost. Reformers ask, 'Was the price too high?' Ignored for years, the ecological crisis gave new impetus to their warnings and brought new converts to their ranks.

Reformers occupy the same suburbs as their more conventional peers. But their materialism is tempered by an overriding concern with the fair distribution of the spoils of technocracy and the impact of technology upon society and the environment. For some, commitment means giving to the United Fund or buying unleaded gas. Others are deeply involved in social reform and environmental rehabilitation movements. In general, they bank on the future, but they would like to have a hand in shaping it.

A small but vocal segment, the Reformers are bent on perfecting the productive mechanism, both technically and socially. Technical improvements have been aimed at eliminating or reducing pollution in its many forms. Socially, the thrust has been toward equality in employment and educational opportunities and improved working conditions.

The implications of this group for business are obvious: reform or be reformed – since the group's power and influence seem to be spreading rapidly. For marketing, pollution control is likely to become big business, but probably not as big as promotion dealing with pollution control. Consumerism, now off and running, will likely extend into more and more areas of marketing activity.

The Counterculture

The Counterculture in some ways represents a throwback to an earlier era. The refugees who compose it exhibit a life style reflecting a personalized, humanized outlook on life. If the tempo of their lives seems somehow slower, it is because the synchronized machinery of technology propels the rest of us at an ever quicker pace.

The Counterculture is frequently mistaken for the Anarchists, or vice versa. At least they look the same – to the Traditionalists, the Liberated, and the Reformers. Their decision to get off the mechanized merry-go-round to seek more direct control over the products of their labor was a response to a growing feeling of nonexistence in the collectivized, complex, and controlling institutions within which most of us live and work.

Interestingly, the hand-wrought artifacts of the Counterculture bring exorbitant prices on the market. Perhaps the more conventional people who buy them are nostalgically reminded of the good old days when life was less complicated. Or perhaps 'straight' people share a common curiosity about the freaks who occupy the side shows along the polished chrome and plastic corridors of affluent America. Whichever, it all works out rather well for the Counterculture. The price of nonconformity is high.

Currently the Counterculture is a small, impoverished group, which merits close attention as a bellwether. Their life style is anathema to profit margins and turnover.

This group supports itself in communes and co-ops, or in other loosely structured family arrangements, maintaining a simplified life-style. They are not truly independent of the dominant culture – the technocracy. But their dependence is confined to necessities and to a few selected, symbolic luxuries. Their highly personalized handicrafts find a ready market, especially among the Anarchists and Do-your-own-thing group. And their demand for individualized products has filtered into other strata of society. The extent to which the Counterculture's life-style finds other advocates is a key marketing variable for the 1970s.

Accelerating change was the hallmark of the 1960s; the decade ahead will see the pace and pulse quicken. With accelerating change will come increased fragmentation of the American social structure.

We have identified and characterized five major social movements emerging on the American scene, each responding differently to the growing insufficiency of traditional institutions and objectives to the altered conditions of modern living. The divergent motives, methods, and goals of these movements have crystallized in varied, often contradictory life-style patterns expressed in diversified configurations of consumption behavior.

What does it all mean for marketing? We have suggested a few possibilities. But for the marketing executive who must plan for a future clouded by revolutionizing change, surveillance is the key. The ability to extrapolate continuities and trends in the confusion of constant change is the only effective antidote for future shock.

References

GALBRAITH, J. K. (1964), *The Affluent Society*, The New American Library, Inc., p. 19; Penguin, 1971.
KELLEY, E. J. (1963), 'Discussion', *Proceedings: Winter Conference, American Marketing Association*, pp. 170 and 168.

14 H. A. Lipson and D. F. Lamont

Marketing Opportunities and Marketing Infrastructure in the Less Developed Countries

Adapted from H. A. Lipson and D. F. Lamont, 'Marketing policy decisions facing international marketers in the LDCs', *Journal of Marketing*, vol. 33, 1969, pp. 24–31.

This article will show marketers how to make proper marketing decisions within the less developed countries (LDCs) of the world. LDCs are those countries which have a per capita national income of less than $500 per year. Their middle class is small; the majority of the people are poor. Markets are highly fragmented in terms of income, social class, language and tribal differences, and other socioeconomic characteristics. The institutional structure needed to integrate these markets is organized on a very inefficient basis or is nonexistent.

Marketers have to deal with these conditions in setting policy decisions that will lead to profits. They are faced with impoverished economies whose governments seek change. National economic plans drawn up to formalize the desire for greater economic prosperity give marketers an indication as to how they can support the public goals of the country in which they are doing business, and at the same time find new avenues for marketing success. Examples of adaptations in marketing policies to fit local governmental and cultural circumstances are presented below from experiences actually encountered within the underdeveloped world. India, Nigeria, and Mexico were selected for presentation simply because they show that the marketing adaptation problem is not bound by geography, cultural differences, or stages of economic growth. The problem exists for markets in Asia, Africa, and Latin America.[1]

Analysis of market opportunities

First, given the paucity of information and its relative unreliability, marketers are faced with the problems of estimating customer

1. The results presented in this paper are a part of a research project carried out in the International Business Program of the Graduate School of Business at the University of Alabama. Two graduate students, John W. Roquemore and Richard H. Kenyon, were responsible for the basic findings on India and Nigeria.

markets from gross data sources. Means are available to do so, and estimates of potential markets through production figures converted into apparent consumption figures provide a marketer with useful analytical information. The knowledge that 5 per cent of India's 550 million population, or twenty-eight million people, have incomes that give them the buying power of the average American should suggest to marketers that it is imperative for them to get in early in India's industrialization and market development. Such a market size in fact represents an affluent market that is just a little larger than the Canadian market. If marketers only had a knowledge of India's per capita national income, they more than likely would have overlooked this 'well-to-do' potential consumer market within the sea of a traditional society.

Second, such national estimates must be tempered with a qualitative understanding of the real regional and cultural differences that exist within the LDCs. The boundaries of most Indian states were drawn to represent the local dominance of a particular subcultural language. Before the war between Nigeria and Biafra, Nigeria had been divided into four regional areas; although in each area one major tribe dominated the others, 200 different languages are still spoken among the fifty million people of Nigeria. In West Africa, language differences reflect such wide cultural differences that only a very few products can bridge the gap successfully. Such simple things as the print on cotton fabrics fail to gain sufficient consumer acceptance for economy-of-scale purposes, because there are so many ideas as to what is right and proper. Market size in Nigeria is so small that marketers develop a market at their own peril if they do not know beforehand the real size of their potential market.

English is used as the *lingua franca* along with Hindi in India and Hausa in Nigeria. Spanish has played the same role in Mexico, but now it is slowly coming into full time use among the remaining three or four million Mexicans who speak different Indian languages. Language, therefore, plays a different role in Mexico for marketers. Marketers can be sure that the areas in which the Indian languages predominate are for the most part outside the developing sectors of the Mexican market economy.

The real opportunities for marketers lie in regional and cultural market segments rather than in thinking about a broad national market opportunity. For each market segment, marketers should determine available income, effective buying power, propensity to buy, economic awareness for consumption increases, and those other socioeconomic characteristics that will give them the size of their potential market within highly fragmented national economies.

Third, an analysis of market opportunities will be complete only when marketers take into consideration the current shifts in governmental attitude on import-substitution industries, incentives for new investment, taxes and social security payments, and the many other items that will markedly affect whether the business operates at a profit or at a loss. Marketers should pay careful attention to changes in the administrative rules governing market entry. For example, by reading India's Second Five Year Plan (1956–1961), marketers found that certain industries were to be the exclusive responsibility of the Indian government. (This group includes munitions, atomic energy, iron and steel, heavy engineering and heavy electrical plant, coal, oil, most mining, aircraft, air transport, railways, shipbuilding, communications, and electrical generation and distribution.) A second group was listed for gradual state ownership. (This group includes some mining, aluminum, machine tools, ferro-alloys and tool steels, heavy chemicals, essential drugs, fertilizers, synthetic rubber, and road and sea transport.) All other industries were left to private-sector enterprises for competitive market behavior. As the plan was carried out, it became apparent that the Indian government's Hindustan Antibiotics factory and Tata's, an Indian private-sector drug enterprise, could not meet the growing demand for drugs; Merck, Sharpe and Dohme was given permission to enter a market that formerly had been closed to foreign private-sector enterprises. A similar situation developed in the production and distribution of fertilizers. The demand for fertilizers increased as the need for Indian agriculture increased, and Armco was brought into the fertilizer business to service the growing demand. These are only two examples of why marketers should carefully study the developmental plans and administrative rulings of the governments of the LDCs.

Market infrastructure

There are several kinds of market resources needed by marketers for effective performance in the LDCs: foreign exchange; internal sources of supply; a transportation network; a wholesale/retail infrastructure; and internal sources for consumer credit.

Marketers who have planned to produce or at least assemble

goods within an LDC using foreign raw materials or semi-finished goods will find that the availability of these foreign materials, whether they are coming from the parent corporation or from elsewhere, is *always* contingent upon the availability of foreign currency. The failure of the nation to sell all of their primary export commodities in the world market will reduce the quantity of foreign currency available for imports. Clear and precise choices as to which industry will receive scarce currency and which will not are often set forth in the development plan and supporting administrative documents. Marketers whose products are low on the priority list will be forced to adjust production runs and market commitments to lower levels until the foreign exchange situation eases. Marketers who rely on the importation of materials that could be made within the LDC will find that their permission to use foreign exchange for these items will not be forthcoming once their firms have sunk their investment dollar in fixed facilities.

In today's world, it is unreasonable for marketers to assume that governments of the LDCs will permit national markets to be supplied from foreign production sources. No marketer should include in his plans long-term dependence on foreign sources of supply. Within a year after Sears opened its Mexican retail operation, a severe currency crisis forced the Mexican government to forbid the importation of almost all goods from the United States. Up until that time, Sears had stocked its Mexican stores from United States sources of supply. Now it was forced to find local sources. The story of how Sears force-fed local manufacturers to produce quality items in standard qualities, sizes, and assortments, and how Sears established a distribution system to wholesale these locally manufactured items to its retail outlets is well known.

Marketers who plan to produce goods in one region of an LDC and who want to market these goods throughout the national territory should carefully analyse the functional usefulness of existing transportation and distribution networks. Although they may exist on paper, their continued usefulness as market resources should not be accepted without question. There are numerous examples of how marketers built facilities on the assumption of being able to service the national territory, only to find after the plant was built that the critical market infrastructure worked occasionally or not at all. For example, slides and washouts close the dirt and gravel sections of the Pan American

Highway and other highways in most Central American countries during the rainy season. Guerrillas in Guatemala have in the past prevented Kerns, whose canning facilities are located between Guatemala City and Puerto Barrios, from shipping their canned products to the capital for resale there or for wholesale distribution throughout Guatemala. The forcing of trucks with foreign registry to unload their goods at the border of each Central American country and then reload them on trucks with domestic registry incurs higher costs for these products. Marketers who plan on using a 'through' system of transportation and fail to judge correctly the kinds of market resources they have available to them may find their products spoiling in the short run and their plants operating at excess capacity levels in the long run. Such miscalculations breed losses rather than profits for marketers.

Consumer installment loans (or hire-purchase agreements) are a function of the willingness of financial institutions to insure such installment payments. The availability of such loans assists mass production and mass distribution, and brings about rapid increases in the standard of living. Twenty years ago, Indians were able to make such agreements so that they could purchase durable goods. Today, a shortage of goods together with a lack of insured installment credit have eliminated this resource for marketers to use in raising India's standard of living. In Nigeria, two West African trading companies, United Africa Company and John Holt, and several independent finance companies extended credit for such durable goods as automobiles, TV sets, refrigerators, and air conditioners. Marketers depend upon such credit to support their own plans for market development, and its absence or potential diminution should be considered before risk capital is expended on an LDC.

In the LDCs, market resources are generally not available in sufficient quantities for efficient and effective business performance. Their unavailability limits the size of final customer markets by impeding marketers from servicing these markets. Thus for marketers operating in the LDCs it becomes a question of what resources they can do without and still service a market of sufficient size for profit-making returns.

If marketers can generate sufficient volume and keep the price high enough to cover higher distributive margins, then the problem for marketers is which market infrastructure activities are they willing to perform themselves in the short run, and which market infrastructure activities are they willing to develop by long-term marketing training of wholesale/retail distributors, warehousemen, and financial men.

Market offerings

Market offerings in the LDCs are designed on the familiar bases of product, terms of sale, communication, and distribution strategies; only the cultural nuances and governmental requirements are different. For example, in terms of product strategies, the product line for Mexican made automobiles has been reduced from twenty-five models to eleven models. GM, Ford, and Chrysler are allowed three models each by the Mexican government. The remainder of the production quota is taken up by Volkswagen and Datsun. The government forced certain automobile manufacturers out of business, and forced others to cut down on the number of models produced or sold in Mexico. It is an attempt by a government to provide some economies of scale for domestic production and thereby lower the price to the final customer.

The market offering will be conditioned also by the supplies available for packaging purposes. Some LDCs lack adequate supplies of wood and paper products. Marketers of milk and soap powders have had to shift their package offerings to clear plastic containers. This has meant that they have had to devise new means for storing these items at retail locations and new ways of labeling the packages themselves.

Brand names, as well as the advertisements used in communicating about and promoting the market offering, must reflect new language and cultural norms, but there are dangers here for marketers. In Africa, when English or French language descriptions were given up in favor of local languages, many Africans refused to buy the products with the new labels for fear that they were getting inferior products. This problem is particularly acute for marketers in the food and beverage industries. Carelessness in handling items that require high levels of sanitation is commonplace in the LDCs. Even Cola drinks, such as Coke, can be carriers of sugar bacteria that can make consumers ill. Tubercular cows pass their disease on to the unsuspecting human when care is not taken to protect consumers. Those who have money will select products they know are safe. Brand names from the United States and Western Europe tell the illiterate but relatively affluent consumers in the LDCs that these products will not endanger their health. To meet the requirements of these consumers plus the new laws of the LDCs, marketers put their market information on packages in both the recognized western language and the locally required language.

How high should marketers set prices? It is the policy of governments in the LDCs to promote higher standards of living. One way to do this is to maintain low retail prices on the basic necessities of life. Carnation was forced to sell its canned milk to the Mexican government's limited-line retail supermarkets (CONASUPO) at prices lower than it charged the privately owned middle-class supermarkets. Naturally, Carnation offset its CONASUPO losses with higher prices to the middle-class supermarkets. The Mexican government was able to utilize the price offering of a firm to redistribute some of the wealth of the country. The Indian government, however, has been unable to do the same thing. Its traditional wholesalers are the dominant economic units in the commodities that make up the basic necessities of Indian life. No amount of persuasion has made these wholesalers change their habits of speculation on the prices of these commodities, and retail markets must continue to provide the consumer with low volume, high-priced necessities of life. Marketers will face continued pressure to price their products at some predetermined rate established by the government. It behoves them to know their costs, and to be willing to make their profits in market segments that are not under price control.

In summary, social behavior and impediments in inter-regional exchange are the givens for marketers in the LDCs. National market offerings are often a fruitless waste of resources; instead, market offerings carefully developed for local and regional markets will be both beneficial and profitable. Sales and advertising campaigns should be geared to local differences in taste and thought. Although the Esso tiger has been a phenomenal success as an advertising theme throughout the world, it is folly in many cases to import on a wholesale basis each and every piece of promotional material developed for the United States market. It is just as great a folly to import these campaigns from the capital city market to other areas within the LDC. Levels of literacy, economic sophistication, and local prejudices differ widely from one region to another in many of the LDCs. Thus, market offerings should be customized to fit into the local scene as well as possible. This means more than changing the language of the copy. It means putting additional clothes on female figures so as not to offend more conservative tastes. It means using dialect variations in so-called national languages rather than the phraseology considered proper in the capital city. Several authors have suggested that there is a place for standardized international advertising among the developed countries. A case can be made for appealing to the market segment within the LDCs that relates more to international themes than national themes. Assuming this to be true, it would further strengthen the point that the tastes of the internationally oriented market segment within the capital city are not the tastes of the bulk of the national market within the LDC. And thus the folly of importing advertising themes from the capital city to the provinces is doubly compounded when this internationalized market segment is used as 'the true national market consumer group'. The care used by marketers in developing market offerings that match real market segments will go a long way to insuring that international marketing is profitable.

15 R. Moyer

International Market Analysis

R. Moyer, 'International market analysis', *Journal of Marketing Research*, vol. 5, 1968, pp. 353–360.

Introduction

International market analysis often concerns two basic tasks: (1) assessing the size of existing markets and (2) forecasting the size of future markets. Domestic market analysts also perform these jobs, but international market researchers face two handicaps that make their job more difficult. First, they must analyse many diverse markets. Each has apparently unique characteristics that make generalizing difficult. The second handicap is the paucity of reliable statistical data for many foreign markets, especially in developing economies.

Consider the first handicap. The world is divided into over 100 sovereign nations; each may be a potential market for products of international firms. Several factors – differing customs, tastes, the trade restrictions, and collection of national statistics – require the analysis of individual countries' markets. Even markets within trade blocs, e.g. the European Economic Community, are usually evaluated as individual countries rather than together as a trade group. Most of these national markets are small compared with the US market. For example, Belgium's gross national product (GNP) is less than 2 per cent of the US total.

These small fragmented markets pose a problem. The relatively low payout in many markets permits only modest market research expenditures in each. If a firm enters many national markets, the total potential may be great; however, the market research necessary for analysing the markets will be either superficial and reasonably priced in relation to the benefits or adequate but expensive.

The second handicap, inadequate data, is more severe than the first, especially in markets outside of the western European/North American region. Many factors contribute to the inadequacy of data: insufficient governmental emphasis on data collection, too few trained market research personnel, respondents' reluctance to divulge information.

Both handicaps require modified research approaches when analysing the small fragmented markets that constitute the underdeveloped world. They put a premium on discovering economic and demographic relationships that permit demand estimation from a minimum of information. Fortunately for the researcher these relationships exist. This article will point out some of these relationships and indicate a few techniques that permit market evaluation (sometimes crudely) within the limits of available data.

The reader should realize that the analysis and techniques described here are relevant principally for researching markets in the less developed countries. For our purposes, the situation in western Europe and other relatively advanced areas of the world (e.g. Australia, Canada, Japan) differentiates them from the underdeveloped countries in several respects. First, markets in most of the developed areas are large enough to warrant more refined research techniques than those suggested here. The payout will usually be great enough to justify the kind of detailed research conducted by American firms in their country. Thus, a US tire manufacturer studying the feasibility of establishing a plant in West Germany might use research techniques and methods of analysis similar to those he would use in the US. Second – and related to the first – most of the economically advanced countries generate relevant industry statistics on which to base an adequate market research effort. Therefore, the need to resort to the crude measures suggested here is diminished in these countries. It is principally in those countries with non-existent or unreliable data and with payouts too small to warrant a large research expenditure that I recommend the techniques and analysis described in the following sections.

The reader should also invest the quantitative measures described here with less than divine authority. Quantifying relationships may be a useful exercise, but they often mask overriding qualitative factors that outweigh the numerical relations. This is especially true when macro techniques are used to analyse micro markets.

Demand patterns

First we need to learn the industrial growth patterns for representative countries of the world to gain insight into consumption

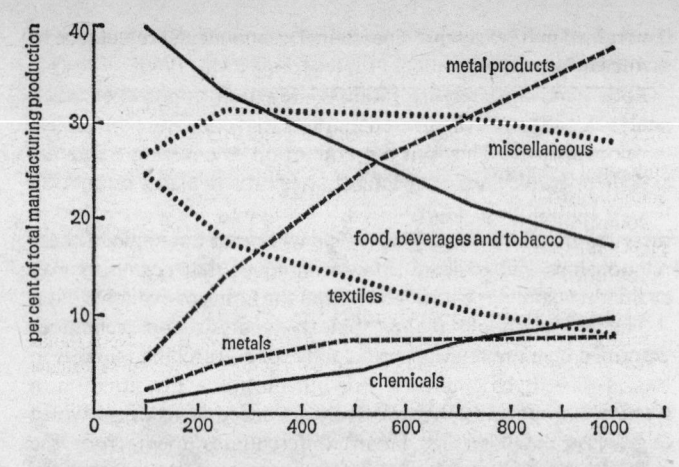

Figure 1 Typical patterns of growth in manufacturing industries[a]
a Based on a time series analysis for selected years, 1899-1957 for seven to ten countries depending on commodity.
b Dollars at 1955 prices.

patterns, our principal concern. Knowing trends in manufacturing production aids market demand analysis in several ways. First, besides inventory changes and net imports or exports, goods produced are goods consumed. Thus production patterns generally reveal consumption patterns, and knowing them helps exporters to assess market opportunities.[1] Moreover, knowing trends in manufacturing production is useful because these industries represent potential markets for US exporters of inputs, e.g. raw materials and machinery, used by industries. Finally, growing industries represent investment opportunities for US firms interested in operating abroad.

The figure broadly reveals growth patterns in large industry categories. It relates the percent of total manufacturing production accounted for by major industrial groups to gross domestic product per capita. At early growth stages when per capita incomes are low, manufacturing centers on the necessities, i.e. food, beverages and textiles, and light manufacturing. As incomes grow these industries decline relatively and are replaced in importance by heavy industries.

1. After adjustments for exports, imports, and changes in inventory levels. Unless there are substantial fluctuations in these three items, production *trends* will mirror consumption trends even though the *absolute* levels of each may never coincide.

Table 1 Imports of major commodity groups by representative countries classified by stage of industrialization, 1965[a]

Stage	Food	Fuels	Industrial materials	Manufactures
Industrial countries[b]	19·2%	10·9%	16·1%	53·8%
Semi-industrial countries[c, e]	15·7	6·5	8·3	69·5
Non-industrial countries[d, e]	17·4	5·1	4·5	73·0

a Expressed as percentage of total imports.

b Belgium–Luxembourg, France, West Germany, Italy, Netherlands, Sweden, Norway, Switzerland, United Kingdom, United States, Canada, Japan.

c Australia, New Zealand, Union of South Africa, India, Pakistan, Argentina, Brazil, Chile, Colombia, Mexico, Israel, Turkey, Yugoslavia.

d Congo, U.A.R., French Morocco, Nigeria, Southern Rhodesia, Indonesia, Iran, Philippines, Cuba, Peru, Venezuela.

e For Chile 1963 data were used; for several of the non-industrialized countries 1962, 1963, or 1964 data were used.

NOTE: The classification of countries follows that used by Alfred Maizels (1963, p. 68) except that the non-industrialized countries have been restricted to a sample of 11.

From *Yearbook of International Trade Statistics*, United Nations, 1965.

Economic growth also creates changes in the import composition with important implications for international marketers. As industrialization proceeds, countries generally develop a predictable import pattern; however, a country's resource endowment may modify this pattern. For example, fuel-scarce economies must import increasing quantities of fuel as they industrialize. We see this occurring today in Latin America. However, much of coal-rich western Europe and the United States launched industrialization without large fuel imports.

Table 1 shows the changing relative importance of imports of various commodities for countries at different industrialization levels. Industrialized countries import relatively more food products and industrial materials than manufactured goods, which are more important for the less industrialized countries. Although the percentage of total imports represented by manufacturers is lower for industrialized countries than for the semi-industrial and underdeveloped countries, the *dollar volume* of manufactured goods imported into industrialized countries far exceeds sales of these goods to poorer countries. In 1965, manufactured imports for the industrialized countries in Table 1 totalled $61·3 billion and for the semi-industrialized and nonindustrialized, $19·2 billion.

Industrial development affects imports of manufactured goods in two ways: (1) on the demand side and (2) from import substitution (Maizels, 1963, p. 63). Developing new industries increases demand for capital equipment and raw materials needed in the new production processes. Moreover, income growth leads to the substitution by consumers of relatively income-elastic goods, e.g. durables, for such income-inelastic commodities as food.

As the following tabulation indicates, reduction in the import-content of manufactured goods is greater for large industrializing countries than for small ones, though there are notable exceptions.

Industrialized countries	1899	1913	1929	1937	1950	1959
Large[a]	9%	8%	6%	4%	3%	4%
Small[b]	—	—	26	18	18	21

a France, Germany (West Germany, 1950–1959), Italy, United Kingdom, United States, and Japan.
b Belgium–Luxembourg, Netherlands, Norway, Sweden, and Canada.
Source: Maizels, 1963, p. 136.

For example, India, large in area and population, has a high import-content of supplies of manufactured goods.[1]

Factors, other than population, that influence the extent of a country's import-content of supplies are, as previously indicated, he stage of industrialization, extent of import restrictions, andt the country's reliance on exports (because of the usual association of high exports with high imports).

Income elasticity measurements

A useful statistic, the income elasticity of demand, describes succinctly the relationship between the amount demanded (consumed) of various goods and economic progress. Symbolically,

$$\frac{\frac{\Delta Q_A}{Q_A}}{\frac{\Delta Y}{Y}}$$

measures the income elasticity of demand for Commodity A where Q represents the quantity demanded, Y is the income, and

[1]. 'Supplies', here and in the tabulation, covers the gross value of production of non-food manufactures and imports of finished manufactures.

Δ refers to quantity changes. The demand for goods with values greater than one is relatively elastic. Goods with values less than one are income-inelastic. The amount demanded of commodities with values less than one rises relatively slower than changes in income levels; as income rises, the demand for goods with higher income elasticity coefficients increases relatively faster than for goods with lower values. This information aids the researcher interested in predicting growth in the demand for particular products or product classes in international markets.

Several cautions should be considered. First, although the usual income elasticity example assumes that income increases, it may also fall in which case the quantity demanded of income elastic goods would fall relatively faster than that of income inelastic products. Second, a high income elasticity coefficient does not necessarily imply high volume markets. On the contrary, greater dollar volume will probably exist in markets for necessities that are consumed in large quantities by the majority of consumers. Nonetheless, the potential for growth in demand as income increases is *relatively* greater for goods with high elasticity coefficients than for those with low ones. Emphasis on the relative responsiveness of demand changes to income changes cannot be overstressed. Finally, empirically derived income elasticity coefficients are probably subject to measurement errors. Therefore, they should be used only as rough indicators of the responsiveness of demand to income changes.

Table 2 summarizes the results of several income elasticity studies that cover both consumer and industrial products and some services and are calculated on a time series and cross section basis. Several conclusions stand out. First, necessities, such as food and clothing, tend to be income inelastic; the demand for durable consumer goods, purchases of which are postponable and made more frequently by high income groups than by low ones, is income-elastic. Capital goods and chemicals are income-elastic, confirming the impression that these commodities are consumed by more developed (higher average income) countries. Second, different ways of computing the elasticities produce different results. Several factors contribute to this result, including errors in measurement, sampling, and drawing samples at different times.

The income elasticity measurements may not apply equally to all income groups. Figures in Table 2 are averages. Another qualification of these elasticity results is that there have been no

Table 2 Income elasticity measurements

Commodity	Cross section	Time series
Food and beverages, excluding alcoholic beverages	0·54[b], 0·53[c]	0·8[a]
Alcoholic beverages	0·77[b]	
Tobacco	0·88[b]	
Clothing	0·8[a], 0·9[a] 0·84, 0·89[a]	0·7[a], 0·8[a]
Textiles	0·5[a]	0·8[a]
Household and personal services	1·19[b]	
Communication services	2·03[b]	
Recreation	1·15[b]	
Health	1·80[b]	
Durable consumer goods		2·7[a]
Furniture	1·61[c]	
Appliances	1·40[c]	
Metals	1·52[c]	
Chemicals		2·1[c]
Machinery and transportation equipment, except passenger cars		1·5–2·0[a]

a From Kastens 1960, p. 42.
b From Gilbert, et al. 1958, p. 66.
c From author's calculations.

price change adjustments in the time series calculations. Prices of goods in relatively new industries, such as chemicals and transport equipment, tend to fall as the industries grow. Thus demand increases for these industries' goods result from a combination of price and income factors. This distorts their income elasticity measurements compared with the elasticities for older industries with relatively more stable prices.

Prices affect the elasticities in several other ways. Relative price differences among major consumption categories (food, clothing, services, etc.) should be greatest among countries at different growth stages than for a single country. Thus a low income country's inhabitants may buy relatively more services (having a high labor content) than clothing (relatively more capital-intensive than services) than is true for low income members of a high income country. But this substitution effect in low income countries is overpowered by the income effect, i.e. the low income country's inhabitants have insufficient disposable income to buy many services *even though* services are relatively cheap. This income effect may therefore result in total expenditure on services in a low income country being less than that in a high income country.

A final impact of prices on expenditure patterns is that, other things equal, the consumption of a relatively low priced good in Country A with per capita income similar to Country B's will exceed consumption in B for the same good at a higher price. The reverse holds with higher priced commodities. Thus Norway with per capita income twice as high as Italy's consumes half as many fruits and vegetables per capita as does Italy, because of different fruit and vegetable price levels in the two countries. Different excise taxes and subsidies will influence prices with consequent impact on consumption levels. Therefore the watchword in using income elasticities is 'caution'. They are useful guides for consumption estimation but are no substitute for careful and comprehensive demand analysis.

Another use of elasticity measurements is in calculating import substitution elasticities mentioned in the previous section. This elasticity measures the responsiveness of imports to changes in domestic variables such as income and, possibly, population.

Consider a model where:
O_i is domestic production of Commodity i
M_i is the import of i
X_i is the export of i
F_i is the domestic final use of i
I_i is the intermediate use of i by other producers
S_i is the total supply of i
D_i is the total demand of i,
then the following equilibrium relations hold:

1. $S_i = D_i$
2. $S_i = O_i + M_i$
3. $D_i = I_i + F_i + X_i$.

Therefore:

4. $O_i + M_i = I_i + F_i + X_i$.

And:

5. $O_i = I_i + F_i + X_i - M_i$.

This is an expanded version of Chenery's (1960) model.

We can define the change in Product i's import ratio to be $\alpha_{i1} - \alpha_{i0}$ where the subscripts 1 and 0 refer either to values at the end and at the beginning of a time span in a time series or values for high and low income countries in a cross section study, α being the fraction of total supply accounted for by imports. Thus we can express the import ratio as:

6. $\alpha_{i1} = \dfrac{M_{i1}}{S_{i1}}$, and similarly for α_{i0}.

Import substitution therefore is:

7. $(\alpha_{i0} - \alpha_{i1}) S_{i1}$.

This can be converted from 6 to:

8. $\left(\dfrac{M_{i0}}{S_{i0}} - \dfrac{M_{i1}}{S_{i1}}\right) S_{i1}$.

From 8 we see that

9. $\dfrac{M_{i0} S_{i1}}{S_{i0}} - M_{i1} = 0$,

in the absence of import substitution. That is, $M_{i0} S_{i1}/S_{i0}$ will equal M_{i1} when no import substitution occurs as income changes, and will exceed M_{i1} if import substitution occurs. The excess measures the extent of the substitution.

Import substitution elasticities may be computed by using either cross section or time series analysis. Chenery (1960, p. 642) made an extensive cross section analysis the results of which are summarized in Table 3. To arrive at import substitution elastici-

Table 3 **Growth elasticities of output and imports**

Sector	Production (1)	Imports (2)	Total supply (3)	Import substitution (4)=(1)−(3)
Investment products	2·24	0·97	1·64	0·60
Other intermediate goods	1·72	0·83	1·38	0·34
Consumer goods	1·32	1·07	1·29	0·03
Total	1·55	0·94	1·40	0·15

Source: Chenery 1960, p. 642.

ties he derived elasticities for total production and imports by using linear logarithmic regression equations that convert the coefficients to elasticities. Per capita value added depends on per capita income and population. In symbols:

10. $\dfrac{V_i}{N} = A \dfrac{Y^{\beta 1}}{N} N^{\beta 2}$.

Appropriate value-added ratios can allow value-added figures to be converted to production.

The regression equation for imports is:

11. $\dfrac{M_i}{N} = A \dfrac{Y^{\alpha 1}}{N} N^{\alpha 2}$.

Chenery uses population as a market size proxy, the assumption being that increases in market size permit scale economies (hence lowered costs) that encourage import substitution. The value of α_2 (not shown in Table 3) for all sectors is -0.281, which tends to validate this assumption.

Import substitution was found to be higher in investment goods than in intermediate goods, and in consumer goods was almost nil; see Table 3, Column 4. The import substitution elasticities also confirm the industrial growth patterns and the growth of imports summarized in the preceding section.

Though Chenery's results allow us to generalize about import substitution elasticities, the analyst interested in a *specific* country ought to calculate that country's elasticity using time series. We will not consider all the factors affecting individual countries' elasticities here. It is sufficient to say that elasticities may vary substantially from one country to another, and that some national economic development plans call for a conscious shift in the ratio of imported goods to total supply. When this is true, the government's tampering with the 'normal' relationship between imports and relevant independent variables probably rules out using even a time series analysis. Here it might be preferable for the analyst to go directly to the development plan for an estimate of import substitution. Where this tampering does not exist, however, time series analysis should be appropriate and useful.

Multiple factor indexes

Those interested in international market research may borrow a technique successfully used in domestic market research, i.e. multiple factor indexes. If conditions prevent directly computing a product's market potential, using proxies to estimate demand may be a satisfactory substitute. A multiple factor index measures potential by indirection, using as proxies variables that intuition or statistical analysis reveal to be closely correlated with the potential for the product under review.[1]

In western Europe the J. W. Thompson Company uses multiple factor indexes to rank markets quantitatively and qualitatively. As factors it uses population, population per square mile, value of imports and exports, private consumption, expenditures, and number of cars, radios, and telephones in use. Weighting the factors equally, it ranks each western European country quantitatively by computing an average index using gross values of the factors just listed. An index using per capita data for the same factors, again equally weighted, provides a qualitative ranking.

Ordinarily market indexes are constructed not to measure total potential but either to rank submarkets or to assign potential *shares* of the total market to each submarket. Erickson (1963, p. 23) constructed such an index for Brazil. Using population, domestic income, and retail store sales, all expressed as percentages of national figures, he measured the potential for consumer goods for each of Brazil's twenty-one states. It has the advantages and disadvantages of *Sales Management*'s Buying Power Index after which the Brazilian index is modelled.

An index of this kind might be used to establish sales quotas and evaluate sales performance, among other purposes. This Brazilian index assigns a potential to the state of São Paulo of roughly 30 per cent of the nation's total. If sales for the product under study fall below the level required by the index and if the product's sales are related to the three-factor index, management has reason to question performance in that submarket. Obviously such a tool must be used judiciously.

Gross indicators like GNP, net national income, or total population are useful in constructing an index but, when possible, one should restrict use of factors to variables that closely fit the product. The better the variables serve as sales determinants of the product for which the index is constructed, the more reliable it will be. For example, determining potential for an electric household appliance might require using such factors as private consumption expenditure on durable goods and the number of wired homes. An index determining potential for boys' outerwear might include an income variable, number of young males in the appropriate age range, and a temperature variable, if data are available. If not, the analyst must use substitute variables.

1. Single factor indexes, also often used, relate the potential of a commodity to the size of a single proxy variable.

Estimation by analogy

Estimating market size with available data is difficult and with inadequate data is even more difficult. Scarce data require resourceful techniques, one of which is estimating by analogy. This can be done in two ways by (1) cross-section comparisons or (2) Merritt Kasten's term, by 'displacing time series in time' (1960). The first technique estimates the market size of a commodity in Country A by computing the ratio of a gross economic indicator, e.g. disposable personal income, for both A and B (for which market data are available) and using this ratio as an estimate of the consumption ratio of the commodity in question.

The time series device uses as a demand estimate for a product in Country A, the demand level for the product in B when B was at the same level of economic growth as A is today. This technique assumes that product usage moves through a cycle, the product being consumed in small quantities (or not at all) when countries are underdeveloped and in increasing (and predictable) amounts with economic growth.

Obviously these techniques have drawbacks. The cross-section approach assumes linearity in the consumption function. Both assume comparable consumption patterns among countries. The following factors can create errors in estimates using either technique:

1. Nonlinearity of consumption functions.
2. Possible lack of correspondence between *potential* for a product and its *sales* because of improper pricing, inadequate credit terms and facilities, defective product quality, inhibiting governmental policies (tariffs, taxes, embargoes), etc.
3. Differences in culture, tastes, and habits that dictate different consumption patterns for two apparently similar countries.
4. Technical factors, e.g. recent inventions that permit a late-developing economy to consume a product earlier in its growth phase than economically more advanced countries.

Regression analysis

Regression analysis may be a powerful tool in predicting market size in all countries, but especially when data are scarce. It also provides a quantitative technique to sharpen estimates derived by the deduction by analogy method just explained.

Cross-section studies using regression analysis benefit from existing predictable demand patterns for many commodities in countries at different growth stages. Just cited were factors that confound attempts to estimate demand in one country from the experiences of another. Despite these obstacles there are still strong international demand patterns that increase the predictive power of the regression technique.

A use of regression analysis is to derive demand estimates by analogy, i.e. by studying the relationship between gross economic indicators and demand for a specific commodity for countries with *both* kinds of data. We then transfer this relationship by analogy to the less developed country where, more than likely, only the gross economic indicators are available. If, however, data relating *directly* to demand for the product in question are available in the less developed country, we would obviously substitute these data for the indirect technique described.

Table 4 summarizes regression results that relate the consumption of various commodities to a gross economic indicator. A linear regression model $y = a + bx$ was used where y is the amount of a product in use per thousand of population and x is GNP per capita. The equations explain from 50 per cent to 78 per cent of the variation in the dependent variable. The simple least-squares slope coefficients are statistically significant at the 0·01 level.

Table 4 **Regression of consumption on gross national product, various products**

Product	Number of observations	Regression equation	Unadjusted R^2
Autos	37	$-21·071 + 0·101x$	0·759
Radio sets	42	$8·325 + 0·275x$	0·784
TV sets	31	$-16·501 + 0·074x$	0·503
Refrigerators	24	$-21·330 + 0·102x$	0·743
Washing machines	22	$-15·623 + 0·094x$	0·736

Sources: *Statistical Yearbook*, United Nations, 1962, and Maizels (1963), pp. 308–9.

Technically, the title of Table 4 incorrectly refers to the consumption of the products it lists. The dependent variable, showing the amount of product in use per capita, is a kind of summary of *previous* consumption. In effect it records the sum of previous purchases, less withdrawals from use because of obsolescence and other reasons. Data are available, however, for the computation of regressions using consumption as the dependent variable, though often these data are difficult to obtain. Ingenuity and a diligent search of data sources, however, are usually rewarding.

From the regression results in Table 4, we may conclude that an increase of $100 per capita in GNP will result, on the average, in an increase of ten automobiles, ten refrigerators, nine washing machines, seven TV sets, and twenty-seven radio sets per 1,000 population. Undoubtedly there is a saturation point for these and other products. Beyond a point (not reached for the five commodities analyzed here) consumption will increase at a decreasing rate, requiring the use of a different kind of equation to describe the relationship.

Factors other than economic growth also contribute to expansion in product demand. We considered these forces previously. The regression for automobiles would have been improved by excluding a few countries' observations. For example, consumption of cars in Switzerland is far less than its level of affluence permits because of an excellent public transportation system, difficult terrain, and the imposition of heavy import duties on cars. Undoubtedly adding price as another independent variable would improve the fit of the equations, although getting this information makes research considerably more difficult.

Some products do not lend themselves to simple regression analysis. For example, a very poor fit resulted for a regression of cement consumption per capita on gross disposable product per capita. Many other variables, including the prices of cement and its substitutes, would have been necessary to improve the results. For paper, however, a reasonably good fit was derived using only gross domestic product as the explanatory variable.[1] Fortunately the consumption of many products can be estimated reasonably accurately by knowing only the income (or GNP) per capita in the countries studied. The demonstration effect undoubtedly leads to this predictable consumption pattern from one country to another.

To use the regression technique to estimate demand an analyst must first compute the regression, using whatever explanatory variables seem appropriate, and provide a close fit. If the unexplained variation is reasonably low, the analyst may use the results as an estimate of current demand in countries for which no

1. Regression results: $0.441 + 0.035x$ $R^2 = 0.66$, statistically significant at 0.01 level.

demand data are available. Getting an estimate of demand requires knowing the value of the independent variable, e.g. GNP. Fortunately these data are readily available on a current basis. The United Nations and others also estimate growth rates, permitting calculation of future GNP levels to predict future demand.

Specifically, assume that we want to estimate the consumption of paper in Country X where this statistic is unavailable. Its present GNP per capita is $200. Using the regression equation in Footnote 1, we calculate present consumption to be 7·4 tons per capita. We may also want to estimate the consumption of paper in that country five years hence when GNP per capita is expected to be $250. Using the same regression equation, we estimate the per capita consumption to be roughly 9·3 tons. Multiplication of this figure by estimated population (also available in UN reports) provides a total consumption estimate for X. This figure may be qualified by using standard error values to provide a *range* within which the anticipated consumption may fall rather than to make a point estimate.

Obviously there are limitations to using this technique as a demand estimator. Not the least of the problems is the assumption that the relationship prevailing in countries for which demand data are available can be transferred to the less developed countries lacking these data.

Input–output analysis

Input-output analysis was used first to describe a country's economic structure and for economic development planning; analysts now recognize the potential of the analysis in international market research as more countries develop I–O tables (see Faucett, 1960, pp. 4, 59). This is especially true in market research for industrial products that lend themselves better than consumer goods products to I–O analysis.

I–O tables permit several kinds of analysis. One can trace the direct and indirect impact on the demand for one's products of changes in demand for other industries' products. One can also determine the extent to which sales are made to final users and, if so, how much the industry depends on sales to governments, households, export markets, etc. Furthermore, the tables reveal the number of industries consuming another industry's products, a valuable datum from the standpoint of planning distribution channel requirements.

The most valuable use of I–O tables in international market analysis is in predicting future output levels for one's customers. A current I–O table summarizes the structure of today's economy. An analyst may ask how a 30 per cent increase in government expenditures would affect the demand for his industry's products. How would doubling the growth rate in vehicle production affect the output of rubber products in Country X? What would be the impact on textile demand of a relative contraction in output of consumers' goods at the expense of capital goods in Country Y (underdeveloped economy)? The possibilities for analysis and prediction from simulating different economic conditions are infinite. I–O's value stems from its being a model that makes it reusable for analytical purposes.

I–O analysis has its disadvantages, too. It assumes that production functions are linear; hence, the technical coefficients are fixed over all output ranges. It thus rules out changes in input-output relationships resulting either from changed production processes or from alterations in output level. Outdated tables for some countries make this drawback even more severe. Unfortunately we know little about the stability of technical coefficients.

Another limitation is the small number of cells in most tables, far fewer than the number of industries in each country. Data may be grouped into so few 'industries' that the input-output relationships are meaningless. Moreover, in many underdeveloped countries' tables, lack of interdependence among industries may leave most cells vacant. Thus only twenty-three of the 306 cells in Tanganyika's (in 1957 before becoming Tanzania) I–O table were filled (Peacock and Gosser, 1957, p. 21).

Nonetheless I–O tables are useful to the resourceful analyst. Their shortcomings should diminish as data become more abundant, the technique better refined, and more countries adopt them. By 1966, twenty-one countries plus the OEEC countries as a group were constructing I–O tables on an annual basis or intermittently; another six countries had them planned or under construction but had no announced plan for periodic compilation of future tables (United Nations, 1966, p. 135).

Dual economy problem

In this discussion I categorized countries as underdeveloped as though each had a relatively homogeneous population. Of course, this is fallacious. Every country has regional income differences, which are often quite pronounced in the less developed countries.

This condition leads to their being described as dual economies. The dual character is evident from a comparison of poor rural areas accounting for a majority of the population in most underdeveloped countries with pockets of relative affluence in the cities.

The contrast may show up in comparisons of average income or purchasing power for different regions of the country. The Brazilian states of São Paulo and Guanabara, for example, in 1959 accounted for 23 per cent of Brazil's population but 46 per cent of domestic income earned and 51 per cent of retail sales (Faucett, 1960, p. 23). The four poorest states, on the other hand, accounted for 13 per cent of the people and generated only 5 per cent of domestic income and 3 per cent of retail sales. The same pattern prevails in other less developed countries.

The dual economy problem requires analysing economies by segments rather than looking only at the whole. One might rule out a country with low per capita income as a potential market for an income-elastic product if he were not going to probe for more than the average income figure for the entire country. This average might conceal the existence of one or more desirable regional markets in which incomes would support the product's sale.

Summary and conclusions

This article briefly describes several techniques to aid international market analysis. It is not meant to be exhaustive. Obviously there are many conventional devices, useful in domestic marketing research, that may be used equally effectively in marketing research abroad, especially in developed economies. Thus consumer surveys, panels, store audits, readership studies, and other techniques familiar in the United States are becoming equally familiar abroad. Indeed several methods discussed here are equally applicable to domestic market research. This would certainly be true for using multiple factor indexes and, to some extent, income elasticity measurement and, more recently, input-output analysis.

But the short-cut research methods of deduction by analogy, analysis of import substitution elasticities, and the use of regression analysis discussed in this article are more applicable in the less developed countries than they are in the developed countries. In the latter, the analyst generally has adequate, if not always abundant, data. In the former, however, the data can be pretty scarce.

References

CHENERY, H. (1960), 'Patterns of industrial growth', *Amer. Econ. Rev.*, no. 50, pp. 624–54.

ERICKSON, L. G. (1963), 'Analyzing Brazilian consumer markets', *Business Topics*, no. 11, p. 23.

FAUCETT, J. G. (1960), 'Input-output analysis as a tool of international market research', *Market Research in International Operations*, Management report no. 53, American Management Association.

GILBERT, M. et al. (1958), *Comparative National Products and Price Levels*, Organization for European Co-operation.

KASTENS, M. L. (1960), 'Organizing, planning and staffing market research activities in an international corporation', *Market Research in International Operations*, Management report no. 53, American Management Association.

MAIZELS, A. (1963), *Industrial Growth and World Trade*, Cambridge University Press.

PEACOCK, A. T. and GOSSER, D. M. (1957), 'Input-output analysis in an underdeveloped country', *Rev. Econ. Stud.*, no. 25, p. 22.

UNITED NATIONS (1966), *Problems of Input-Output Tables and Analysis*, pp. 135–6.

16 L. T. Wells, Jr

A Product Life Cycle for International Trade?

L. T. Wells, Jr, 'A product life cycle for international trade?',
Journal of Marketing, vol. 32, 1968, pp. 1–6 (some footnotes deleted).

The lowering of barriers to international trade has resulted in many opportunities for American companies to profit from exports. Clearly, the businessman needs ways of analysing the potential exportability of his products and, equally important, tools for predicting which products are likely to be threatened by import competition.

Until recently, the manager was dependent on the explanations of trade offered by the classical and neo-classical economists. Their reasoning generally led to the conclusion that each country will concentrate on exporting those products which make the most use of the country's abundant production factors. The economic theory is elegant – it can be stated mathematically or geometrically and it can be manipulated to yield, under certain assumptions, answers to questions such as what is the value of free trade to a country, or what are the costs and benefits of certain restrictions. So long as the problems posed are of a very broad nature, the theory provides a useful way of analysing them. However, when the theory is applied to the detailed problems facing the businessman it becomes of limited value.

The trade cycle model

A new approach to international trade which appears most promising in aiding the business executive is closely related to the product life cycle concept in marketing. The model claims that many products go through a trade cycle, during which the United States is initially an exporter, then loses its export markets and may finally become an importer of the product. Empirical studies of trade in synthetic materials, electronic products, office machinery, consumer durables, and motion pictures have demonstrated that these products follow a cycle of international trade similar to the one which the model describes.

According to the trade cycle concept, many products follow a pattern which could be divided into four stages:

1. Phase 1: US export strength
2. Phase 2: Foreign production starts
3. Phase 3: Foreign production competitive in export markets
4. Phase 4: Import competition begins

A brief look at the reasoning underlying each of these stages will give some clues which will help the businessman to identify the stage in which particular products may be. The concept can then be an aid in predicting the product trade performance to come and in understanding what actions the manager can take to modify the pattern for certain products and to profit from different stages of the cycle.

Phase 1: US export strength

What kinds of new products are likely to be introduced first in the United States? It can be assumed that American entrepreneurs have no particular monopoly on scientific know-how or on very basic technical ability. What they do have, however, is a great deal of knowledge about a very special market – one which is unique in having a large body of very high-income consumers. Products which satisfy the special demands of these customers are especially likely to be introduced in the United States. Moreover, due to a monopoly position of the United States as a supplier of the new products which satisfy these unique demands, they offer the best opportunities for export.

Empirical studies have failed to show a very simple relationship between demand and invention. However, there can be little doubt that certain products are simply more likely to be developed in America. Automatic transmissions for automobiles promised to be pretty expensive additions to cars. If an inventor considers the chances of his brainchild's being purchased by consumers, a US inventor would be more likely to pursue an automatic transmission than a European. The European inventor would more probably concern himself with ideas suitable to European demands. He might respond to high fuel taxes and taxes on engine displacement by developing engines which produce more horsepower per cubic inch. He might develop better handling suspensions in response to the road conditions. An inventor usually comes up with products suitable to his own market.

It is even more likely that the final product development leading to commercial production will be achieved by an entrepreneur responding to his own national demand.

Even if an American is most likely to be the first to produce a high-income product, why does he not set up his first plant abroad where labor is cheaper? Certainly for many products the cost of materials and of capital is not sufficiently higher in Europe to offset the advantages offered by cheaper labor. Moreover, the burden of tariffs and freight are light enough now for many items. And the uncertainties of manufacture abroad are diminishing as more American companies gain experience. There are, though, very rational reasons why the American entrepreneur might prefer to start manufacture at home.

At the early stages of a product's life, design is often in a constant state of flux. There is a real advantage which accrues to a manufacturer who is close to the market for his products so that he can rapidly translate demands for design changes into more suitable products. Moreover, these changes often require the availability of close communication with specialized suppliers. Hence, the instability of product design for new products argues for a location in the United States – near to the market and close to a wide range of specialized suppliers (see Hirsch, 1967). The entrepreneur is less likely to be concerned with small cost differences for very new products. The existence of a monopoly or the significant product differentiation at the early stage of the product life cycle reduces the importance of costs to the manufacturer. The multitude of designs and the lack of standard performance specifications make it very difficult for the consumer to compare prices. Also, in the early stage of the product life cycle the consumer is frequently not very concerned with price. Success comes to the manufacturer who can quickly adjust both his product design and marketing strategy to consumers' needs which are just beginning to be well identified.

At this point, the American manufacturers have a virtual monopoly for the new product in the world market. Foreigners who want the good must order it from the United States. In fact, wealthy consumers abroad, foreigners with particular needs for the product, and Americans living abroad seem to hear about it very quickly. Unsolicited orders begin to appear from overseas. US exports start to grow – initially from the trickle created by these early orders – to a steady stream as active export programs are established in the American firms.

Phase 2: Foreign production starts

Incomes and product familiarity abroad increase, causing overseas markets eventually to become large enough that the product which once appealed primarily to the US consumer has a broad appeal in the wealthier foreign countries. Not only does a potential foreign producer now have a market close at hand, but some of his costs will be lower than those of the US producer. Imports from America have to bear duty and overseas freight charges – costs which local products will not carry. Moreover the potential foreign producer may have to invest less in product development – the US manufacturer has done part of this for him. Some measure of the size of his potential market has been demonstrated by the successful sale of imports. Favorable profit projections based on a demonstrated market and an ability to underprice imports will eventually induce an entrepreneur in a wealthy foreign market – usually first in Western Europe – to take the plunge and start serious manufacture. Of course, this manufacturer will, in some cases, be an American subsidiary which starts production abroad, realizing that if it does not, some other company will.

However, the calculations that yield favorable costs projections for competition with imports from the United States in the foreign producer's home market do not necessarily lead to the conclusion that the foreign producer will be a successful competitor in third markets. For many modern manufactured goods he is likely to be at a serious disadvantage due to the small size of his plant in a market where he also must bear the burdens of freight and tariffs. Scale-economies are so important for many products that the US manufacturer, with his large plants supplying the American market, can still produce more cheaply than the early foreign producers who must manufacture on a significantly smaller scale.

During this second stage American exports still supply most of the world's markets. However, as foreign producers begin to manufacture, US exports to certain markets will decline. The pattern will probably be a slowdown in the rate of growth of US exports. The slowdown in the rate of growth of exports of home dishwashers in the last few years as European manufacturers have begun production provides an example of a product in this phase of the cycle.

Phase 3: Foreign production competitive in export markets

As the early foreign manufacturers become larger and more experienced their costs should fall. They will begin to reap the advantages of scale economies previously available only to US manufacturers. But, in addition, they will often have lower labor bills. Hence, their costs may be such that foreign products become competitive with American goods in third markets where goods from both countries have to carry similar freight and duty charges.

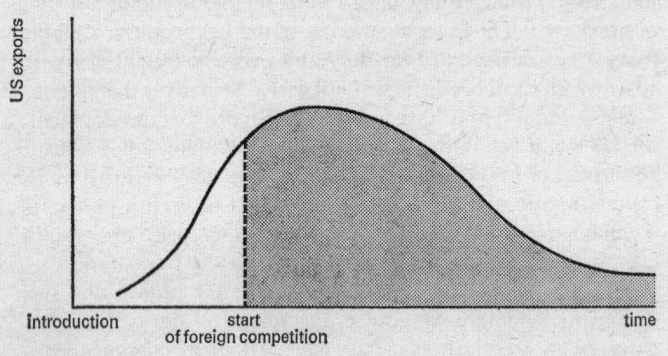

Figure 1 Export cycle

During this stage, US producers will be protected from imports in their domestic market where they are not faced with duty and overseas transportation costs. However, foreign goods will gradually take over the markets abroad which were previously held by American exports. The rate of growth of US exports will continue to decline. The success of European ranges and refrigerators in Latin America points out that these products are in this phase.

Phase 4: Import competition begins
As the foreign manufacturer reaches mass production based on his home and export markets, his lower labor rates and perhaps newer plant may enable him to produce at lower costs than an American manufacturer. His cost savings may be sufficient that he can pay ocean freight and American duty and still compete with the American in his own market. This stage will be reached earlier if the foreign producer begins to think in terms of marginal costs for export pricing. If he believes that he can sell above full costs in his home market and 'dump' abroad to use up his excess capacity, he may very quickly undercut the US producers pricing on full costs.

During this final stage, US exports will be reduced to a trickle, supplying very special customers abroad, while import competition may become severe. The bicycle is a product which has been in this phase for some time.

The cycle

Thus the cycle is complete – from the United States as a strong exporter to the stage where imports may capture a significant share of the American market. Figure 1 above shows schematically the US export performance for an hypothetical product.

The early foreign producers – usually Western Europeans – will face a cycle similar to that of the US manufacturer. As still lower-income markets become large enough, producers in these countries will eventually become competitive – displacing the dominance of the early foreign manufacturers. The manufacture

Table 1 **Ratio of value of 1962–1963 exports to value of 1952–1953 exports**

Necessity		*Discretionary*		*Luxury*	
Refrigerators	0·47	Automobiles	0·99	Movie Cameras	4·14
Ranges	0·87	Electric Clocks	1·04	Freezers	0·74
Radios	1·42	Still Cameras	4·66	Air Conditioners	3·59
Irons	1·56	Washers	1·35	Slide Projectors	4·66
Televisions	1·04	Vacuum Cleaners	1·78	Dishwashers	8·50
		Mixers	1·25	Outboard Motors	4·18
		Record Players	1·81	Recreational Boats	4·40
Average	1·07		1·84		4·32
				$F=7·0$ (Significant at 0·95 level)	

Note: Adjustments for freezer exports to Canada and 1963 still camera exports raise significance to 0·99 level. See Wells, 1966.

Source: Classification of products from James Gately, Stephen Gudeman, and George Moseley, 'Take-off phenomenon', unpublished paper submitted to Consumer Behavior Research Seminar (Harvard Business School, 27 May 1965). Export data from US Department of Commerce, Bureau of the Census, FT 410 Reports.

of products moves from country to country in what one author has called a 'pecking order' (Hufbauer, 1966).

So far, there are only relatively few examples of the less developed countries becoming exporters of manufactured goods. The classic example is standardized textiles. Another interesting example is the export of certain standardized computer components from Argentina. However, the current growth rate of over 12 per cent per year for exports of manufactures from less developed countries may indicate that they will soon become an important factor for the American businessman.

How different products behave

Obviously, the export patterns are not identical for all products. Three variables were critical to the argument supporting the trade cycle concept: the uniqueness of the appeal of the product to the US market, the reduction in unit costs as the scale of production increases, and the costs of tariffs and freight. Differences in these variables will be very important in determining how a particular product behaves as an export or import – and thus what the profit opportunities or threats will be.

High-income products

The advantage of the United States in export markets in certain products was said to be dependent on the uniqueness of the appeal of the product to the American consumer. The cycle would be more 'stretched out' if this demand is particularly unique. For such products, the US manufacturer will probably remain an exporter for a longer period of time and can postpone his fears of import competition.

It is possible to categorize some products for which the US demand is 'unique':

Luxury function. Certainly products which perform functions people are willing to do without until they are comparatively wealthy have a particularly large demand in the United States. Movie cameras and room air-conditioners come immediately to mind. In fact, a classification of consumer durables into luxury, discretionary, and necessity shows a remarkable correlation with the US export performance of the products. Exports increased 330 per cent over a ten-year period for the luxury products, compared to an almost 84 per cent increase for the discretionary items and only a 7 per cent increase for the necessity products (see Table 1 above).

Expensive to buy. Products that cost significantly more than other products which perform similar functions appeal primarily to a high-income market. Electric knife-sharpeners are an example of this type of product. A study by Time Marketing Service[1] showed that 21·5 per cent of households with incomes of over $10,000

1. Time Marketing Services, *Selective Mass Markets for Products and Services*, Time Marketing Information, Report No 1. 1305.

(where the heads were white collar, college educated) owned electric knife-sharpeners. In contrast, only 11·6 per cent with incomes under $10,000 owned them.

Expensive to own. Similarly, products that are expensive to maintain or to operate compared to alternative products which perform similar functions are uniquely suited to a high-income market. The American automobile provides an example. The disadvantage of its high fuel consumption more than offsets the advantages of more space and higher horsepower for most low-income foreign consumers.

Labor saving. Products which save labor by substituting a relatively large amount of capital are particularly appealing to the American market. The high cost of labor, a function of high American incomes, makes it very attractive to buy items such as heavy road building equipment and computers which substitute capital for labor.

Of course the businessman can influence the appeal of his products through his product policy. For example, he can build larger or smaller cars, automatic record players or simple ones.

Scale economies

The trade cycle is also influenced by the amount of savings in cost, which can be achieved by increasing the scale of production. If a small plant is equally as efficient as a large one for a given product, a foreign producer will start to manufacture while his market is still relatively small. US exports will not be as successful, and import competition will probably soon begin.

The effect of scale economies is well illustrated by the cases where a product goes through several stages of manufacture. In refrigerator production, for example, low costs can be reached in assembly operations at a much lower volume than in the manufacture of compressors. This difference shows up in the performance of US exports for one period where exports of completed refrigerators fell drastically, but exports of compressors for inclusion in refrigerators assembled abroad held their own.

Tariffs and freight

If tariffs or other trade barriers overseas are high for a particular product, foreign production is encouraged. Hence US exports will receive early competition from foreign production. Developing countries have frequently raised tariffs to encourage local production while their markets are still small. However, if the American tariff is high, it follows that the United States manufacturers need worry less about import competition.

High freight costs, usually for products which are heavy or bulky compared to their value, tend to discourage trade. Not only will foreign production occur earlier, but foreign competition is unlikely to become a serious threat in the US market. In the extreme cases of very high transportation costs, trade never occurs, or occurs almost entirely along borders where a foreign source is closer than a domestic one. For example, trade in gravel has never been significant because of transportation costs.

Exceptions to the cycle

Not all products can be expected to follow the cyclical pattern described. The model says little about products which do not have a particularly strong demand in the United States. In addition for some products the location of manufacture is tied to some particular natural resource – agricultural, to certain types of land; mining and initial processing, to areas containing the mineral. The manufacturing processes for some products such as the traditional handicraft goods have only slightly increasing returns to scale. Moreover, some products appear to remain sufficiently differentiated so that price discrepancies play only a slight role. For example, American cigarettes have continued to command a price-premium in Europe.

There are also manufactured goods for which even the US market is not large enough to allow significant scale economies. Such products tend to be produced in various locations close to market clusters, and no one area achieves a large cost advantage. Trade tends to be more on the basis of product differentiation or specialization. However, as demand in the United States grows, a standard version may be produced in quantity, bringing the cost down so that the product moves into the cycle under discussion.

High-performance sports cars and sail boats may be examples of this type product. Until recently, much of the production for such sports cars was located in various areas of Europe and was based on small production quantities. Recently both of these products have seen some large-scale manufacture in the US and significant cost-reductions. General Motors led the way with mass manufacture of the Corvette. More American manufacturers will probably enter the high-performance sports car market and compete with the virtually hand-produced, expensive European sports cars.

The trade cycle and business planning

Obviously, no simple model can explain the behavior of all products in international trade. However, the trade cycle model does appear to be useful for understanding trade patterns in a wide range of manufactured goods. Although no such model should be used by the businessman without a careful examination of individual products, it does provide some very useful hints as to which products might be exportable and which might suffer import competition. The concept can give some clues as to the success of various product policies.

Market segmentation

The model provides some insights into the role which market segmentation can play in increasing exports and protecting against imports. Design modifications can be made for certain products which can change the appeal of the product to different kinds of customers and thus modify the trade cycle. In fact, the manufacturer often makes such changes for reasons unrelated to international trade but rather as a response to changes in the nature of his home market. As the American consumer becomes wealthier and more sophisticated, and as domestic competition becomes more severe, the manufacturer often makes his products more automatic, more powerful, more luxurious. The marketer may be trying to differentiate his product from those of his competitor, or he may simply be responding to the demands of a wealthier consumer. These changes may make the product more suited to the growing incomes of the American customer, but they will also affect its exportability. The item may become too expensive for the majority of foreign consumers, hastening competition from foreign-produced goods.

This gradual product sophistication may, however, provide some protection against imports in the United States. No doubt, the size and automatic features of the American automobile have had a special appeal to the high-income American market and have consequently held back the flow of imports. The product design has, however, had another effect: simpler, cheaper foreign cars have been able to capture a part of the US market more concerned with economy of operation and lack of style obsolescence than with luxury, fashion, and automatic features – second cars, student cars, etc.

The American automobile industry did not respond to imports by trying to produce a real economy car in competition with the Volkswagen and Renault, but rather produced a middle-range product (the compacts) which competed with Volvo and Peugeot, for example. The move was probably a wise one. No doubt, the producers of the economy cars abroad had reached cost savings from scale economies equivalent to anything the US producers could hope to obtain. Moreover, they had lower labor costs. By choosing to attack the middle range, the American manufacturers chose a market where they could have a scale advantage for a time, until the higher-income segment of the European market was so large that middle-range cars would be more important. Perhaps the US manufacturers simultaneously created a more exportable product for the future.

For products where design sophistication consists of adding special features to a basic model, export versions can be produced simply by eliminating some of the extras. Thus, some producers can extend the exportability of their products while simultaneously satisfying the more sophisticated needs of their home market.

The existence of segmented markets leads to Americans' exporting and importing the same product: exporting large automobiles to high-income consumers abroad while importing small, economy cars; exporting large refrigerators while importing small ones for campers and summer homes. The relative competitiveness of the United States in 1965–6 in the higher-quality versions of a product stands out well in the case of home freezers. Prices were contrasted for comparable home freezers of different sizes in Germany and in the United States. For each model the lowest-priced unit was chosen for comparison. The larger models were cheaper in the United States and the smaller models in Germany. American manufacturers did not yet need to worry about imports of large freezers, but they were already beginning to experience competition from smaller models.

Product roll-over and foreign investment

Of course, the point is finally reached for many products where design changes can no longer make the American product competitive abroad or safe from imports. The US firms may follow two strategies for survival: a continual product roll-over, shifting resources to new products more suited to the unique demands of the American market; and manufacturing abroad to take advantage of lower production costs and to save tariffs and transportation charges. The strategies are not mutually exclusive, but both require advanced-planning and constant surveillance of the future of individual products and assessments of the company's capabilities.

Conclusion

Companies can no longer afford failure to analyse opportunities for profit offered by exports and the possible threats to their own market posed by imports. The trend of international events indicates an increased importance of trade to businessmen. In response to this changing environment, the manager must have a continuing program to analyse the future directions of international trade in his products so that he may plan early enough for appropriate policies. The product cycle model provides a useful tool in this analysis.

References

HIRSCH, S. (1967), *Location of Industry and International Competitiveness*, Clarendon Press.

HUFBAUER, G. C. (1966), *Synthetic Materials and the Theory of International Trade*, Harvard University Press.

WELLS, L. T. Jr (1966), 'Product innovation and directions of international trade', unpublished doctoral thesis, Harvard Business School.

Part Five
Marketing Strategy: One-Up on the Marketing Mix

To synchronize marketing strategy and market structure is the key challenge in marketing management. Part Five is addressed to marketing strategy, and so, to varying degrees, are Parts Six to Eight. We ask the indulgence of the reader for the fact that while the readings in this part do touch on broader issues of strategy they are focused on the instruments of the marketing mix, i.e. on product, price, promotion and distribution. This is to make certain that each of these areas is given coherent treatment. Again, we emphasize that marketing strategy represents something vastly more significant than a random mix of the marketing instruments. The crux is the wholistic effect achieved when the instruments mutually enforce each other, as indicated in Part One. In Part Eight, the concluding part of the book, we shall return to the planning of general strategy in international marketing.

Reading 17, by Keegan, is an integrated treatment of product and promotion (communication) in multinational marketing. An array of conceptually different product-promotion combinations is presented with useful practical examples. Reading 18, by Stone, is a down-to-earth discussion of product simplification in marketing to the LDCs. While it is true that products especially adapted for materially primitive conditions are often scorned by the large poverty-stricken groups in the LDCs (presumably for reasons of pride) it is equally clear that these nations do represent a vast potential market for simplified goods. The article gives some successful examples and suggests that British ingenuity is still abroad.

Reading 19, by Cateora and Hess, serves a purpose already by relating pricing policy to business objectives – a rule all too often neglected by price-makers in practice. The discussion of price escalation in industrial marketing will be particularly instructive to readers not yet experienced in export (or import) operations.

Anglo-Saxon readers have reason to be interested in what is said about the effects of value-added taxes – unfamiliar as these taxes may be they are a wave of the future. We may note that the trend is toward non-cumulative varieties of the turnover tax, which generally have less upsetting effects on domestic distribution structures as well as on international trade. Reading 20, from *Business Week*, deals with pricing and other marketing problems under so-called run-away inflation, a topic of utmost practical importance completely neglected in the marketing literature.

One of the major problems in international marketing strategy planning is to decide when a strategy of homogenization (trying to capitalize on similarities between markets) and when one of heterogenization (capitalizing on, or adjusting to, differences between markets) is likely to pay off. This issue is especially acute when considering regional market arrangements, such as the EEC. Reading 21, by Ryans, summarizes the literature in this area as far as promotion planning is concerned. It also suggests that the observable trend towards market homogenization in various parts of the world notwithstanding, the time has not yet come (if, we would say, it ever will) to infer that a single global promotion strategy generally is advisable, perhaps excepting a few standardized products, such as soft drinks and gasoline.

Reading 22, by Ikeda, deals with a distribution system in transition. The general trading companies are, of course, the most outstanding feature on the marketing scene of Japan, the world's third largest trading partner.

17 W. J. Keegan

Five Strategies for Multinational Marketing

W. J. Keegan, 'Five strategies for multinational marketing',
European Business, January 1970, pp. 35–40.

Success lies in market response to a product offering. Although many companies have highly satisfactory product planning approaches for their domestic markets, very often the multinational product planning is left undone. This lack of planning for international markets is one of the major factors inhibiting the growth and profitability of international operations today.

Table 1 **Multinational product-communication mix: strategic alternatives**

	Product strategy	Communications strategy	Product examples	Product function or need satisfied	Conditions of product use	Ability to buy product
1.	Uniform	Uniform		Same	Same	Yes
2.	Same	Different	Bicycles Recreation Transportation	Different	Same	Yes
3.	Different	Same	Gasoline Detergents	Same	Different	Yes
4.	Different	Different	Clothing Greeting cards	Different	Different	Yes
5.	Invention	Develop new communications	Hand-powered washing machine	Same		No

The purpose of this article is to identify the *five strategic alternatives available to international marketers* and to show how to decide which strategy to use. Since the communications used to advertise and promote a product are such an integral part of the product itself, we shall include this factor in our analysis. Table 1 summarizes the proposed strategies.

Strategy one: same product, same message worldwide

As a company begins to move into foreign markets, there are good arguments for pursuing a uniform strategy of international marketing. This approach involves offering exactly the same product with the same advertising appeals to each national market. The uniform approach has a number of advantages. Firstly, and by no means the least, is its simplicity. Its demands upon executive and marketing time are minimal. It requires no original analysis or data generation, only execution or implementation. Since the product itself is unchanged, engineering and manufacturing costs that would be incurred by product changes are reduced to zero. In sum, it is the *lowest cost international product strategy*.

Another reason for a uniform strategy is the scarcity of good ideas. When a new one comes along, a wise manager tries to exploit it as much as possible. A case in point is Avis Rent-A-Car. They have used their 'We Try Harder' theme in America and in Europe – both times with success.

Many companies have followed this approach, with varying degrees of success. There is a story told in a well-known Belgian biscuit company about the company's nineteenth century founder. A relative of the company's founder had shipped some of the company's biscuits to China. The biscuits were very well received, and the relative wrote to Belgium saying that the Chinese liked the biscuit very much and that there was an excellent market for the company's product in China but that one modification would be required. Unfortunately, the company's white package was the color of mourning in China. If the package were changed, he wrote, there would be a substantial market. The founder replied with the hauteur of nineteenth century commercial pride, 'If the Chinese wish to eat our biscuits, they will take them in a white package.' Needless to say, the uniform strategy failed in this case.

In more recent times, companies such as PepsiCo have employed the uniform strategy. PepsiCo has sold exactly the same product, with the same advertising and promotional themes and appeals used in the United States, in each of the more than 100 countries in which it operates.

Coca-Cola sends to all its local managers a suitcase packed with materials including a bible which gives all the ads to be printed in color, those to appear in black and white, the number of times it can be full page or half page, and so on. The suitcase specifies each photo, every line of copy to be used, the tapes of music to be played over the radio. The local managers can do nothing on their own without first clearing it with headquarters in Atlanta.

These two companies' outstanding international performances are often cited in justification for this strategy.

Unfortunately, the uniform strategy does not work for all products. Chrysler has attempted to sell its Dodge Dart in Spain but the price and size of this product in the Spanish auto market have placed it in a category where potential is small and competition great, so that the sales performance of the Chrysler product has fallen far short of targets. Another US company spent several million dollars in an unsuccessful effort to capture the British cake mix market with their American-style fancy frosting and cake mixes, only to discover that Britons consume their cake at tea time, and that the cake they prefer is dry, spongy, and suitable to being picked up with the left hand while the right manages a cup of tea. Another US company that asked a panel of British housewives to bake their favourite cakes discovered this important fact and has since acquired a major share of the British cake mix market with a dry, spongy cake mix.

The uniform product-communications-price strategy has an enormous appeal to most multinational companies because of the cost savings associated with this approach. Two sources of savings, manufacturing economies of scale and eliminations of product R and D costs, are obvious. Less apparent, but still important, are the substantial economies associated with standardization of marketing communications. For a company with worldwide operations, the cost of preparing separate print and TV-cinema films for each market is enormous. PepsiCo international marketers have estimated, for example, that production costs for specially prepared advertising for foreign markets would cost them $8 million per annum, which is considerably more than the amount now spent by PepsiCo International for advertising production for its international markets. Still another source of savings of the uniform strategy is its marketing and managerial simplicity. Since a company's whole market department, and much of its general management, is focused on such questions as which product to offer, at what price, and with what kind of advertising appeals uniform strategy obviates the necessity for rethinking the answers and reduces the need for expensive manpower in each branch.

While the cost advantages of a uniform strategy are unmistakable, cost reduction is not as important as profit maximization. As shown above, the uniform strategy in spite of its immediate savings may in fact prove to be financially disastrous.

Furthermore, even companies such as PepsiCo who have had a generally successful experience with a uniform strategy are now beginning to conclude that while they have done well, they can do even better if they adapt their marketing mix.

Strategy two: same product-different communications

When a product fills a different need or is used differently under conditions similar to those in the domestic market, the only adjustment required is in marketing communications. Bicycles and motorscooters are illustrations of products which often fit this approach. They satisfy needs for recreation in the United States and for basic transportation in many parts of the world. Outboard motors are sold mainly to a recreation market in the United States, while the same motors in many countries are sold mainly to fishing and transportation fleets.

In effect, when this approach is pursued (or, as is often the case, when it is stumbled upon by accident) a product transformation occurs. The same physical product ends up serving a different function or use from its original one. An actual example of a very successful transformation is provided by the US farm machinery company which decided to market its US line of suburban lawn and garden power equipment in less developed countries as agricultural implements. The company's line of garden equipment was ideally suited to their farming tasks and most importantly, it was priced at almost a third less than competitive equipment – especially designed for small acreage farming.

There are many examples of food product transformation. Many dry soup powders, for example, are sold mainly as soups in Europe and as sauces or cocktail dips in the United States. The products are identical; the only change is in marketing communications. In this case, the main communications adjustment is in the labeling of the powder. In Europe, the label illustrates and describes how to make soup out of the powder. In the US, the label illustrates and describes how to make sauce and dip as well as soup.

The appeal of the same product-different marketing strategy is its relatively low cost of implementation. Since the product is unchanged, R and D, tooling, manufacturing setup, and inventory costs resulting from additions to the product line are avoided. The only costs of this approach are in identifying different product functions and reformulating marketing communications (advertising, sales, promotion, point of sale material, etc.) around the newly identified function.

Strategy three: different product, same communications

A third approach to international product planning is to extend without change the basic communications strategy developed for the home market, but to adapt the home product to local conditions. The different product-same communications strategy assumes that the product will serve the same function in foreign markets under different use conditions.

Esso followed this approach when it adapted its gasoline formulations to meet the weather conditions prevailing in market areas but used without change its basic message, 'Put a Tiger in Your Tank'. Since the tiger is an almost universal symbol of power, Esso was able to use its campaign in Europe, America, and Asia.

There are many other examples of products which have been adjusted to perform the same function internationally under different environmental conditions. International soap and detergent manufacturers have adjusted their product formulations to meet local water conditions and the characteristics of washing equipment with no change in their basic communications approach. Agricultural chemicals have been adjusted to meet different soil conditions and different types and levels of insect resistance. Household appliances have been scaled to sizes appropriate to different use environments, and clothing has been adapted to meet fashion criteria.

Strategy four: dual adaptation

Certain market conditions indicate a strategy of adapting both product and communications. As a result of different market conditions and the product's serving different functions, this combines strategies two and three.

US greeting card manufacturers have faced this in Europe, where a greeting card provides space for the sender to write his own message in contrast to the US card, which contains a prepared message, or what is known in the greeting card industry as 'sentiment'. The conditions under which greeting cards are purchased in Europe are also different from those in the United States. In Europe, cards are handled frequently by customers, which makes it necessary to package the greeting card in cellophane.

To sell instant coffee in England, Nescafé had to use this strategy. Their traditional instant coffee, developed in Switzerland and sold on the Continent, did not sell well in the United Kingdom. Their local marketing managers made tests and found that most Englishmen prefer a light, almost blond coffee. Their coffee-drinking habits had been developed during World War II, with the presence of American troops; consequently their taste in coffee is similar to the American one.

In marketing the new blend, Nescafé found that coffee is viewed as a non-traditional drink. As is well known, everyone drinks tea; those who choose coffee, like the young, are looking for something different. To reflect this, their publicity spots were made more aggressive.

Strategy five: product invention

The adaptation and adjustment strategies are effective approaches to international marketing when customer needs and the conditions under which products are used are similar to those in the home market. Unfortunately, this is not always the case, particularly in the less developed countries which contain three-quarters of the world's population. For these markets, the strategy should be invention or the development of an entirely new product designed to satisfy customer needs at a price within reach of the potential customer. This is a demanding, but – if product development costs are not excessive – a potentially rewarding product strategy for the mass markets in the middle and less developed countries of the world.

Although potential opportunities for invention in international marketing are legion, the number of instances where companies have responded is disappointingly small. For example, there are an estimated 600 million women in the world who still scrub their clothes by hand. These women have been served by soap and detergent companies for decades, yet only last year did one of these companies attempt to develop an inexpensive *manual* washing device.

The effort was launched by the vice-president of Marketing-Worldwide of Colgate Palmolive who asked the leading inventor of modern mechanical washing processes to consider 'inventing backwards' – to apply his knowledge not to a better mechanical washing device but to a much better *manual* device. The device developed by the inventor is an inexpensive (price under $10), all-plastic hand-powered washer that has the tumbling action of a modern automatic machine. It is one of the most efficient converters of mechanical energy to a hydraulic washing action yet developed and is reported to have been very favorably received in Mexican test markets.

How to choose a strategy

The best strategy is one which optimizes company profits over the long term. Stated more precisely, it maximizes the present value of cash flows from business operations. Which strategy for international markets best achieves this goal? There is no general answer to this question. Rather, the answer depends upon the specific product-market-company mix.

Some products demand adaptation, others lend themselves to adaptation, and others are best left unchanged. The same is true of markets. Some are so closely similar to the home market as to require little change. Other markets are moderately different and lend themselves to adaptation, and still others are so different as to require adaptation of the majority of products. Finally, companies differ not only in their manufacturing costs, but also in their capability to identify and produce profitable product adaptations.

Product-market analysis

The first step in formulating international product policy is to analyse each product. How is the product used? Does it require power sources, linkage to other systems, maintenance, preparation, style matching, and so on? Examples of mandatory adaptation are products designed for sixty cycle power going into fifty cycle markets, or products calibrated in metric measures going to the Anglo-Saxon markets. Products that require upkeep should be changed to reflect the different maintenance standards and practices, and products used under different conditions than those for which they were originally designed must be adapted.

Even more difficult are the product adaptations which are clearly not mandatory, but which are of critical importance in determining whether the product will appeal to a narrow segment rather than a broad mass market.

European companies frequently neglect adaptation of distribution and communications. Too often, companies believe they have adequately adapted their international product offering when they make mandatory adaptations of the physical features of a product (i.e. converting 220 volts to 110 volts) but extend their home market communications approach and rely upon export channels for distribution. The effect of such practice is to leave excellent products far short of their true market potential. Perhaps the most impressive example of what a company can do if it does commit itself to the full development of advertising and distribution programs is Volkswagen of America. It has developed a one billion dollar plus business basically by *taking a given product and exploiting its potential to the limit with a communications program specifically designed for the US market*, and a dealer organization whose quality and coverage have been widely admired in the industry.

Company analysis

Even if product-market analysis indicates an adaptation opportunity, each company must examine its own product-communications development and manufacturing costs. Clearly, any of the product strategies must survive the test of profit effectiveness. The often repeated exhortation that in international marketing a company should always adapt its products, advertising, and promotion is clearly superficial, for it does not take into account *costs* of adapting products and communications programs.

What are adaptation costs? They fall under two broad categories – *development* and *production*. Development costs will vary depending on the cost effectiveness of product/communications development groups within the company. The range in costs from company to company and product to product is great. Often, the company with international product development facilities has a strategic cost advantage. The vice-president of a leading US machinery company spoke recently of this kind of advantage:

> We have a machinery development group both here in the States and in Europe. I tried to get our US group to develop a machine for making elliptical cigars that dominate the European market. At first they said, 'Who would want an elliptical cigar machine?' Then they grudgingly admitted that they could produce such a machine for $500,000. I went to our Italian product development group with the same proposal and they developed the machine I wanted for $50,000. The differences were partly relative wage costs, but very importantly they were psychological. The Europeans see elliptical cigars every day, and they do not find the elliptical cigar unusual. Our American engineers were negative on elliptical cigars at the outset and I think this affected their overall response.

Analysis of a company's manufacturing costs is essentially a matter of identifying potential opportunity losses. If a company is reaping economies from large-scale production of a single product, then any shift to variations of the single product will raise manufacturing costs. In general, the more decentralized a company's manufacturing setup, the smaller the manufacturing cost of producing different versions of the basic product. Indeed, in the company with local manufacturing facilities for each national market, the additional manufacturing cost of producing an adapted product for each market is zero.

A more fundamental form of company analysis occurs when a firm is considering in general whether or not to explicitly pursue a strategy of product adaptation. At this level, analysis must focus not only on the manufacturing cost structure of the firm, but on whether the firm is capable of identifying product adaptation opportunities and of converting them into profitable products. The ability to identify possibilities depends to an important degree on the creativity of people in the organization and the effectiveness of information systems in the organization. The latter capability is as important as the former. Nescafé was able to find the right blend of coffee for the English only because of its well-developed marketing departments and their close connection to headquarters. The existence of salesmen, for example, who are creative in identifying profitable product adaptation opportunities is no assurance that their ideas will be translated into reality by the organization. Information, in the form of their ideas and perceptions, must move through the organization to those who are involved in the product development decision-making process and this movement, as any student of information systems in organizations will attest, is not automatic. Companies which lack perceptual and information system capabilities are not well equipped to change products, and either should concentrate on products which can be left alone or should develop these capabilities before turning to a product adaptation strategy.

Summary

The choice of product and communications strategy in international marketing depends on three key factors: (1) the product itself, defined in terms of the function or need it serves; (2) the market, defined in terms of the conditions under which the product is used, the preferences and ability to buy of potential customers; and (3) the costs of adaptation and manufacture of these product-communications approaches. Only after analysis of the product-market fit and of company capabilities and costs can executives choose the most profitable international strategy.

18 P. Stone

The Massive Market for Simplicity

P. Stone, 'The massive market for simplicity', *British Industry Week*, 25 April 1969, pp. 24ff.

On a scruffy doorway near Covent Garden Market is a sign saying 'Intermediate Technology Development Group'. What goes on beyond a door on the second floor suggests that all is not yet lost for British enterprise. ITDG is a limited, non-profit making company. Its main product is a catalogue of British companies and their wares, aimed at small scale enterprises in the developing countries.

In some parts of the world, what ITDG is trying to encourage in Britain exists naturally – because it is obvious that it should. For example, in Japan the Toyo Kogyo motor company used to produce a three-wheeled truck for the home market. When Japan began to prosper, the market for the cheap, slow three-wheeler practically disappeared. So the company sought out southeast Asian countries which were at an appropriate stage of economic development and mounted an export drive in those countries. Its three-wheeler still sells.

Halfway between a bicycle and a car, the three-wheeler was an example of 'intermediate technology'. In the same way, a horse-drawn mower and reaper, representing the halfway stage between a sickle and a combine harvester, might be the ideal thing at a certain stage in a country's economic evolution. One British manufacturer still draws an income from such a machine, thanks to ITDG.

But intermediate technology is not the same thing as old-fashioned technology that we have now abandoned. In agriculture, for example, many machines which gave good service in nineteenth-century England were made by casting metal. Now lighter, stronger versions may be built by welding rolled sections. The design will have been modified to suit modern production methods – but the machine will still be put to the same use.

Immense potential

The less-developed countries are growing at 5 per cent a year on average. Some, like Pakistan, are growing far more rapidly. They constitute an expanding market in which it is possible to sell a wide range of manufactures without the need to invest in speculative R and D or to adopt sophisticated designs. The potential demand surge from these countries is immense; British exporters should establish themselves now, with a view to future prosperity.

That is only part of the reason why the existence of ITDG is an encouraging sign. The way in which the company came to be formed suggests that the British may not have lost the ability to triumph in spite of their own Government and, more difficult, their own economists.

Such economists as Lord Balogh and Mr Kaldor have long been active in the field of aid to the underdeveloped countries. Even before economists were employed by the British Government, international organizations like FAO and UNESCO offered challenging jobs to men prepared to help the poor nations. The accepted emphasis was placed on the provision of an infrastructure – steel plants, railways, chemical plants and the like. All these were big projects demanding large amounts of scarce capital and technical resources. The idea of expending capital on lesser things was frowned upon, because capital is generally less productive if dispersed. This 'industrialization first' orthodoxy led to the neglect of the agricultural sector although, to be fair, Lord Balogh himself has always been a strong advocate of agricultural development.

However, commonsense suggested that a slow build-up of agricultural wealth by the introduction of simple technology – moving from sickles to scythes – might be a sensible step. Two people who believed that were Mrs Julia Porter and Mr George McRobie. In the summer of 1965 they called a conference at the Overseas Development Institute, a body which often seems to function as a lightning conductor by allowing dissatisfaction with British aid policy to earth itself without upsetting the Ministry. The first meeting of bankers, economists and businessmen resulted only in an agreement that the subject should be discussed further.

Meanwhile, a well-known but definitely not mainstream economist for the National Coal Board, Dr E. F. Schumacher, had written an article for the *Observer* advocating similar views and defining 'Intermediate Technology'. The article had languished on the *Observer* spike for a year until, one August weekend, the main lead fell through and it was pushed into the gap. The response was astonishing. Apart from a deluge of letters, African prime ministers actually rang up and demanded: 'Who is this Schumacher? He must come to my country . . .' Mrs Porter and McRobie joined Schumacher and set up an organization to propagate their unfashionable but very sensible views.

At that point, the hopeful spark might simply have flickered out. Attempts to change the perspectives of governments and international bodies usually expire on the outer palisades, where lack of money and evident lack of progress combine to exhaust even the most idealistic.

But, by lucky chance, the British National Export Council (BNEC) was about to send off a mission to sell British agricultural machinery in Nigeria. It was suggested that much of the machinery was too sophisticated for Nigeria's stage of development. With the help of the National College of Agricultural Engineering, a list of hand- or animal-operated agricultural machinery was compiled and despatched in a hasty three weeks. The response to these machines was far warmer than that accorded to the expensive combine-harvesters which British agriculture considers necessary.

From that time, theoretical arguments on the merits of concentrating capital expenditure rather than frittering it away on intermediate technology became increasingly irrelevant. ITDG simply responded to demands from the developing countries.

Advertising revenue

Obviously a much enlarged catalogue was the next logical step, and this provided a way to raise funds. Suitable manufacturers were invited to advertise in the catalogue at the rate of £10 a half-page. Butyl Products took four pages to give a handy guide to building your own reservoir; most companies took less. One company now advertises a windmill pump for £120 complete f.o.b. – 'remember there are no running costs'. One company advertises ploughshares in both French and German, another displays its harrows with a photograph of two superb English Shire horses. There are advertisements for irrigation packs, wheelbarrows, small engines and generators, pulleys, looms, printing machines and tractors. Animal-drawn tool bars can be bought for as little as £10.

So far, 7000 copies of the catalogue have been either distributed to or bought by banks, company operatives, importers, government offices and other bodies in developing countries.

When a response comes, it can be embarrassingly large. By 1950, Bamletts of Thirsk, which appears to have had the distinction of making the last animal-drawn reaper and mower in Britain, was down to making one or two a year. Now that the idea of Britain as a supplier of intermediate technology has caught on, things have changed. Esso Petroleum contacted ITDG with an enquiry about 1000 animal-drawn reapers and mowers for Turkey. Tanzania and Pakistan wanted them too. Bamletts sold a licence to a company in Pakistan and is now drawing royalties from a design that seemed obsolete ten years ago. If the Turkish order materializes, the company will have to set up a new production line.

Moulding policy

Gardening tools form a good part of the equipment requested and such devices as spring-loaded forks and spades ought to sell well. However, ITDG realizes that peasants have profound suspicions of anything too new. Although the spring-loaded spade may be the suburban gardener's answer to digging a small plot with minimum exertion, a peasant used to, say, the mattock, will find the change far too great. ITDG has therefore helped to promote the development of a more efficient mattock, with an extra handle for added leverage.

What does ITDG do next? Again, circumstances are moulding policy. ITDG now gets many enquiries not only for hardware but also for advice and information. What is needed is a clearing house for technical enquiries. That need is now being investigated with a view to establishing 'Inter-tech', which would have two functions. One would be as a base for consultancy, in order to promote the field application of low-cost intermediate technologies, the other would be to run a London-based office to handle enquiries from abroad and find British companies, research associations and the like which could provide the answers. Whether products were sold would then be for the interested parties to decide between themselves.

Successful path

ITDG treads a somewhat tortuous path between being businesslike and being charitable. It is determined, however, to lean as far as possible towards commercial behaviour; the 'rate for the job' is a firm policy. One interesting pointer to future development is VITA, or 'Volunteers for International Technical Assistance', an American non-profit-making organization which provides spare-time assistance from a bank of specialists. Its budget for 1968, when it handled 2000 enquiries, was $210,000. It also defines key problems for concentrated development effort. The result of one such effort, the VITA solar cooker, is now 'in wide demand throughout Africa'.

On the British domestic scene do-it-yourself has become an industry on its own, or at least a market with a clearly definable identity. It is familiarly known as the DR market and many have made a lot of money from it. On the international scene the same could happen to intermediate technology. Perhaps the ITDG will turn out to be as successful in its own area as Barry Bucknell has been in his.

19 P. R. Cateora and J. M. Hess

Pricing in International Markets

Excerpted from P. R. Cateora and J. M. Hess, *International Marketing*, Richard D. Irwin, 1971, pp. 667–710.

Pricing objectives

Two basic choices are available to a company in setting its price policy. It may view pricing as an active instrument for the accomplishment of marketing objectives, or it may consider prices to be a static element in business decisions. If the former viewpoint is adhered to, the company will utilize prices to accomplish certain objectives relative to a target return or profit from overseas operations or for the accomplishment of a target volume of market share. If the second approach is followed, the company will likely be content to sell what it can in overseas markets and look on this as bonus volume. Obviously the second alternative is hardly adequate for enterprises with operations in foreign countries and is more likely to be the viewpoint taken by a firm which exports only and which places a rather low priority on foreign business.

Companies' policies may be framed in terms of control over final prices, or the company may be more interested in the net price received by the business. In the latter case, the producer may not attempt to control the price at which the product is ultimately sold; in the former, price is considered to be an important strategic element of the marketing mix and the company will want to accomplish all possible control over the end price. Some firms, however, that follow a price control policy in their domestic business have found that they were unable to control end prices in foreign markets, and therefore have reoriented their thinking to 'mill net pricing', e.g. to prices which they receive for their goods when they are shipped from the plant.

Approaches to international pricing

Regardless of whether the orientation is toward control over end prices or over net prices, the company will have a policy relative to the net prices that must be received. Both cost and market considerations are important; the company will not sell goods below cost of production and cannot sell goods at a price which will not be accepted by the market. Firms which are not extremely active in overseas marketing and many firms which produce industrial goods orient their pricing almost solely on a cost basis. Firms which employ pricing as part of the strategic mix, however, will be aware of such alternatives as market segmentation from country to country or market to market, competitive pricing in the marketplace, and other market-oriented pricing factors.

Even firms which orient their price thinking around cost must determine whether they are going to use variable cost pricing or full cost pricing in costing their goods. In variable cost pricing, the firm is concerned only with the marginal or incremental cost of producing the goods that are sold in overseas markets. Such firms regard foreign sales as bonus sales and assume that any return over their variable cost makes a contribution to net profit. These firms may be able to price most competitively in foreign markets; but because they are selling products abroad at lower net prices than they are selling them in the domestic market, they may be subject to charges of dumping. In such case they open themselves to antidumping tariffs or penalties, which takes away their competitive advantage. Companies which follow the full cost pricing philosophy insist that no unit of a similar product is different from any other unit in terms of cost and that each unit bear its full share of the total fixed and variable cost.

In domestic marketing, both variable cost and full cost policies are followed, but there is probably not so much use of variable cost pricing as there is in international marketing. The international firm which uses variable cost pricing is ultimately confronted with the question of whether it regards itself as a marketer exporting from one country into another or as a world marketer. If the firm regards itself as a world marketer, it is more likely to think in terms of full cost pricing for all markets. There is always the question, however, of whether a firm should price below full costs if it will increase profits and if it has no other alternative access to certain markets. These are all questions of policy which must be resolved by the firm.

A sample policy

The policy of the Eimco Corporation relative to international pricing is reproduced below. This statement illustrates the complexity of establishing a price policy for a firm which operates differently in various countries and which sells numerous types of products. It also represents an example of a concise, well thought out, general pricing policy for international operations.

A pricing philosophy for this kind of a multiple operation *could* be so complex and sensitive to external situations as to be thoroughly unworkable. Therefore, we chose a rather simple formula which has succeeded for us so far. It was prompted by the fact that many of our customers are themselves engaged in activities around the world and are likely to use our machines in any country.

Where the same product is made and offered for sale by the domestic company and one or more of its subsidiaries, each company is free to compete with the others, although they are substantially geared to market in separate areas. Pricing among our various subsidiaries is generally based on the real costs of each, and there is no attempt to hold to a universal factory price. Our licensees are largely restricted to specific areas where they determine their own pricing policy, which includes the cost of a technical fee or royalty to us.

Eimco maintains its factory list prices in selling its standardized products throughout the world. Except in special circumstances, its dealers may not add a markup of their own but must look to their regularly established discount or commission for their compensation. In other words, regardless of where our machines are made or sold, they will be priced to a customer at the established factory list price of the producing company plus the cost of transportation and related charges.

The pricing of our tailor-made process machinery follows somewhat the same pattern. Prices are primarily geared to the cost of manufacture in the country where they are made and to the usual overheads of that division, plus a markup which is calculated to give a fair and reasonable return (Seakwood, 1961).

Cost factors

Regardless of the strategic factors involved and the company's orientation to market pricing, every price must be set with cost considerations in mind. At a minimum, prices over a long run must cover costs if a business is to survive. Full costs do not have to be covered in every market. However, as long as company sales as a whole do cover all costs in international marketing, even the determination of the cost of goods sold may occasion much debate. In the case of intracorporate transfers, such transfers may be based solely on direct production costs (variable costs only) or may include profit plus general administrative costs, research and development costs, and other overhead items. In determining producer company overheads, management must be careful not to include factors which would unduly raise prices abroad and thereby reduce sales volume. Sometimes domestic marketing sales and advertising costs are included in the base price of the goods, but because such costs are reincurred in the foreign markets they should not be included in the basic cost determination.

Technically, operations in a given market may contribute profit as long as goods are sold at a price above variable cost, but in reality most companies insist that at least some of the other costs mentioned above be included.

A number of costs which are unique to international marketing or which are exaggerated in international marketing should also be borne in mind by the pricing executive. Some of the major categories are taxes and tariffs; middleman and transportation costs; and financing and risk costs.

Taxes and tariffs

'Nothing is surer than death and taxes' has a particularly familiar ring in the ears of the international trader because taxes include tariffs, and tariffs are one of the most pervasive features of international trading. Taxes and tariffs affect the ultimate price which the consumer must pay for a good, and in most instances it is the consumer who bears the burden of both. Sometimes, however, the consumer may benefit when manufacturers who are selling goods into foreign countries reduce their net return in order to gain access on a competitive footing to a foreign market. Whether he absorbs them or passes them on, taxes and tariffs are of interest to the international businessman.

A tariff, or duty, is a special form of taxation, and like other forms of tax, it may be levied for the purpose of protecting a market or for raising governmental revenue. A tariff is a fee charged when a good is brought into a country from another country. The level of the tariff is typically expressed as the rate of duty and may be levied as specific, ad valorem, or in a combination of these forms. A specific duty is a flat charge per physical unit imported, such as fifteen cents per bushel of rye. Ad valorem duties are levied as a percentage of the value of the goods imported, such as 20 per cent of the value of imported watches. Combination tariffs include both a specific and an ad valorem charge, such as $1 per camera plus 10 per cent of its value. Tariffs and other forms of import tax serve to discriminate against all foreign goods. Fees for import certificates or for other administrative processing can assume such levels that they are in fact import taxes, but such fees, and most other direct taxes, do not discriminate against foreign goods. Many countries, for example, have purchase or excise taxes which apply to various categories of goods, value added or turnover taxes which apply as the product goes through a channel of distribution, and retail sales taxes. Such taxes may increase the end price of the goods rather significantly but, in general, do not discriminate against foreign goods nor detrimentally affect foreign goods.

Indirect taxes, such as income tax, and excise taxes may influence decisions concerning the legal form of operation or the country in which to produce. Generally, however, such taxes are calculated in the basic cost of production of the goods and do not significantly or directly affect the pricing policy of a firm. Such taxes are accounted for in different ways. Under current GATT rules, it is a practice to permit indirect taxes on goods to be rebated at the time of exporting; direct taxes may not be rebated. Some individuals have argued that if the mix of the US taxes were varied to reduce direct taxes and increase indirect taxes, American goods would be more competitive in the world marketplace. One study, however, has indicated that US prices could not be reduced more than 2 per cent at the border as the result of such manipulations (Aliber and Stein, 1964). In general, then, tariffs are the primary discriminatory tax which must be taken into account in reckoning with foreign competition. All the various taxes, however, must be considered when attempting to establish retail or industrial selling prices.

Middleman cost

The diversity of channels used to reach the market and the lack of standardization of the middleman's markups may leave the typical producer in a position of not knowing what his product ultimately sells for.

Channel diversity is difficult to cope with, but the fully integrated marketer operating abroad may also find that he is faced with a large number of unanticipated costs because the marketing and channel of distribution infrastructure is so undeveloped. In addition to the wide variations in the cost of international shipping and internal transportation costs, the marketer may incur extra expenses for warehousing and for handling of small shipments, and he may have to bear increased financing costs when dealing with underfinanced middlemen.

Since no convenient source of data on middleman costs is available, the international marketer must rely on experience and marketing research to discover what his middleman cost will be. For example, the Campbell soup company found their middleman and physical distribution costs in the United Kingdom to be some thirty percent higher than in the United States. Among other reasons, extra costs were incurred because soup was purchased in such small quantities – English grocers typically purchase 24 can cases of assorted soups (with each can being hand packed for shipment). In the United States, a typical purchase unit is 48 can cases of one variety, and they are purchased by dozens, hundreds, and carloads. Such small purchases in Europe forced the company to include an extra wholesale level in its channel to facilitate handling of such small orders. Purchase frequency patterns also run up billing and order costs; both wholesalers and retailers purchase two to three times as often as their US counterparts. Sales-call costs become virtually prohibitive. These and other distribution cost factors caused the company to change both its price and price patterns, but also forced a complete restructuring of the channel system.

Financing and risk costs

The differences in financing international marketing activities contrast with domestic financing essentially in magnitude rather than type. Because of the time lags involved for both the seller and the buyer, international business transactions may tie up capital for considerable lengths of time. Such capital tie-ups increase the cost of financing not only for the seller, but in some instances for the buyer as well. In some countries, for example, when an import certificate is obtained for certain goods the purchaser may have to deposit funds for the purchase of the goods or equipment. In the case of custom-made machine tools or equipment, the funds may be tied up for as long as six months or a year. Such a cost is particularly significant in countries where interest rates are high. In some South American countries, for example, interest rates of 3 per cent a month are not unusual. Assuming an interest rate of even $1\frac{1}{2}$ per cent, a six-month commitment can, in effect, add 9 per cent to the cost of the goods for the ultimate purchaser.

Other than the normal risks encountered in business, some of which may be intensified internationally, inflation and exchange-rate fluctuations constitute significant financial risks which may affect the price of goods, the terms which are offered, the cost of doing business, and even the manufacturer's method of pricing goods and publicizing price changes.

The effects of inflation on cost must be accounted for. In countries with rapid inflation, selling price should be related not only to the cost of goods sold, but to the cost of replacing the items. Goods are often sold below their cost of replacement plus overhead and sometimes are even sold below replacement cost. In these instances, the company would be better off not to sell the products at all. When payment is likely to be delayed for several months or is worked out on a long-term contract, inflationary change must be figured into the price.

To do business in nations with runaway inflation, such as Brazil, which has experienced inflation at rates as high as 86 per cent per year, companies have learned that they can adjust to the situation by being constantly alert to the rate of change and modifying their prices to match the pace of the inflation. Pharmaceutical manufacturers in Brazil have prices which are fixed by law; yet these manufacturers are faced with wage and material cost increases that cannot be circumvented or absorbed into the production cost. Such companies move as rapidly as possible to secure governmental approval for price increases which will keep pace with inflation.

The problems of exchange-rate fluctuation pose fewer hazards because a number of devices are available for counteraction. Prices, for example, may be quoted in the currency of the home country or in terms of some stable monetary unit, such as the US dollar. When such a contract is unacceptable to the purchaser, the foreign exchange risk may be modified through the process of hedging.[1] Companies with foreign operations have few ways to protect themselves in attempting to repatriate foreign profits; however, the foreign operations are usually in tune with local inflation and exchange rates, so this problem, too, can be minimized.

Innumerable other cost variables could be identified depending on the market, the product, and the situation. The cost, for example, of reaching a market with relatively small potential may be high. Extreme competition in certain world markets can raise the cost or lower the margins available to world businessmen. Even such small things as the payoffs that may be necessary for local officials can introduce unexpected cost to the unwary entre-

1. 'Hedging' relates to the process of selling or buying foreign currencies in a manner to offset exchange fluctuations.

preneur. In any case, experience in a given marketplace will provide the basis for compensating for cost differences in different markets. With experience, a firm which does its pricing on a cost basis operates in a realm of fairly measurable factors.

Price escalation

Businessmen or others traveling abroad are often surprised to find that goods which may be relatively inexpensive in their home country are priced 'outrageously' in other countries. Because of the natural tendency to assume that such prices are a result of profiteering, manufacturers often resolve to begin exporting to 'crack' these new foreign markets. Excess profits may in fact exist, but more often added costs are the cause of the disproportionate difference in price. What the uninformed or inexperienced marketer does not understand, however, is the rapid rise of prices which sometimes take place when goods enter foreign markets. Such price increases are here termed price escalation. Specifically the term relates to situations where the ultimate prices are raised by shipping cost, tariffs, longer channels of distribution, larger middlemen margins, and special taxes.

The following sections show how cost and tax variations cause prices to rise differently in various markets under alternative circumstances and offer some possible methods of coping with the specific type of price increases called price escalation.

Sample effects of price escalation

Table 1 illustrates some of the possible effects these factors may have on the end price of a consumer item. Because costs and tariffs vary so widely from country to country, a hypothetical but realistic example is used; the student should realize that fluctuations can be wider than those illustrated. For example, tariff rates and international transportation charges are held constant in this example; if they should vary, the end price would vary also.

Table 1 assumes that a constant net price is received by the manufacturer; it further assumes that all domestic transportation is absorbed by the various middlemen and reflected in their margins. In the first three foreign examples, it is assumed that the foreign middlemen have the same margins as the domestic middlemen. In some instances foreign middleman margins will be lower, but it is equally probable that foreign middleman margins will be greater (as is assumed at the retail level in the fourth foreign example). In fact, in many instances middlemen will use higher

Table 1 Sample causes and effects of price escalation

	Domestic example	Foreign example 1: assuming the same channels with wholesaler importing directly	Foreign example 2: importer and same margins and channels	Foreign example 3: same as 2 but with 10% cumulative turnover tax	Foreign example 4: long channels larger retail margins, no turnover tax
Mfg. net	$ ·95	$ ·95	$0·95	$0·95	$0·95
Transport, c.i.f.	x	0·15	0·15	0·15	0·15
Tariff (20%)	x	0·19	0·19	0·19	0·19
Importer pays		x	1·29	1·29	1·29
Importer margin when sold to wholesaler (25% on cost)	x		0·32	0·32 + 0·13 turnover tax = 0·45	0·32
Wholesaler pays landed cost	·95	1·29	1·61	1·74 0·58 + 0·17 turnover tax = 0·75	1·61
Wholesaler margin (33⅓% on cost)	·32	0·43	0·54		0·54
Local foreign jobber pays	x	x	x	x	2·15
Jobber margin (33⅓% on cost)	x	x	x	x	0·72
Retailer pays	1·27	1·72	2·15	2·49 1·25	2·87
Retail margin (50% on cost)	·63	0·86	1·08	+ 0·25 turnover tax = 1·50	1·92 (66⅔% on cost)
Retail price	1·90	2·58	3·23	3·99	4·79

Note:
1. All figures in $ US
2. x = This cost is not applicable in this example.
3. The table assumes that all domestic transportation is absorbed by the middlemen.
4. Transportation, tariffs, and middleman margins vary from country to country, but for purposes of comparison only a few of the possible variations are shown.

wholesale and retail margins for foreign goods than for similar domestic goods. Such a differential contributes an additional source of price escalation.

Notice that the retail prices for the product range from $1·90 domestically to $2·58 in the most optimistic foreign example (example 1), $3·23 when an importer is involved (example 2) through $3·99 when a cumulative turnover tax of 10 per cent is added (example 3) and finally to $4·79 when the channel is longer and the retail margin is greater (example 4). Remember that in all five examples the net price received by the manufacturer is $0·95. The variation in the retail price illustrates the difficulty of price control by manufacturers when they are dealing with overseas retail markets. No matter how much the manufacturer may wish to market his product in a foreign country for a price equivalent to $1·90 US, he may find that he has little opportunity for such control. Even assuming the most optimistic conditions of foreign example 1, the producer would need to cut his net by nearly one third to absorb freight plus tariff so that the goods could be priced the same on the foreign and domestic markets.[1]

The National Housewares Manufacturers Association of the United States sponsored a trade mission to Germany, France, Italy, and the United Kingdom. The report of this mission provides numerous examples of price escalation. It was reported that in Italy 'a combination electric can opener with a US cost of approximately $5·98 and a retail range of $8·88 to $9·88 was priced in a Milan department store at the equivalent of $24.' Tariffs, transportation and other costs causing such price escalation may put foreign manufacturers at a distinct competitive disadvantage. Again, many US appliances in France were reported to be from 20 to 100 per cent higher in price than comparable French-produced merchandise. A French automatic toaster, for example, was priced at $15, with a very similar American one priced at $22.

Strategic approaches to price escalation

Although the manufacturer may not be able to control the end price of his goods as closely as he would like, he can employ several strategic approaches designed to counteract the problem of price differentials. Large, well-financed manufacturers may

1. To compute, work backward from the retail price. Retail price minus (retail margin, wholesaler margin, transportation and tariffs) equals manufacturers' net.

have a number of alternative approaches, but the small firm which is merely engaged in occasional exporting has less flexibility.

A company may attempt to offset tariffs and transportation charges by accepting a lower net price for goods sold in foreign markets. This often is not an acceptable alternative; in the first foreign example in Table 1, the manufacturer would have to be willing to accept sixty-seven cents rather than ninety-five cents a unit to maintain the same retail price in the foreign as in the domestic market. Freight absorption has the same effect and serves essentially the same function as a price reduction in that it lowers the net price received by the producer or exporter.

The type of price reductions mentioned here may be viewed by the importing country as dumping and thus may be subject to being offset by countervailing tariffs which would nullify the intended price advantage.

Tariff differentials can sometimes be at least partially overcome by modifying the product in such a way to bring it into a different rate category or by shipping components and assembling them in the foreign country where they are to be sold. This alternative assumes a fairly well-developed market and is suitable only when assembly costs represent a rather large part of the total product cost or where components can be shipped under substantially lower tariff rates than completed products.

The manufacturer may find that tariff and transportation barriers are so great that he needs to go into overseas production in order to remain competitive in the foreign market. This, of course, is a logical alternative only if the manufacturer is adequately financed, if raw materials and labor are available in the foreign country, and if the market will support such a productive facility.

If the manufacturer can find ways to shorten the channels of distribution or to distribute products directly to customers or consumers, this may keep prices under control. The process of eliminating middlemen is as costly in international markets, however, as it is in domestic markets, and although channels may be shortened, marketing functions are not eliminated and marketing costs may not necessarily be lowered. Many countries have what is called a turnover tax which is levied on goods as they pass through the channel of distribution. Each time a good changes hands, it is taxed. In some countries, such as France, the tax is levied in such a way that it is noncumulative; that is, tax is paid only on the difference (value-added) between a middleman's and selling prices. A good sold by a manufacturer to a wholesaler for $7 would be taxed seventy cents if the tax rate were 10 per cent. Thus the cost to the wholesaler must be $7·70. If the wholesaler sold it for $9·50, the tax would amount to 10 per cent of the $1·80 margin, so it would be eighteen cents, making the wholesaler's selling price $9·68. The 'normal' rate of the French value-added tax (VAT) is 20 per cent of the sale price, including the VAT itself. It ranges from 6 per cent on basic foodstuffs to 25 per cent for luxury items. Such items as bread and milk are exempt.

Prior to 1970 all European Economic Community countries except France had a turnover system of taxation, but all have agreed to go to a VAT system. The new system will employ a higher rate of tax but will tax only the value added at each transfer. In general, such taxes have tended to raise the total tax bill, but the effects are difficult to assess because every country in Europe has a somewhat different taxing system. The VAT, incidentally, is often refunded to manufacturers when they export goods, thereby serving, in effect, as a tax subsidy for exports.

In some countries, the turnover tax is cumulative. In such countries the total selling price is taxed each time goods change hands. To follow the previous example, the tax on the sale from the manufacturer to wholesale would be seventy cents with the wholesaler costs being $7·70. The wholesaler who marked the price up to $9·50 would have to add 10 per cent of that price, ninety-five cents, making his selling price $10·45. In countries where turnover is cumulative, the tax alone provides special incentive for developing short distribution channels. Some nations, however, attempt to lessen such effect on distribution patterns by assessing the tax at different rates. The normal turnover tax rate is about 4 per cent, but in certain carefully defined circumstances wholesalers may be taxed at a rate of only 1 per cent. In Table 1, example 3 assumes a cumulative turnover tax of 10 per cent which in that example is incurred three times – when the importer sells to the wholesaler, when the wholesaler sells to the retailer and when the retailer sells to the consumer. The tax in that example totalled fifty-five cents or slightly over half of the manufacturer's net price. Shorter channels could have reduced the tax considerably.

References

ALIBER, R. Z. and STEIN, H. (1964), 'The price of US exports and the mix of US direct and indirect taxes', *Amer. Econ. Rev.*, September, p. 703.

SEAKWOOD, H. J. (1961), 'Pricing considerations in the international market', *Pricing, The Critical Decision*, American Management Association, Inc., p. 78.

20 Business Week

When Cruzeiros Spiral – Think Dollars

'When cruzeiros spiral – think dollars', *Business Week*, 13 March 1965, pp. 107–109.

This Reading is included as illustrative of marketing problems under inflationary conditions; at the request of the original publisher we emphasize that naturally it does not purport to be descriptive of Brazil seven years later.

Corn Products Co., a multinational company with sixty-four plants in twenty-seven countries, prides itself on its ability to operate anywhere in the world – even under the most adverse conditions.

Right now, in Brazil, where it has three plants, the conditions Corn Products must cope with include an inflation rate that topped 80 per cent last year – and that's about as adverse as any company treasurer would want a condition to get.

But Corn Products has a long experience in dealing with inflation. In other Latin countries where it operates – among them Chile, Colombia, Argentina, and Uruguay – inflation currently is running as high as 40 per cent annually.

To deal with this kind of situation, Corn Products has devised a many-pronged strategy to keep profits up and growth constant. What it tells its overseas managers to do is to think in dollars – not cruzeiros or pesos.

'Each managing director of an overseas affiliate understands that he represents a dollar economy whose dividends are paid in dollars,' says Corn Products Honorary Chairman John R. Rhamstine. 'His goal is a dollar return.'

Rhamstine adds: 'We do not speculate in foreign exchange, but we utilize every known means of protecting our investment and profits from deterioration because of currency devaluation.'

The long term

Thinking in dollars doesn't mean that Corn Products expects to repatriate dollar profits from every overseas operation every year.

In Brazil, its three plants make industrial and consumer products that range from starches and syrups to mayonnaise, soups, and animal feeds. But under that country's currency exchange restrictions, Corn Products hasn't taken any profits out of Brazil for three years.

'We're in business for the long term,' says one top company official. 'We can afford to wait.'

Running up the figures

To keep tabs on how it is doing amidst inflation, Corn Products' Brazilian affiliate prepares frequent supplementary reports on prices, earnings, and other balance sheet data, using the Brazilian cost-of-living index as a correction factor to translate cruzeiro figures into dollar equivalents.

'Exchange rates don't necessarily represent the true value of the currency,' explains James W. McKee, Jr, Corn Products controller and former managing director of the Brazilian affiliate. 'But it has been our experience in Brazil that over the long pull the rates of exchange follow the trend of the cost-of-living index.'

Since the index is adjusted monthly, it eliminates to a large extent the extreme fluctuations that result from changes in the exchange rates. It has the further advantage that it 'tends to reduce unpleasant surprises in reports to management,' McKee adds.

Using this method, McKee says, Corn Products is able to determine whether it is keeping prices up on a dollar replacement basis. But it attaches no dollar figure to sales: instead, it watches only the trend of physical volume of sales. On this basis, the company boosted sales in Brazil 78 per cent between 1959 and 1964.

Another phase

Keeping track of operations in dollar terms and actual sales volume is only the start of Corn Products' strategy to beat inflation. As a part of Corn Products' technique of multinational operations, McKee has systematically compiled from the experience of affiliates in all countries a set of guides for making a profit in an inflationary economy. The most important tools are frequent price increases and the borrowing of money.

The faster the rate of inflation, the more frequent the price increases. Early last year, most companies in Brazil were boosting their prices every three to five weeks; automobile makers were automatically hiking prices 7 per cent on the first of every month.

It's better for a company to make small, frequent price hikes like this, than to jolt customers with the large price increases that sooner or later would be required to pass on rising raw material costs.

Guessing game

One problem, though, is that customers tend to put in big orders just before a price increase and cut back their purchases afterwards – paying only when it is time to place a new order. To offset this, companies in an inflationary economy like Brazil's tend to give shorter and shorter notice of price hikes – with the result that customers try to anticipate the increase.

'It becomes quite a game, trying to outguess each other,' says McKee. 'Some companies found that if they boosted their prices on the first of each month, they would sell only in the last few days.'

Keeping bad debts down

One peculiarity of rising inflation in an economy like Brazil's is that losses from bad debts are generally very low, since customers can eventually pay what they owe in cheaper cruzeiros, if they wait long enough. The problem is to get them to pay promptly. While credit terms may be a maximum of thirty days, accounts receivable may run as high as sixty days.

'Such a level of accounts receivable wouldn't be tolerated in the States,' McKee observes.

One way to keep receivables down is to offer discounts for early payment – in Brazil or anywhere in the world. But the effective discount rate has to be more attractive to the customer than his cost of borrowing money elsewhere.

'A customer who has to pay 7 per cent interest per month would prefer to pay on due date rather than with discount, if we were to use terms – similar to the US – of thirty days net with 2 per cent for payment in ten days,' McKee says. 'Last year, when interest rates outside were running 5 per cent per month, we raised our cash discount rate to an effective 7 per cent per month.'

The borrowing ploy

A company operating in an inflationary economy must also borrow money, in order to protect its capital. Theoretically, a company would be fully protected if it could borrow all its working capital.

In Brazil, the most common means of borrowing include expanded supplier credits, discounting of accounts receivable, using receivables or inventories for collateral, promissory notes, depositing inventories in bonded warehouses and discounting warrants.

Some companies in Brazil use less conventional means of 'borrowing' money. For example, Brazilian corporate income taxes are not on a pay-as-you-go basis; returns for the previous year are filed in April, with payment due from July through November. By shifting the close of its fiscal year to, say, February, 1965, a company could get a one-time advantage from not having to pay taxes on 1964 income – normally due in 1965 – until July of 1966.

Difficulties

The higher the rate of inflation, the harder it is to borrow long term money. Some banks in Brazil will lend money on 24-hour call. Outside of normal financial channels, other businesses that are looking for a better return on their funds than they could get from a bank may also lend money on call.

In many countries – not only Brazil – companies usually must have a number of banks as credit sources. It may even be necessary, according to McKee, to maintain standby credit lines that are used from time to time to keep them active, and absorb the interest charges.

'The banks want a lot of movement in the accounts,' McKee says. 'This not only is a form of advertising to the people receiving their checks, but it enables them to keep a more liquid position when checks are not always presented immediately.'

3 Protecting the profits

For companies like Corn Products, which buy farm commodities, there's an advantage in the easier availability of agricultural credit over industrial credit from government agencies. It may be possible to obtain credit from a government agricultural bank that will be passed on directly to suppliers.

By such methods, Corn Products has managed to keep afloat and make a profit in Brazil. To keep those profits from being eaten up by inflation, it has been putting most of them into fixed assets.

'Generally, it is recognized that once funds have been invested in fixed assets, the inflationary loss is stopped,' McKee says. 'This is based on the premise that values of real estate and equipment tend to increase at the same rate as the devaluation of the currency.'

New plants

Expanding by this means, Corn Products has built two new factories in Brazil in the past five years, including a new $10 million plant at Mogi Guacu that was completed early last year. In the same period, it has expanded its number of employees from 1,000 to 1,800.

Such investment requires advance planning, however, to provide a use for profits as they are accumulated. Companies that have just finished a program of plant expansion invest in other things, such as inventory or advertising as a means of increasing future earnings.

Easy sales

Selling is no great problem in a rising inflation such as Brazil has had in recent years, when people spent money to convert their depreciating cruzeiros into consumer goods, or into investment in hard goods or real estate. But now, the rate of inflation is falling in Brazil under the impact of the Castelo Branco government's austerity program. As a result, some of the rules for dealing with inflation have to be revised.

'In this situation', McKee cautions, 'you have to be careful not to have large loans at rates you don't want to pay.'

In addition, demand eases off in a period of declining inflation, since people still making payments on previous purchases can't afford to make so many new purchases. In such a leveling-off period, extended credit terms may be essential to help sales.

An eye on everything

Most of all, what's needed in dealing with inflation is a manager with good financial acumen, one who is prepared to forget some of the rules for operating in a more stable economy.

'The man on the spot has to be fast on his feet,' McKee says, 'and he has to watch what is going on – in the markets, in the economy, and in his own planning.'

21 J. K. Ryans, Jr

Is It Too Soon to Put a Tiger in Every Tank?

J. K. Ryans, Jr, 'Is it too soon to put a tiger in every tank?', *Columbia Journal of World Business*, March–April 1969, pp. 69–75 (some footnotes deleted).

Foreign tourists motoring across France are surprised to see a sign with a familiar theme: 'Mettez un Tigre dans Votre Moteur.' Tourists in other parts of Europe and around the world may expect to see the same theme in other languages. Esso carried its 'Put a Tiger in Your Tank' campaign to a vast marketplace in the appropriate languages of the various countries.

What these travelers are seeing is a classic example of the use of the common approach to international advertising; an approach that is the source of considerable current debate in international marketing circles. Briefly stated, this controversy centers around whether common advertising themes or even advertisements themselves – with proper translations – are as effective as separate messages and advertisements developed specifically for individual national markets.

Although the common advertising approach has been a subject of discussion for some time, the apparent success of various firms, including Esso with its world-wide 'Tiger' campaign, has focused attention upon its use. Traditionally it has been more or less accepted that nationalistic differences prevented the use of similar copy and advertising themes on a multinational basis. The impact of the 'Tiger' campaign, however, along with the advantages of using a common approach, are leading other firms to examine the feasibility of universal advertising themes.

When they do so, they run into any number of barriers which must be overcome. In addition to the obvious language barriers between countries or regions, there are cultural, taste and environmental differences, media availability differences and developmental differences – standard of living, discretionary income and other economic considerations.

Most experienced international advertisers and advertising agency executives – even the outspoken proponents of the common approach – recognize these barriers to varying degrees. Yet the potential cost savings from a universal approach and the opportunity to maintain a common global image or theme are most attractive. Two strongly divergent points of view have created controversial dialogue among respected experts in the field. An executive for a large US agency without overseas affiliations, for example, may claim that adapting campaigns along national lines is unnecessary and that a universal approach developed by a single centralized agency is best, while an executive in a small national agency located abroad and unaffiliated with a US agency may say that advertisers should use domestic agencies in each area and direct their advertising specifically to that area.

One theme

A number of writers and practitioners have for years been particularly outspoken in favoring the common advertising theme approach. Among them are Arthur C. Fatt, Chairman of the Board of Grey Advertising, who has stated that despite obvious language and cultural differences, peoples of the world have the same basic wants and needs. He says that most '... people everywhere, from Argentina to Zanzibar, want a better way of life for themselves and their families ...', that the desire to be beautiful, to be free of pain, to be healthy, etc., is universal. He suggests that a successful campaign in one area of the world – utilizing a theme that would appeal to the basic wants or needs of the individual – could reasonably be expected to produce similar results in other areas of the world if the language is translated into the local idiom.

Fatt (1964 and 1967) points out that today's rapid international communications, particularly television, increased international travel, and the growth of the truly international brand name have given even greater impetus to the trend toward a common advertising approach.

Another advocate, Erik Elinder, though agreeing with the concept of a universal approach, has been principally concerned with its development at an all-European rather than at a worldwide level. Speaking from his years of experience as a Swedish advertising executive and as the Chairman of the Board of the Swedish Sales Institute, he says that many of the problems often associated with the common approach, such as language differences, are actually 'lightweight'.

Elinder (1964 and 1965) cites the success that the international editions of the *Reader's Digest* have shown in varied markets, as well as the worldwide popularity of best sellers, films, etc., to support his view that similarity in sales appeals can also be successful. Further, he points out that a large percentage of Europeans now travel extensively on the Continent and that television, magazine and newspaper coverage extends beyond national borders – two factors important to firms seeking to reach markets in several countries and to maintain advertising continuity.

There are others, of course, who favor the universal approach, such as Nicholas E. Keller, managing director of McCann-Erickson Europe. Keller uses the Esso 'Tiger' campaign to demonstrate how the same basic idea with very few modifications can be used in multimarkets (Kurtis, 1967).

Advertisers supporting the common approach fully emphasize the advantages of presenting the same trademarks, brand names and logotypes in many and varied markets. Such a universal approach permits the advertiser to maintain the same 'image' in every country and prevents confusing the 'border-crossing tourist' as he seeks the firm's product in a different market. Perhaps even more important to some advertisers, however, is the potential cost saving of the universal approach. The extra costs of using separate artists, separate copywriters and the higher mechanical costs involved in preparing entirely different campaigns and individual advertisements for each country where their advertising is to appear are an important incentive to the advertiser for using the universal approach.

Probably the most active opponent of the universal approach is John M. Lenormand, a Paris advertising agency executive. Lenormand has stated (1964) that to achieve a universal approach a common denominator would have to be found that would have the same impact '. . . for South Americans, Swedes, Germans, and Spaniards, not to mention Flemings and Sudeten Germans.' According to Lenormand, such a common denominator has not been found.

Like other critics of the universal approach, Lenormand cites many additional obstacles to achieving successful common advertising. He points out that problems arise due to differences in mentalities, customs, religious beliefs, living standards, laws, media, etc. These problem areas, along with language barriers, literacy rates, varying distribution channel structures and the lack of truly international advertising agencies, are the ones most frequently mentioned by those either opposed to the common advertising approach or dubious about its present applicability.

Generally, opponents of the common advertising approach point to dissimilarities between countries and even between regions in the same country to support their opinion. Most of these differences are cultural or environmental. For example, the status of women in several tropical African countries where they are considered chattel, differs from their status in Western countries. In such an environment, advertisements appealing solely to women, as are frequently found in Western societies, would mean ignoring the fact that it is the man who makes the final approval of the purchase. Basic differences between Far Eastern cultures and European cultures have also been noted. Others refer to cultural variations between Latin Americans and Spaniards or French Canadians and French Swiss who speak the same basic languages. German villagers from Schleswig-Holstein and Bavaria have difficulties in communicating with one another.

Cultural differences, however, are not the only obstacles to the use of common advertising. Areas vary widely in terms of availability of media and media capabilities. There are some regions where magazines and newspapers are 'available', but where their facilities are so inadequate that illustrative matter is not satisfactorily reproduced. Similar criticisms can be made regarding other media in specific world areas. Differences in the amount of discretionary income and the standard of living among countries and regions are still another argument against the technique.

A recognition of the obstacles does not necessarily make one an opponent of the common approach. In fact, proponents and opponents alike recognize these problems to varying degrees. Rather, the question seems to be whether these differences are considered insurmountable at one extreme or to be of minimal importance at the other. There is some agreement that a universal or at least a 'European' style of advertising is coming, but many of those who have adopted this point of view also see the need for further research and experimentation before such an approach is widely adopted by advertisers.

One theme – with differences

Between these polarized views is a broad middle ground of opinion: principally those who believe that some degree of uniformity of advertising theme is needed, but agree that individual area differences must also be recognized. An often used approach by such companies is to let an international advertising agency – an agency with branches in key locations around the world – handle both their domestic and non-domestic advertising. This permits the advertiser to have as much uniformity as he desires, while at the same time the local nationals employed by the international agency in each of its branches can indicate those characteristics of the advertising theme, campaign or individual advertisements that are not appropriate in their particular area. Others prefer to employ separate advertising agencies in each country or region in which they operate but furnish these agencies with a theme, trademark and/or campaign developed by the company's home office or its domestic agency. This is done to insure that some similarity in advertising will be maintained and local differences recognized.

Much of the success of using an international agency to handle varying degrees of uniformity depends upon the abilities of the nationals it employs in various areas, the degree of centralization in the agency and consequently the freedom the nationals may have or feel they have to question or change themes, etc. Some agencies have wholly-owned branches, while others have only partial ownership or perhaps just an exchange arrangement with their 'branches', which are really independent foreign agencies. Also, since the development of uniform themes, trademarks and even individual advertisements involves creativity, many criticisms from the branches may simply reflect disagreement with some creative aspects of the theme or campaign and not with its suitability in the nationals' markets.

The use of separate agencies in each area increases the problems of maintaining some degree of uniformity in advertising. The tendency for the local agency to want to develop its own original approach tailored to its market and its unwillingness to accept a theme developed elsewhere are problems that again have to be recognized.

Another approach some advertisers employ is to seek the advice of nationals in their own overseas branches or their representatives in various countries or regions in attempting to develop a uniform theme that can successfully be used multinationally. These branch officials or representatives may be asked to submit suggestions or ideas, examine advertising proofs, coordinate efforts or work closely with a local agency in their area.

Obviously, companies have devised a variety of ways to obtain the advantages of the common advertising approach and still take into consideration the cultural, economic and other differences among global areas. In some instances, recognition of the differences has been more or less token, while in other instances considerable efforts have been made to adapt the uniform themes to particular local differences.

The product and the market

In most of the dialogue regarding the common advertising approach, two key considerations are generally either ignored or only briefly noted. These considerations are the product to be marketed and its place in the market.

The nature of the product may be the single most important factor in determining whether or not it is feasible for a firm to employ a common or universal approach in its multinational advertising. Certainly, there are low-priced, non-durable goods fulfilling basic needs that have broad potential markets. Firms selling such products may not be too concerned about many of the differences among global areas. Coca-Cola, for example, has successfully appealed to a broad market and become a byword among consumers around the world. However, Coca-Cola is so low-priced and appeals to such a basic biological need – thirst – that its potential market includes a large number of consumers wherever it is introduced.

Virtually all durable goods producers and most non-durable goods producers are not blessed with such a broad potential market for their products. Questions relating to the product and its market need to be considered to determine whether or not the common approach is desirable. One would have to assume that all consumers either within a single country or region or worldwide were basically the same to give a simple yes or no answer to the question of using the common advertising approach to reach a mass market.

There is a school of thought that states that people everywhere are basically the same and that a truly universal appeal will be successful in any market. One needs only to compare the literacy differences between Somaliland and Sweden, or familiarize oneself with cultural differences between countries or within countries to realize that consumers are not all alike. Even the strongest proponents of the common advertising approach would agree that there are national or regional differences between peoples.

Perhaps more realistically, some writers, such as Elinder, see the advent of the all-European consumer (or an all-Western European consumer). They point to increased inter-European tourism and the growth of television – particularly Eurovision – as leading toward such a consumer. Yet, if one is familiar with rural France or Portugal, for example, he will find a degree of provincialism that raises doubt about the early arrival of the all-European consumer.

Consumer categories

Rather than a single all-European consumer or worldwide consumer for the mass marketer, one can suggest at least three broad categories of consumers based solely on their potential receptivity to the common advertising approach:

International sophisticate
Semi-sophisticate
Provincial

Though not exhaustive, this grouping identifies some of the consumer characteristics that separate those who might be somewhat responsive to a good universal approach from those who would find such an approach meaningless or might even be repelled by it – regardless of the product.

International sophisticate

Although the term 'jet set' has perhaps been overstressed by gossip columnists and the press in general, there are at least a few people that might be termed 'world citizens' in most countries and particularly in the Western World. These people would be equally comfortable in St Moritz and Acapulco and are frequently multilingual. Such individuals, regardless of home base, would probably be as responsive to a universal campaign as would anyone with their same economic background and interests in the advertiser's own country.

This is a relatively small group of world citizens, but the growth of another, larger group that might be called the 'international sophisticate' has more relevance to most advertisers considering using the common advertising approach. This group of middle- or high-income consumers includes those who have a genuine interest and awareness for products, fashions and cultural activities in countries other than their own. This may be reflected by their having traveled extensively in various countries; by their familiarity with the international editions of publications or such international publications as *Paris Match*, *Der Stern*, etc., or perhaps even by their being in an area where television programming from other countries is available. Regardless of the ways this multinational interest has been obtained or is expressed, the most important characteristic of this group is their appreciation and 'feel' not only for the cultures, but also for their peers in other countries.

The growth of the international sophisticate has generally occurred in Europe, the United States, Canada and Japan. Travel between various European countries, as well as between Europe and the US, has increased dramatically in the last decade. However, this is more a reflection of the effect, rather than the cause, of the growth of the international sophisticate, who is apparently a product of greater disposable personal income, better education and an environment that offers the greatest promise for the advertiser seeking to be truly universal in his advertising approach. Such consumers would be expected to be highly responsive to a good campaign theme, whether it originated in the United States or Switzerland or Japan.

Semi-sophisticate

In addition to the 'sophisticate', there is a much larger group of people found in varying numbers around the world that might be called the 'semi-sophisticates'. This group includes many of the burgeoning number of middle- and high-income individuals found in the United States, Western Europe, Japan, Canada and South America. In this group are found the people with an increasing discretionary income and a growing but as yet unmotivated awareness of the world around them. Through limited travel, television or documentary programs, reading or a variety of other ways, these people have begun to become interested in other lands and cultures.

This increased interest may manifest itself in the curiosity to sample a few inexpensive products from 'abroad' or to own Danish furniture actually produced in Denmark or a Toyota from Japan. Often this willingness to try such products may be due only to the desire for the status such unique products may afford. On the other hand, it may be due to a growing appreciation of other cultures and a willingness to sample goods from those areas. It is important to the advertiser, however, that such semi-sophisticates have no hesitancy to purchase at least certain types of items produced outside of their own country.

Consumers of the semi-sophisticate type are found in both urban or rural areas. They are more apt to be located near metropolitan cities because of their wider range of varied interests.

In terms of advertising, they can be made receptive to an international approach. However, they probably would be even more receptive to advertising demonstrating the use of this 'foreign' product in their own environs and indirect references to the advantages (mainly status) of having something unique. Further, they might well miss any subtleties included in the universal advertisement, and care would need to be taken to insure that no such subtleties are included in advertisements.

Provincial

Whether city or rural dwellers, the 'provincials' have one characteristic in common: a lack of interest, appreciation or 'feel' for the non-domestic. For some, this may be due to a strong spirit of nationalism that affects the way they perceive anything from the outside. Others may simply be unaware of things outside their sphere of interest and may be too involved to develop a new sense of awareness. Still others may lack the opportunity to become involved with things outside their locale, region or country.

Provincials range the full continuum in terms of wealth and education. This group includes a range from those who are wealthy and well-educated, who abhor anything from beyond their political boundaries or area of interest to an illiterate peasant too involved in the battle for survival to notice the world. Even more important for some geographic areas, however, this group includes many middle-income individuals who feel their own country to be self-sufficient in all its aspects and simply have no interest in other nations.

Because of their introverted attitude, some consumers of this type may purchase imported products without realizing that these products are non-domestic. For this reason, many firms have initiated programs, such as changing their brand name if it indicates or implies the country of origin, to prevent their products from being clearly identified as non-domestic products in areas outside their home country.

This is a large group. Most obviously it would not be responsive to the universal advertising approach. For some, the subtleties would be too great or the message too foreign for their frame of reference. For others, they would simply have no interest in any product unless it was tied closely to their own habitual needs and wants. Finally, some would be antagonized by any product from the outside and their nationalistic feelings would build an impenetrable perception barrier to the advertiser's message.

There are undoubtedly other categories and many sub-categories of world consumers in terms of their receptivity to the universal advertising approach. They all add up to the conclusion that a simple one-world consumer does not exist at this time. Firms must exercise caution in adopting the same or similar advertising in multiple markets, especially if they are seeking a mass market. For the firm seeking clearly distinguishable market segments in terms of socio-cultural, socio-economic and demographic qualities, a thorough job of identifying the characteristics within various markets might lead to a central theme that would be appropriate. Even this may be difficult if their desired segment includes consumers of the provincial type. Yet, nationalistic tendencies may be overcome to some extent if the problem is recognized.

Few, if any, would disagree with the view that advances in communications, education, etc. will ultimately create an atmosphere where the common advertising approach will be the rule rather than the exception. However, adoption of such an approach today is premature and advertisers should make use of it with caution.

References

ELINDER, E. (1964), 'How international can advertising be?', in S. Watson Dunn (ed.), *International Handbook of Advertising*, McGraw-Hill.

ELINDER, E. (1965), 'How international can European advertising be?' *Jour. of Mark.*, April.

FATT, A. C. (1964), 'A multi-national approach to international advertising', *International Advertiser*, September.

FATT, A. C. (1967), 'The danger of "local" international advertising', *Journal of Marketing*, January.

KURTIS, C. (1967), 'Ads need a different touch in each country of Europe', *Herald Tribune International*, 9 June.

LENORMAND, J. M. (1964), 'Is Europe ripe for the integration of advertising?', *International Advertiser*, March.

22 Y. Ikeda

Distribution Innovation in Japan and the Role Played by General Trading Companies

Y. Ikeda, 'Distribution innovation in Japan and the role played by general trading companies', *Management Japan*, vol. 4, no. 2, 1970, pp. 17–21.

Preface

The winding and narrow lanes in a typical Japanese castle town – this is the very thing which symbolizes the structural characteristics of the distribution system in Japan. With roads and streets being widened and highways being constructed in various local cities, and with these cities being transformed into smaller replicas of Tokyo by uniform city planning, it can be said that the Japanese high growth economy is now gradually moving from its 'era of production orientation' to an 'age of distribution and consumption'.

If the communication and production systems of a nation may be compared to the nerve and muscle systems of a man, the distribution system can be said to correspond to the circulation system. Setting aside the importance of the man's character and physique, it is obvious that one cannot expect a healthy circulation system without a sound constitution.

On reflection, the geographical situation in Japan can be singled out as one of the most effective factors contributing to the secret of modern Japan's rapid growth from the middle of the nineteenth century.

Firstly, a central nerve with a comparatively high level of culture has made it possible to form a spinal cord running the length of the Japanese archipelago and has aided the formation of a nation-wide communications network.

Secondly, the good coast line, coupled with the abundant availability of water, has also prompted Japan's industrialization. Thirdly, although the distribution system was primitive in its early stages, it was able to support this rapid industrialization being aided by the favorable shipping industry and also by the wise policies of the Meiji Government toward the railway system. However, it is apparent that mass production, mass consumption, and mass distribution have recently had a great impact on the circulation system of our economy, so that distribution policies may well influence the future direction of Japanese economic growth. Therefore, the role played by general trading companies, which have played the main part historically and structurally in the Japanese economic society, is becoming increasingly important.

Distribution innovation in Japan

Since 1956 when the famous catch phrase of 'the postwar period is over' was created, the Japanese economy completed its rehabilitation and began to climb the steps towards development.

With the expansion of production capacities, the problem of commercial distribution was taken up because of the need to establish a volume sales store, such as supermarkets, in order to cope with both mass production and mass consumption. Furthermore, the manufacturers themselves were forced to establish their own marketing policies in line with trend of mass age. Consequently the so-called 'marketing boom' appeared in that period.

As a result, the progress in eliminating wholesale merchants in the distribution innovation gave rise to the theory that general trading companies would decline in importance as the tendency for trading companies to become more like commission merchants advanced and their financial influence was relatively lessened with the increase of industrial capital. It cannot be denied that this theory came as a warning signal to general trading companies, which have traditionally tended to be more manufacturer-minded than market-minded.

However, this assumption, with its emphasis on commercial distribution innovation, failed to give full consideration to the potential demand of the market not only for lower prices and bulk sales but also for diversification, as the income of the general public increased. Even in the marketing innovation aspects, only the necessity for cost reductions as in the fields of packing, transportation, and storing, as seen in the move toward containerization or palettization, was pointed out.

Although there were very few intellectuals who realized that the aims of genuine distribution innovation were far away and that the obstacles lay even deeper, the general trading companies, which were raised in the circumstances particular to Japan, could feel this fact instinctively. In any case, the present distribution innovation, in both commercial and merchandising, is advancing in the directions of:

1. Grouping of distribution.

2. Diversifications of distribution.
3. Simplification and shortening of distribution channels.

The role of general trading companies in distribution

The general trading company is a peculiarly Japanese system brought about by the characteristics of the Japanese society. Therefore, any discussion on the role of the general trading company should be based on its elements of birth and traditions.

Traditional role

Although there are many specialized trading companies in foreign countries, a policy of seclusionism of old Japan and the characteristics of the Japanese language account for the fact that the general trading company has become strong only in Japan.

When the social ranking system of 'warriors, farmers, artisans, and merchants' and various other systems of old Japan were abolished by the Meiji Government, the conceptual distinction in production fields such as agriculture and industry and businesses engaged in the sales of their products was left unchanged – a pattern which exists as the framework of the modern merchandising and commercial distribution systems.

In the meantime, trading companies began to establish their foundations as general trading companies. At the outset, they functioned as wholesale merchants and as markets increased, they engaged in such other activities as buying and selling products in both domestic and overseas markets, financing, foreign exchange, commodity hedging operations, insurance, transportation, storage services, and market research.

Thus, Mitsui and Co., a leading general trading company of prewar Japan, widely developed its business activities and came to control the main parts of the economy from natural resources to finished-products being aided by its huge financing ability and communications and recorded the sales which surpassed the national budget of Japan at the time.

After World War II, although general trading companies belonging to the Zaibatsu like Mitsui and Mitsubishi were ordered by the Allied Occupation Forces to disband into hundreds of smaller companies, new moves for greater economy amalgamation began, in keeping pace with the reconstruction of the Japanese economy.

The newly-created general trading companies are radically different in style from those of the prewar period. However, setting aside their scale and role, the scope of business activities has grown to such an extent that it has surpassed its prewar level, as the need for distribution and technical innovations began to attract attention owing to the fact that the industrial emphasis shifted from light industries to heavy and chemical industries in the 1960s.

The new role of general trading companies

It is true that the number of medium and small wholesale companies has declined with this new movement. Distribution innovation has brought about diversification, grouping, and simplification of the distribution channels, causing extensive reorganizations in the traditional aspects of merchandising as well as commercial distribution. On this point, it became quite obvious that the existence of a trading company would be vulnerable if it kept strictly to the traditional distribution functions. Thus, the general trading company further expanded its operations by taking full advantage of its information networks, administration and coordination.

As for the diversification and multiplication of distribution, the general trading company is trying to form new distribution channels of the so-called 'one-stop shopping' type through large distribution channels of groups of various items, instead of dealing through the conventional distribution channels specializing in single items (producers to wholesalers, including first and second stages; to retailers to consumers). On the other hand, exerting its maximum capabilities as general trader, it has increased its significance from both the national and social points of view, creating a complete channel of distribution consisting of production to processing to transportation insurance to storing to distribution consumption functions, and displaying its financing and buffering functions for credit risks at the same time.

In short, the functions of the general trading company within the framework of Japanese industries could be described most effectively as the three vital 'tions' of communication, transportation, and distribution. However, as stated above, the function of developing natural resources may be added to the role of the general trading company as the economy and society progress. Various functions of the general trading company to meet the needs of the new era include:

1. Development and import of resources from overseas.
2. Overseas joint ventures.
3. Import and export of new technical knowledge.

4. Lease enterprises.
5. Development of growth and future industries.

These are all based on Japanese economic growth and the aid to developing countries. It is certain that general trading companies have contributed greatly to the expansion of international trade as well as the growth of Japan's international trade, but it is also true that 50 per cent to 55 per cent of the total sales turnover is from the domestic marketing business. Therefore, in this article, I would like to elaborate, on the role of the general trading company concentrating mainly on the field of domestic distribution.

As noted earlier, the traditional roles of the trading company include the agent's functions such as wholesale, hedge-selling, merchandising adjustment, financing, transportation, and insurance. However, new roles have since been added, such as organizing industries and supplying merchandise, funds, and information to form a total system making full use of its coordination and thus to contribute to the more efficient progress of the national economy and the whole of Japanese society. In view of this, the general trading company has come to play an important role in the Japanese economy as it has ceased to be engaged merely in the wholesale business.

The general trading company is also playing an important part in organizing the domestic market, and some such specific measures include:

1. Grouping and reorganizing of wholesale businesses.
2. Collaboration with volume sales stores (e.g. department stores and supermarkets).
3. Links with or construction of shopping centers.
4. Construction of marketing bases and distribution and processing centers.
5. Construction of food kombinat.
6. Establishment of and tie-ups with affiliated companies in the fields of production, sales, warehouse, transportation, and future industries.

Specific distribution policies of the general trading company
Grouping and reorganizing of wholesale businesses

The most fundamental point to distribution innovation in Japan can be said to lie in the need of improving the very traditional system of the multi-stage middle marketing system. The idea is to carry out innovation in the field of organization in order to lower distribution costs by linking producers with consumers closely, re-arranging and reorganizing the existing groups of wholesalers and agents, and also aiming to integrate the distribution channels of various single items into larger ones.

Collaboration with volume sales stores

In order to cope with the demands of the era, an era in which the economic pattern is shifting from a production orientation to a consumption orientation, the general trading company is in a position to become a so-called mass-merchandiser directly linked with such larger retail shops as supermarkets and department stores, with manufacturers, or with farmers, so that better quality merchandise can be made available to consumers at lower prices.

If necessary, the general trading company should also act as wholesaler, warehouser, and transporter in a new system to assist these retail stores to improve their structures through forming chains and expanding their operations by rendering them real estate, capital, and leasing assistance.

Links with or construction of shopping centers

It is expected that the general trading company should not only tie up with existing shopping centers, as in the case of large retail shops, but also construct its own shopping centers at suitable locations to operate under its own management or to be leased. Although there are few shopping centers being run by general trading companies in Japan, it will not be long before the shopping centers managed by general trading companies or their affiliated companies are to be established, judging from the outstanding results of such shopping centers in the US.

Construction of marketing bases and distribution and processing centers

The innovations in transportation and communication have made it necessary to construct coastal distribution bases in order to cope with the increased imports of raw materials and consumer goods from all over the world. In addition, the construction of large depots to distribute the goods to inland markets from these coastal bases has become necessary in order to ensure a smooth flow of goods and low distribution costs.

At the same time, with regard to semi-finished products, the general trading company is expected to perform its new wholesale role as a bulk supplier to meet the heavy demand by constructing a combination of processing and distribution centers in and around areas of consumption.

Construction of food kombinat

In order to raise the nation's standard of living with regard to food supplies, the general trading company is to construct a food kombinat where food, feed, oil, and their raw materials developed overseas are to be imported and other raw materials, semi-finished products, or finished products bought from farmers and their organization or grown on a consignment basis are to be processed, stored, and distributed.

Establishment of and tie-ups with affiliated companies

It is necessary to establish new companies either with other companies in the same group of enterprises, or independently in order to expand the sales of goods manufactured in the same group and also to aim at the growth and future industries (such as the development of atomic energy, ocean development, development of oil resources, urban development, housing, leisure, education, medical treatment, and related industries). In these cases, overseas subsidiaries, affiliated companies, and other joint venture companies are also expected to contribute when necessary.

Conclusion

As seen in the foregoing, the roles of the general trading company are constantly changing as time passes. However, it must be pointed out that the general trading company as a complex industry is entirely different from the US conglomerate in which the latter has grown through external factors such as taking over or increasing its holdings in other enterprises, while the former has progressed through its own internal factors like the expansion of its own functions, which has brought about a natural and unique form of enterprise.

While continuing to contribute to the betterment of the Japanese economy and social life, the general trading company in Japan is still expected to play its role as an organizer in a consistent international distribution system realizing that its character and duties as a leader lie in the international field.

Part Six
Small Business and International Marketing

The special problems of small and medium-sized business in international marketing is the province of Part Six. The two most critical problems are seen as whether or not to engage in international marketing (or to enter a new market abroad) and, if the answer is positive, what channels of distribution to use. Small business typically encounters a third major problem in beginning export operations, namely financing. We have not included readings on this matter, as the institutional conditions (export banking facilities, government credit and risk insurance, etc.) vary so tremendously between countries. Expert advice should be sought in this area in the individual case.

Reading 23, by Sweeney, is a case history of why and how a small American high-technology firm decided to enter the European market. 'Offense is the best defense' was an important part of the commitment decision. Moving with the international product life cycle in computer accessories was another, closely tied in with future profit opportunities. The article is also instructive in highlighting the differential advantages enjoyed by small companies in international markets as well as domestic. Reading 24, from *Business International*, greatly facilitates consideration of entry into a (new) foreign market by systematically inventorying all types of commitment, from the modest filling of occasional unsolicited export orders to the most ambitious: the creation of a wholly owned manufacturing-marketing subsidiary. In between the two there is a vast range of alternatives, arranged in approximate order of financial and/or risk commitment.

Before making any type of commitment decision (beyond the routine filling of whatever export orders that may come in spontaneously) management is wise to keep in mind two important points of practical experience. First, that going international rarely is a successful escape from domestic problems.

In other words, domestic operations should generally be fairly well 'under control' before venturing abroad. Second, to assure a wise decision on when and where to commit what resources to international operations there is virtually no substitute for the well-prepared personal visit by top management to the foreign market(s) under consideration. This is simply because international commitments tend to be major commitments, and they invariably represent entrepreneurial decisions.

Readings 25-27 deal with problems of distribution. Reading 25, from the OECD, deals with various forms of export cooperation between small businesses. It considers cooperation between firms representing complementary, unrelated and competing products. The important point is also made that joint activity need not be confined to (or even include) sales but can also comprise other functions, such as marketing research, advertising, trade fairs and physical distribution. Reading 26, from *Business Europe*, is a case study of successful 'piggyback' arrangements practised by the Schick Safety Razor Co., an American firm entering the German market. Piggybacking involves the utilization of the distribution organization owned by another manufacturer rather than independent distributors or a self-owned sales setup.

Reading 27, by Beeth, is a lively piece on the dos and don'ts of finding and keeping good distributors in international marketing. It is based on many years of personal practical experience in American and Swedish companies marketing all around the world.

23 J. K. Sweeney

A Small Company Enters the European Market

Excerpt from J. K. Sweeney, 'A small company enters the European market', *Harvard Business Review*, vol. 48, no. 5, 1970, pp. 126–32.

Inviting as Europe is for many smaller US companies seeking markets, few of them seriously consider doing business there. Mostly they assume that only the giants on *Fortune*'s '500' can venture into that marketplace.

The recent experience of my small company in setting up subsidiaries, first in England and then in France, suggests, however, that the little fellow – with careful research, planning, and perhaps some unorthodox moves – can successfully enter Europe. While we do not consider our European education by any means complete, we do think we have learned a good bit about doing business there. As a result, I have some observations and suggestions for other small companies eyeing Europe.

Our company, Computer Machinery Corporation, was quite small when we 'went multinational' in 1969 by opening a sales and production facility in England. We had just seventy-five employees and only $2 million in total capital.

Today, with about 475 employees and more than $6 million of invested capital, we are stronger than when we launched our overseas operation, but of course hardly a computer industry giant. Nevertheless, partly because of the experience and confidence we have gained from our English venture, we have opened a sales and service facility in France, and we expect to start operations in West Germany and Italy in 1971.

Why go multinational?

Nearly eleven years ago, an article in the *Harvard Business Review* cited these conditions as stimulating the entry of US companies into overseas markets:

> Especially in the case of our more mature industries, high market penetration, high saturation points, and more than adequate productive capacity give promise of a further competitive profit squeeze. Even

when there have been major volume increase, as is true for many industries, costs have often risen faster than prices, creating declining returns on sales and investment...

Many companies that lack production sources abroad are encountering fiercer competition – not only in their export markets but in the United States market – both from foreign corporations and from American competitors that have established production sources abroad...

No longer able to measure their competitive position by studying their domestic competitors, a significant number of American companies must today make their plans for capital expenditures and for market penetration with a full knowledge of what both their domestic and their overseas competitors are likely to do (Clee and di Scipio, 1959).

These reasons to engage in overseas operations are just as strong, if not stronger, today. Moreover, many of the factors which are driving the larger corporations to multinationalism are pressing just as forcefully on smaller US companies.

CMC's purpose in entering the world marketplace was to forestall this potential 'fiercer competition' by establishing a foothold before the competition got its chance to do so. To accomplish this, the company in actuality had, and has in the foreseeable future, only one market outside the United States: Western Europe. Minor ones for our kind of business, such as Japan, are too small or too difficult for us to enter.

Europe, of course, is historically the location most favored for an overseas venture by a US company. Still, there are good reasons for smaller companies to be wary of Europe. One is their inexperience in the ways of doing business in the area; until quite recently, this has been generally true of the larger US companies too.

What makes inexperience so dangerous for smaller companies is the fact that they cannot afford to make many mistakes. Slips that would hardly cause a 3M or an RCA any worry can spell disaster to a little company with limited resources.

The profit-and-loss sheet is another reason small companies think twice about going abroad. In CMC's case, it would have made more economic sense to stay out of Europe – at least for the time being. As a loss operation, it is a drain on our comparatively limited capital.

If immediate profit and loss questions had been the only consideration, CMC would not be in Europe today. But our market research showed that Europe represents a sales potential of fully 50 per cent that of the United States.

Our principal product is designed to replace key punches, and we knew how many computer systems were installed in the United Kingdom. Our sales personnel canvassed computer users on the list to obtain the number of key punches in use.

The compelling reason for our entering Europe now – in addition to broadening our market 50 per cent – was to capitalize on our innovative advantage. We consider our products to be well ahead of competitors', both the large and the small companies. But in our fast-moving field – data entry systems and input equipment – this could change rapidly.

If one or more of our larger competitors – or even those our size – became established in Europe before we did, we might never be able to penetrate that market. Our move into Europe, although expensive now, would be more expensive – and riskier – later.

Look at the market

Despite the Common Market, reciprocal tariff reductions, and similar factors, Europe has more of a geographic than a business unity. From one country to another, great variations exist in laws, monetary policies, transportation facilities, attitudes toward work, and the degree of government involvement in business. Thus the businessman who is a whiz in Spain may be totally lost in Germany. This point seems obvious, but time after time it is overlooked by big US companies as well as small ones.

Furthermore, even when a particular European country represents a tremendous potential market for one's wares, its immediate neighbor may have little or no call for them. For example, CMC's market research in the computer field revealed that England, France, West Germany, and Italy offer us significant markets. England, France, and Germany are about equal-size markets, while Italy represents about two-thirds the potential of any one of those countries.

On the other hand, the Scandinavian market is only about one-third to one-half that of the big three. The potential for computer sales in Spain, Portugal, and the Benelux countries is insignificant at present.

Taking everything into consideration, we decided to set up first in England because its market for our products is as large as any and its language and laws are similar to ours. England is different enough to get your feet wet, yet similar enough to the familiar US business environment so that you do not get in over your head.

A good deal of care must be taken in researching the European market to make sure there is real demand for your product *in its present form*. Not only in Europe, but around the world, markets are quite disorderly. Particularly in consumer goods such as automobiles, household appliances, and clothing, customers demand different sizes, shapes, textures, colors and other configurations.

Fortunately for the computer industry, markets throughout the world tend to be quite similar with respect to product demand. We have IBM to thank for that; the company has stamped the entire industry with its image – an image that remains the same no matter what corner of the world IBM enters. True, computer applications vary, and there is often a greater lack of sophistication in operations outside the United States. But, like its ubiquitous eighty-column card, IBM remains constant and thereby gives order to what could easily be chaos.

Wages for the European workingman are still lower than they are here. Salaries for technical and managerial personnel are less too. But European professionals are increasingly demanding and receiving compensation parity with their American counterparts.

Enter the little fellow

A small US company operating in Europe has some advantages over a larger one. Because the little fellow has far less impact on the host country, he is more likely to be left alone by the government than is the giant whose every move generates economic repercussions.

Understandably, labor unions, too, pay little attention to the small company, probably viewing it as being not worth the effort. CMC, for the dollar volume involved, is not labor intensive. Its ratio of hourly workers to salaried professionals is quite low in the United States and even lower in Europe.

In their approach to Europe, CMC's executives are somewhat unconventional. We first of all totally endorse the view that our overseas ventures are not 'foreign'; their location outside the United States is incidental. We are determined to view all our eventual overseas operations in exactly the same light as our domestic ones. If belt tightening becomes necessary, for instance, we will not cut back on European operations without doing the same at home.

Therefore, we have done something too few companies do: we made an absolute commitment to the overseas operation. Once we decided that Europe was worth entering, we concluded that the success of the venture depended greatly on our being wholehearted and unhesitant about it.

When any company's management discusses establishing its first subsidiary in an overseas area, someone inevitably asks: 'If it doesn't work, how do we get out?' That remark betrays an attitude that can almost by itself doom the enterprise. The question of retreat came up in discussions at CMC, as I knew it would. My answer was that, once committed, we should no more be thinking of ways to back out of Europe than of ways to dissolve the parent company.

If, for example, we are losing money overseas, we will simply have to work to achieve a turn-around, just as we would try to do at home. If the subsidiary is worth starting up in the first place, it *must* be worth whatever effort is necessary to make it a success. I am convinced that once a company retreats under fire from Europe, the chances are good it will never return.

To speed the start-up process, we patterned the English subsidiary after the parent company. For motivational and political reasons, however, we are insisting that the English operation be as independent as possible in pursuing its objectives. We have not merely hoisted a Union Jack over a group of Americans, as many companies do. We have set certain guidelines and goals and turned the subsidiary's management loose.

We are convinced that the best way to run our overseas – and domestic – operations is to select high-quality people, motivate them, and let them run their own show. Most of the money they generate will be theirs to reinvest in their operation. We are handling our new French subsidiary in much the same way.

We are giving unity and direction to our European subsidiaries in several ways. First, there is financial control, which follows the practices so well understood these days that it is unnecessary to go into them. Secondly, we have set up Computer Machinery Corporation International, a coordinating organization comprised of all our overseas subsidiary managers and appropriate executives from headquarters. This group meets frequently to exchange ideas and to coordinate corporate activities and product development.

Because communication is vital to a diversified company such as we intend to be, we have hired a man to be communications coordinator and have made him a vice-president of CMC International. He is the information conduit between headquarters in California and the overseas operations. He sees to it that questions are answered promptly and reports from Europe are prepared on time and moved quickly to their destinations.

When starting up

Here are some pointers to consider concerning the critical period before the new operation is actually launched:

Adopt a low profile. Investigation convinced us that our chances of success depended heavily on our ability to blend into the business environment of the host country. We have made every effort to find out its rules and practices and to abide by them scrupulously. Whether these rules are 'right' or 'wrong' is immaterial; you either play by your host's rules or find it very hard to play at all.

One of America's largest companies has found this out. Best known as a diversified manufacturer of home appliances and electrical equipment for industry, it swaggered into France and began operating exactly as it did in the United States.

To head the operation, it brought in the kind of American who does not know one end of a wine bottle from the other. Having little or no foreign business experience, this poor fellow committed a series of gigantic mistakes that would have been quite funny if they had not been so costly.

At the other extreme, IBM has done a fine job of blending into France. The French government has a very active policy aimed at stimulating exports. IBM has brought its practices into line with this policy and is consistently that country's number one or two exporter. IBM has done this in very clever ways, and the French government gives it much credit for favorably affecting France's balance of trade. (In Europe, IBM has about 65,000 employees, ten manufacturing plants, and four research centers. The company has conscientiously tried to fit into the business climate in every country it has entered.)

CMC is determined to do the same. For example, consider one thing we are doing to accommodate ourselves to France. Frenchmen, to a man, want the entire month of August off for *les vacances*. We could try to fight this, as some companies have. But we are sure it would be more trouble than it is worth. Besides, there is a very practical reason for not taking issue with the custom: the Frenchmen you want to do business with are all on vacation, so you cannot get much done in August anyway.

Work closely with government officials. Long before our English subsidiary was anything but an idea, we contacted the subgroup in the British Ministry of Technology dealing with computers and related equipment.

On one of the regular visits of their representatives to US manufacturers, we invited them to our facility. We brought out a cardboard mock-up of what we were going to make and told them all about our plans to open up in England. We put special emphasis on our desire to do business there and our intention to employ British nationals and become a UK export company.

It must have been hard for them to take us seriously – ten Americans in business only a few months talking about starting a manufacturing operation in England. But we wrote faithfully every month to bring them up to date on our overseas plans. Whenever we said we would do something, we made sure we did it – or had a good reason to tell them why we could not. On preliminary trips to the United Kingdom, we called at the Ministry of Technology to let the people there know how we were coming along.

In this way, they got to know us and we them, and – more important – we made them aware that our word was good. That accomplishment has been helpful several times already, and it should be of inestimable value in the future.

Think twice about using agents. Most companies in the capital goods field, including computers, start out overseas with sales agents. Sometimes the agents are distributors, sometimes trading companies – there are all sorts of possible arrangements. After carefully looking them over, CMC's management decided that the agent route was definitely *not* the way to enter Europe.

Whether business goes well or poorly, agents often become a problem. If the product succeeds, most manufacturers, envisioning greater profits, want to set up their own European sales network. The manufacturer's contract with the agent may make this extremely difficult – and costly – to do. On the other hand, if the product fails and the manufacturer wants to dissolve his agreement, the agent may demand the fat compensatory payment that is frequently part of his contract.

Setting up your own sales force right away, is that the best approach to establish yourself in Europe? Generally, *yes*; but a sales force alone is not the whole answer. Once you establish a sales network and start doing business across borders, you run into a plethora of protective tariffs, extra costs, and competitors. Thus it soon becomes very attractive – if not essential – to manufacture in Europe.

We foresaw possible problems with agents or with a European sales force without European manufacturing. This prompted us to start right off with a combination sales and production facility. We have not regretted that decision.

The personnel problem

As part of the plan to maintain a low profile overseas, we will hire only nationals wherever we go. This is true not only in the case of workers and technical personnel, but also managers, including the head of the operation. There are a number of obvious (and not so obvious) reasons why this is a good practice:

1. If the managers we hire are good businessmen, they will be far more effective in their familiar environments than most transplanted Americans could be for quite some time – maybe ever. The subtle nuances of doing business that often trip up Americans are second nature to nationals.

2. Hiring nationals is the best way to overcome the language problem. Americans face a hard decision in choosing a second language: should it be French, German, Spanish, Russian, Italian, or what? There is no choice for Europeans: English is *the* second language. Obviously they can communicate in their own language better than an American. And, if they are carefully chosen, they will be effective enough in English to report clearly and concisely to the US parent company.

3. You may avoid sending one or more of your key managerial or technical persons overseas permanently. Thus you can prevent weakening the parent company – especially if it is a smaller one. Also, few Americans are happy when obliged to make extended tours of duty abroad with their families.

4. Having nationals in management positions is very helpful, if not downright essential, in the government dealings that inevitably are a major element of doing business overseas. Nationals are more likely to know which government official to see, how to get to see him, and what to say. Moreover, governments are far more cooperative with companies that employ nationals as managers. It is an understandable, though

often overlooked, part of nationalism. Every person we employ in the United Kingdom is British, and every person we have hired in France is French.

Admittedly, CMC's approach here is unorthodox. But it makes sense politically. And it makes sense operationally. A Frenchman, for example, can deal much more effectively with other Frenchmen, at both higher and lower levels. A business operation typically encounters enough problems without the extra headaches caused by national prejudices and language barriers.

Pool of talent

How do the countries we are operating in shape up as a reservoir of managerial and technical talent? According to our way of thinking, quite well. The combined population of England and France is half that of the United States. But these countries do not offer their people anywhere near half the business opportunities that the United States does. So much of their managerial and technical potential is yet to be tapped.

As far as the computer industry is concerned it is not correct to say that everyone is far behind the United States. True, we are ahead in materials technology and computer applications. But other countries possess equal – or superior – theoretical and design capabilities.

Take the Russians, for example. Some years ago, I was in the Academy of Sciences in Moscow. It is like all our colleges lumped into one, a gigantic central facility. Around the room that housed their computers I could see warm soldering irons for patching and boxes of computer components that would be considered antiques in the United States. Yet the Russians I spoke to talked absolutely brilliantly about computer theory. They knew everything we knew, maybe more.

We in CMC's management have kept that incident in mind when searching for persons with experience or untapped talent to staff our foreign subsidiaries.

The difficulty of finding, keeping and motivating good managers in this country is no less a fact in Europe. I started out looking for a fellow with whom I could work to head our English facility. We took a great deal of time in settling on the man because he is absolutely critical to our success there.

We paid far more attention to what candidates had accomplished in the real business world than to where they went to school. European titles, fancy schools, and memberships in various high-sounding organizations are not as good a measure of a businessman as the positions he has held and what he has achieved in them.

Further, we carefully checked the references of the candidates under serious consideration. While there is no reason to suspect there are more phonies in Europe than the United States, there is also no reason to believe there are fewer.

Finally, we selected a man who had not only had sales management experience with General Electric Company, Ltd, but experience as a computer programmer. He is a good negotiator and a good leader, and is ambitious. The opportunity for stock options with a US company appealed to that ambition.

After our experience in looking at candidates to head the UK subsidiary, incidentally, I have become convinced that US companies must do much more to develop in their European managers a willingness to take risks. They have failed to do this because until recently there was no advantage to risk taking in Europe. There was not much capital to accumulate, so taking chances offered a greater probability of failure than success.

Most small companies must take risks to compete with the larger ones. This is doubly true in the computer industry, where there are young small companies and old big ones; but no such thing as an *old small* one.

Reference

CLEE, G. H. and DI SCIPIO, A. (1959), 'Creating a *world* enterprise', *Harvard Business Review*, November–December, pp. 77–8.

24 Business International

Alternative Ways to Penetrate a Foreign Market

'Alternative ways to penetrate a foreign market', *Business International*, in *100 Checklists: Decision Making in International Operations*, 1970, pp. 6–8.

Whether a company is approaching a foreign market for the first time or has been operating in it for years, periodic reviews of the techniques used in it are necessary to keep ahead of changing conditions and to update corporate objectives in that market.

Factors that call for such periodic examinations include interregional shifts, urbanization and suburbanization, technology, transportation, competition, social pressures, local expertise, changing buying patterns and selling outlets, and, of course, government actions and rules and regulations.

Company policies may dictate certain basic operating patterns or preferences, but local conditions and laws may demand important modifications. A company that is rigid in its style of operations, i.e. choosing to invest in a market only as a majority owner or selling only through its own sales force, may be passing up opportunities for great profits. None of the many possible routes to market penetration should be overlooked in a company's periodic review of its approaches. Below is a checklist of the major market routes, from the simplest to the most committed.

Domestic export sales

1. Fill unsolicited orders from independent export/import houses that buy and sell for their own customers.
2. Sell to foreign government buying offices, and buying groups of other foreign organizations located in the domestic market (e.g. The Afro-American Purchasing Center Inc. of NY and Amtorg Trading Co.) and qualify for listing on approved government buying lists.
3. Bid on tenders solicited by foreign governments or private organizations (some may be limited to local or regional companies).
4. Sell to foreign subsidiaries in domestic market products for shipment to parent and other overseas subsidiaries.

5. Sell to domestic customers products for shipment to their overseas subsidiaries.
6. Display and take part in trade fairs and exhibitions.

Indirect export sales

1. Hire the services of a combination export managing (CEM) firm, which in effect becomes your export department. (You get involved only to the extent and with products desired.)
2. Hire the services of an export/import house. It takes over the responsibility for exporting and distributing your product overseas, but leaves you with little control or ability to keep abreast of the market. Can be vital in small and remote markets.
3. Arrange to have another company market your product through its overseas marketing channels, particularly when it is well established abroad and its products are complementary to your own (also called 'piggybacking' or 'mother hen').

Direct export sales through outside distribution channels

1. Join forces with other manufacturers of your product line and export under a group, industry, or association. US companies can do this via Webb-Pomerene Associations (Export Trade Act of 1918), which are designed to enable small firms to engage in foreign trade (cutting costs and competing effectively against overseas cartels) without running into antitrust snags.
2. Organize your own export department, staff it with your own export salesmen and sell via middlemen in the foreign market. This may be to a commission house or purchasing agent, resident buyer, broker, auction house, export/import merchant or jobber (takes title to your merchandise); or independent agents and distributors (sells on commission).
3. Negotiate export barter sales via a third party entrepreneur (or direct with foreign purchaser).
4. Form an export consortium with other manufacturers to supply turnkey and large-scale development projects.

Direct export and sales through local company sales organization

1. Create a regional sales branch office and/or subsidiary.
2. If a US company, organize a Western Hemisphere Trade Corporation to engage in export within the western hemisphere; it can obtain concessional tax rates for these activities.

3. Create a national sales branch office and/or subsidiary.
4. Organize a joint selling company with a:
   (a) Local partner.
   (b) Unrelated third-country manufacturer.
   (c) Related third-country subsidiary.
5. Establish own sales force and distributors using:
   (a) Domestic salesmen.
   (b) Expatriate salesmen.
   (c) Third-country nationals.
   (d) All three.
6. Use company sales force as well as 'missionary' salesmen for:
   (a) Certain customers.
   (b) Particular areas.
   (c) Particular outlets.
7. Set up regional distribution centers or warehouses.
8. Set up national company distribution centers or warehouses.
9. Hire services and rent facilities of public warehouses.
10. Use combination of company distribution centers and public warehouses.
11. Lease warehouse space in unrelated company warehouses.
12. Organize an overseas franchise system using independent franchises or a combination of company and independents.
13. Team up with another equally strong manufacturer (or several) whereby you each distribute and sell noncompetitive products through company showrooms or dealers in:
    (a) The same country.
    (b) Different countries.

Licensing, assembling and manufacturing

1. License patents and/or unpatented know-how in return for:
   (a) Royalty payments and fees.
   (b) Equity.
   (c) Royalty and equity.
2. License patents and/or unpatented know-how for a flat sum payment, e.g. East European deals, and licenses of obsolete processes.
3. Obtain licenses of foreign patents and/or unpatented know-how for use in third countries (and domestic market).

4. Arrange to cross-license equipment of a manufacturer who in turn produces under license your equipment. Each to be sold in respective markets.

5. Contract out manufacture of products to be sold:
   (a) Under your company trademarks and brand names.
   (b) Under private label.
   (c) For small and/or test runs.

6. Operate under a management contract that gives you management responsibility.

7. Set up a consortium with three or more partners, with the company:
   (a) Assuming management responsibility.
   (b) Being passive partner.

8. Purchase an equity interest in an existing manufacturing or assembly operation with:
   (a) 100 per cent equity
   (b) Controlling interest } acquired with { Cash. Technology. Parent stock.
   (c) Minority interest

9. Set up manufacturing or assembly operations in a free trade zone or free port.

10. Purchase assets of an existing foreign corporation, buying some or all assets for cash, stock or a combination of the two.

11. Organize a joint venture with a local partner, holding equity through a third-country corporation (a base).

12. Join with a third-country partner in a new manufacturing/assembly operation:
    (a) Unrelated third-country manufacturer.
    (b) Related third-country subsidiary.
    (c) Private financial partner, e.g. Edge Act Corp.
    (d) Public institutional financial partner, e.g. IFC.

13. Create a joint venture with local interests in a new manufacturing/assembly operation:
    (a) Fifty-fifty ownership – with joint management.
    (b) Majority-owned – with management responsibility.
    (c) Minority-owned – with or without management responsibility (i.e. with, if partner is a bank, government).

14. Create a manufacturing/assembly operation wholly owned by a third-country holding (base) company.

15. Create a wholly owned manufacturing/assembly operation.

25 OECD

Basic Considerations in Connection with the Establishment of Export Marketing Groups

'Basic considerations in connection with the establishment of export marketing groups', in *Export Marketing Groups for Small and Medium-Sized Firms*, OECD, 1964, pp. 13–19.

Range of products

If manufacturers are to derive advantage from a coordination of their export functions, it is of major importance that their export cooperation should be properly planned. The production programme and markets of each individual firm must be analysed in detail before firms decide to cooperate in promoting their export sales.

The question of selecting the range of products to be marketed by the group is of paramount importance. The rational selection of the range of products greatly influences marketing efficiency and, consequently, export costs.

It may have considerable bearing on the proper selection of the range that the products are consumed together. This is exemplified by the Danish Theta[1] Group for marketing textile materials for interior decoration in the USA, and the Belgian Epsilon Group for the exportation of textile machinery. In the latter case this point is so important that the group sometimes enters into co-operation with foreign manufacturers so as to be able to offer a complete range of machines to certain types of factories.

Sometimes, better export results are achieved when all products are sold through the same channels of distribution. This is the case where marketing efforts are mostly directed towards distributors and not towards end-consumers. This fact has been taken into consideration by the Gamma Group in Belgium, which is endeavouring to select a range that can be sold through the same type of retail shops.

Since manufacturers cooperating in export promotion remain independent, their interests may clash when their products can be used readily as substitutes for one another. How much importance

1. Greek letters are used to conceal the true names of marketing groups which have been mentioned in this report, all of which exist.

they should attach to this particular point depends on the extent of their export cooperation. If their cooperation includes only market information, advertising and service, the fact that the participating firms are offering rival products does not usually entail any adverse consequences. If, on the other hand, cooperation also includes a centralization of order booking and distribution, then the actual allocation of orders to rival firms may entail difficulties. However, firms should consider the consequences before ceasing to cooperate on the grounds that their products can be substituted for one another. As tastes differ, consumers often wish to see a whole range of products before they decide to buy. It may, therefore, be an advantage to include in the same collection products appealing to different tastes.

As a consequence of difficulties experienced in connection with the distribution of orders, manufacturers are frequently advised not to centralize the booking of orders and distribution when their products may be substituted for one another. In spite of this fact many such firms find it beneficial to perform these export functions on a joint basis.

The problem may be solved by excluding rival products from the joint range. The Delta Group in Switzerland is an excellent example of how this can be done in practice. This solution does not prevent firms from marketing their full range of products in the local market, though it would naturally be advantageous if the specialization of export sales could be reflected in production.

Same or different industries

Another major question is whether the export group is to be made up of firms in the same industry or in several different industries.

It is not possible to give a general answer to this question. The division into industries is generally based on products or raw materials used and does not necessarily provide an adequate basis for determining the scope of the export group. Sometimes, however, the division into industries is reflected in the wholesale and retail trades, the products of one industry being sold through the same channels of distribution. Export cooperation among firms in the same industry can therefore result in improved marketing possibilities. Furthermore, products of the same industry frequently differ so much from one another that rival firms may perform their export functions on a joint basis.

In several countries the channels of distribution carry products from several industries. This development is a result of the efforts to improve marketing efficiency by combining products that are bought together, cost approximately the same, are sold in different seasons, etc. A case in point is furnishings that are now being sold to an increasing extent from the same shop, whereas the products were formerly distributed through several different types of retail outlets.

Such a development may suggest the establishment of export groups consisting of firms in several different branches of industry. An adaptation to developments in the furnishings trade may result in export groups of furniture and textile manufacturers.

In the producer goods industry export groups are often established for the purpose of covering complementary requirements for products outside the individual range of one industry; e.g. complete equipment for hospitals. Such groups are frequently established ad hoc. This does not prevent the firms concerned from distributing their products concurrently through wholesale and retail channels in the same markets, either alone or in cooperation with other firms.

In many cases, therefore, it is inadvisable for an export group to handle the products of one particular industry alone. The factors influencing the selection of products for a particular range will determine what branches of industry are to be included in the cooperation.

Fields of cooperation

An export group may be established for the sole purpose of procuring detailed market information, even though it is nowadays possible to obtain this from public institutions, trade organizations, chambers of commerce, etc. It is, however, necessary to adapt these data to the particular interests of the manufacturers in the group. Moreover, such a desk-research may be the beginning of more extensive cooperation in future.

The advantages of cooperation become more apparent when a group undertakes field research on a joint basis. Such research is difficult and calls for larger investments which are easier to finance if undertaken jointly. Export market analyses are frequently supported financially by public authorities, provided a group of firms will benefit from them and itself contributes financially.

If cooperation includes sales promotion, the economic advantages become still more obvious. Advertising may well be undertaken collectively, even though the participating firms continue individually to canvass their own customers.

If manufacturers do not want to restrict their cooperation to prestige advertising but to extend it to the promotion of individual products, such products should be advertised under a common name of brand which should also be used by the individual firms in their own sales propaganda on the packages, etc. Collective advertising can only be fully efficient however when group exports are centralized. This may include a central export office and the use of joint channels of distribution on the export markets. In fact, export cooperation will be much more economic and successful if products are sold and distributed through a joint export office. A thorough coordination and centralization of all export functions thus becomes possible and enables firms to get a better return for their marketing costs. It is usually advisable to locate the export office in the home market so as to facilitate the close cooperation between managers of member firms, but if a group concentrates on a single foreign market with a large turnover it may be expedient to establish the sales office in that market.

In order to derive full advantage from export cooperation, it is necessary to establish joint marketing channels in export markets as well. An export group is able to procure the best channels of distribution in the individual markets owing to the advantages presented by this type of cooperation to foreign distributors.

Normally, any export group should begin its life carefully with a selection of possible and, in the long run, desirable functions. Desk-research, collective advertising, and sales promotion form the basis for marketing groups abroad. Field-studies, branded goods policy, and product development might follow later when the cooperation has proved successful. A full marketing service should always be the goal when looking ahead as export groups must offer their members collectively the same competitive weapons as are available to the larger firms individually. In later stages, of course, the group can and should include other fields like buying, harmonization of production and basic technical research, to name a few.

Number and types of markets

The proper choice of the market or the markets which the export group should consider entering is of major importance for the success of the cooperation. If the potential member firms of the group have not been active at all in exports, the choice is relatively simple as biased personal preferences will not influence the decision so easily. A thorough study of the potentials of promising markets has to be made and preference should be given to that market or partial market where satisfactory results can be achieved most economically.

Even the combined strength of twenty or thirty firms will not perform miracles. Activities have therefore to be restricted in the first stage to two or three foreign markets which should be homogeneous and similar to each other. This would prevent different marketing approaches, especially in sales promotion and advertising, which could prove very costly and would therefore quickly discourage the group. Furthermore, it would be advantageous if the markets were located in the same regional area, like the Benelux countries, the Scandinavian countries or Austria and Switzerland, for in the beginning it would not seem advisable to spend time and money on markets so geographically apart as, for instance, Northern France and Southern Italy.

It has to be assured also that the chosen market will offer equal opportunities for the products of all participating firms, particularly if assortments are heterogeneous, and that the same sales organization and the same channels of distribution can be used. The choice of markets is therefore interdependent with the types of firms in the marketing group – and vice versa.

If potential group members have already been actively engaged in export marketing and have established sales, then the choice of market becomes more complex because these firms might want to: (a) have those markets included, hoping thereby to strengthen their position with the help of the whole group even if this choice might prove disadvantageous for the rest, or (b) have those markets excluded, as they are already well established there and are more interested in new market areas, while their prospective partners are especially interested in profiting from the experience gained by these firms.

Again, only a market survey can serve as a basis for the final decision in order to ensure that the best possible market chances for the majority of member firms shall be exploited. Firms which cannot agree to such a decision should be left out. It seems better to limit the number this way than to start off with compromises, which will hamper the commercial success of the marketing group.

Some existing export groups – like the Delta Group in Switzerland – have tried to solve this important problem by constituting sub-groups for those member firms who are only interested in certain markets and regions or in certain specified outlets like department stores or government buying. This certainly is a useful solution, but it seems doubtful whether such a choice is feasible at the beginning of the enterprise when too many complications may jeopardize the efficiency and success of the export activities. It should, therefore, be considered as a second stage when the spreading of activities to new markets is planned.

International export cooperation

Export cooperation between smaller firms of different countries does not seem yet to be very common, but is obviously growing in importance. If the selection of partners is made carefully enough, not only is such cooperation as good as export marketing with firms of the same country, but it can bring even faster and more profitable results. The foreign partner already has his sales organization established, knows the trade outlets and market conditions well, and has established a reputation of his own which can be of great advantage to the manufacturer who enters into cooperation with the firm, but the risks involved are naturally greater than with manufacturers of their own country who are well-known to the firm. A close look has to be taken, therefore, at the following points which could mean failure or success in cooperating with the foreign partner or partners:

1. Position of firm in market (reputation, strength, channels used, market coverage).
2. Production facilities and capacity of the firm.
3. Liquidity, financial resources and management ability.
4. Marketing policies.
5. Assortment range.

The last item is especially important, as lack of harmonization in assortments can easily lead to misunderstandings, unwanted competition with partners, overlapping of efforts and failure of the cooperation.

It is easier for manufacturers to cooperate if their products are complementary to each other. If their production programmes overlap they must endeavour to specialize in such a way that the individual product is manufactured in one factory only, with a resultant lowering of manufacturing costs. An Italian manufacturer of motor-scooters may, for instance, enter into cooperation with a Dutch manufacturer of bicycles and bicycle-trailers by selling the Dutch products through the same channels of distribution as the motor-scooters. In this way the marketing costs are distributed over a larger number of products, and the Dutch manufacturer derives advantage from a well-established marketing organization on the Italian market. Similarly, the Dutch manufacturer includes the Italian motor-scooters in his marketing organization and the Italian manufacturer derives a corresponding advantage in Holland.

This type of cooperation can be expanded to other countries in which two manufacturers wish to promote their export sales. By employing a joint marketing organization they will be able to reduce the cost of market research, sales promotion and actual distribution.

Cooperating firms, of course, run the risk that one of the participants may take up the manufacture of the products of one of the others after sales in the product are rising. This risk is particularly serious in the case of international cooperation, as it may be difficult to take legal proceedings, but the risk may be reduced by arranging for the payment of substantial penalties in case the agreement is broken.

Firms in different countries may also work together in more restricted fields. A French, a German and a British shirt-maker may, for instance, cooperate on advertising their cotton shirts in preference to shirts made of synthetic fibres. Firms also frequently combine in arranging specialized international exhibitions. If cooperation is only to comprise a general publicity campaign, then it is of no consequence that the ranges of products be identical. Collective quotations for large contracts are also frequently submitted. Such contracts often comprise products that are not made by a single manufacturer alone, or are of a volume that exceeds the productive capacity of a single manufacturer. The Belgian Gamma Group for textile machinery cooperates with manufacturers in other countries both as regards exhibitions and quotations for large contracts.

How does one get started?

On examining what it is that makes manufacturers want to cooperate on exporting, the main reason usually found is marketing difficulties, often engendered by keener competition with imported goods. There is no doubt that, in many cases, manufacturers would have been better able to counter such competition if they had begun to cooperate at an earlier stage. The problem, however, is who should take the initiative in getting firms to cooperate in time on export functions?

When export cooperation is to be a voluntary effort, a proposal to this effect put forward by a potential member of the export group will probably meet with the best reception. If the initiator is a businessman who enjoys the respect and confidence of his trade, the idea of cooperation will stand a good chance of success. The French Beta Group and the Swiss Delta Group were both started this way.

However, managers of small and medium-sized firms may feel that they will suffer loss of prestige if they take the initiative and call for export cooperation. Sometimes it is also difficult for them to realize soon enough that changed market conditions often necessitate marketing cooperation if they are to continue as independent firms.

It is therefore important to establish that, when a firm calls for export cooperation, it may be a sign of foresight and adaptability. Naturally, a firm that systematically analyses, for example, consequences of the present market integration, is in a better position to take the initiative in promoting export cooperation than a firm that makes a similar proposal against a background of marketing difficulties.

Many firms are not aware of the advantages of export cooperation and information should therefore be supplied by trade associations and public export authorities. Most trade associations already help members by supplying market information and acting as advisers on export questions. Consequently, they possess excellent qualifications for estimating the competitive position of the industry. On the basis of these estimates the associations may initiate export cooperation between members. Such information should be distributed at meetings and courses of the trade associations, through publicity, and articles in periodicals and other papers.

Trade and other business associations may operate as the organizational centres of export groups. Such is the case with the French Alpha Group, which comprises many small industrial firms. Even if one does not go that far, associations may often make their secretariat available for the drafting of articles of association and the execution of other formalities in connection with the establishment of a group. In some trade associations the secretariat carried out regular office work during the export group's initial period of operation.

In Belgium one of the largest trade associations makes both offices and staff available to members for permanent cooperation on important export functions. The trade association of textile manufacturers in Denmark helps to establish export cooperation by presenting basic information on markets where a joint export drive seems possible.

In several countries the public authorities regard export co-operation between small and medium-sized firms so essential that they have encouraged joint efforts in various ways.

Firms or associations who have taken the initiative in starting export groups have done so because of marketing conditions necessitating active cooperation. Also, they have used results from market research, where such has been carried out, as well as figures from official statistics, to prove the necessity for a joint export drive. Proposals for cooperation should, furthermore, show the economic advantages and set out how it could be carried out.

Before the initial meeting, all special problems of cooperation should be discussed with the individual firms. It has proved to be useful if, at the initial meeting, a representative of an already existing export group be present to speak on his group's experience and to answer questions. However, the lead must come from one or two active men. They must provide the leadership especially necessary when a new organization gets started. Many examples can be found in recent business where similar organization succeeded because a few enthusiastic members carried their colleagues with them. Again, voluntary chains and retailer buying groups present valuable case material in this respect.

26 Business Europe

How Schick Sharpened Dull Sales Techniques to Cut into German Market

'How Schick sharpened dull sales techniques to cut into German market', *Business Europe*, 6 September 1968, pp. 281–282.

The successful German experience of Schick Safety Razor has recently proven that one practical way of making a new and costly sales network pay off rapidly is to sell the products of other manufacturers on a commission basis. Known as piggybacking in American business terminology, the system of sharing a sales team with other manufacturers may appeal not only to firms that have one or a few product lines but also to companies whose many product lines cannot be sold through a single distribution network.

By opting for piggybacking as a method of selling its products in Germany, a highly competitive market with many regions, after two unsuccessful attempts at cracking that market, the California company has been able to: establish a large distribution network that covers all parts of Germany; cover a portion of the high fixed costs of its sales organization with the sales commissions received from its partners; and increase rapidly its share of the market.

For companies that use another firm's sales network to launch a product in a new market, piggybacking helps cut distribution costs to a minimum. In fact, these firms need only pay sales commissions to their partners and bear the cost of advertising. But there is one caveat: Such companies will not have much control over the degree to which their partners' salesmen push their products.

Before adopting the piggybacking technique, Schick used the conventional method of employing an independent distributor. It soon became clear that, although the distributor was aggressive and well established, his sales staff was too small to call regularly on all cosmetics retailers in Germany.

Unhappy with the results, Schick canceled its contract with the dealer and entrusted distribution of its products to the German sales subsidiary of Sweden's Barnängens Tekniska Fabriker, a chemicals and light metals company that manufactures, among other products, the Vademecum line of toiletries. One of Schick's reasons for choosing Barnängens was that the Swedish firm markets its articles through food stores as well as through specialized cosmetics shops. At first, Schick's German sales rose substantially, but the situation suddenly soured when Barnängens launched a flower preservative that proved to be a best seller. Barnängens salesmen concentrated their efforts on this new product, for which orders were easy to land, rather than on the harder-to-sell Schick toiletries.

Having again failed to penetrate the German market satisfactorily, Schick set up its own sales subsidiary and hired as manager a former executive of its major competitor, Gillette. Schick then faced the basic choice of either:

1. Keeping initial costs at a minimum by recruiting a small sales force and later expanding it; or
2. Hiring a large staff and launching a major sales effort immediately – a riskier but more promising long term solution.

Choosing the second alternative, Schick hired some fifty salaried salesmen. The company estimated that this sales force would be large enough to visit all retailers once every two months, if it marketed no more than three product lines.

But Schick soon realized that, in view of the heavy sales expenses involved, it might be five years before its German subsidiary could turn a profit. Fortunately, American Cyanamid was then seeking an independent distributor for its Breck hair cosmetics. Although Cyanamid had its own sales organization in Germany to market pharmaceutical products, its salesmen were concentrating on pharmacies and physicians, rather than on cosmetic shops. In early 1968, Schick and Cyanamid found a solution to their distribution problems by signing a piggybacking agreement under which Schick became exclusive agent for Breck products in Germany (see below).

During the initial phase of the partnership, Breck products are being market-tested in the Hesse province only, but they are soon to be sold throughout Germany. Cyanamid, which under the contract bears the advertising expenses, is spending all sales proceeds minus commissions on advertising.

Pleased with the experiment with Cyanamid, Schick has recently taken a further step in piggybacking. Last week, the razor firm signed a contract with Associated Products (AP) of New York under which Schick will handle German distribution of the cosmetic articles manufactured in AP's Lyons plant.

Schick's sales figures are an eloquent testimonial to the merits of piggybacking. In one year, the razor company's share of the German market has grown from 3 per cent to 7 per cent, a growth that might not have been achieved with a small sales force.

Schick-Cyanamid piggybacking setup

The Schick-Cyanamid contract provides that Schick sell Breck cosmetics in its own name but for the account of Cyanamid – i.e. the products remain Cyanamid property until they are sold. Schick agrees not to sell its own similar products or similar products of a third company. Should any question arise concerning 'similarity' of a new product, Cyanamid must be consulted before a marketing decision is made.

The contract stipulates that Schick receive a higher commission during the launching period. (As a rule, German agents' commissions in the field of cosmetics are about 25 per cent of sales, as their high fixed costs range between 10 per cent and 16 per cent.) Cyanamid is authorized to check Schick's accounts with an independent auditor and to withdraw Breck cosmetics from the market if sales are disappointing. Should Schick be taken over by a third company, Cyanamid has the right to cancel the contract immediately.

27 G. Beeth

Distributors – Finding and Keeping the Good Ones

G. Beeth, 'Distributors – finding and keeping the good ones'. This article is based on a chapter of a forthcoming book to be published by the American Management Association.

This article is mainly concerned with distributors (including agents) of industrial equipment. Thus, not all of the conclusions are applicable to distributors in other fields. Generally, we have in mind 'sole' distributors, that is, an exclusive distributor for each country.

The importance of having the right distributor

Most international companies looking at the actual range of performance of their foreign distributors find that it does not fall within, say, 80 per cent to 120 per cent of what they would expect from carefully determined market potential figures. Instead, performance varies from zero to over 200 per cent of the expected, and the difference in performance between distributors is enormous. Finding excellent distributors is therefore all-important.

But even with your best efforts, you will never have a group of only excellent distributors. With careful and hard work, you can have a few excellent, many medium, and some mediocre distributors ... and a few worthless ones whom you are always trying to replace. There is no way to hit 100 per cent.

We may take as a rule of thumb, that in most countries with only *small* markets there are in each field:

0 or 1 excellent distributors,
0 or 1 medium distributors,
1 or 2 mediocre distributors,
and the remaining distributors are worthless to you.

In most countries with *bigger* markets, yet not markets so big that they warrant a subsidiary, there often are in an industrial equipment field:

1 or 2 excellent distributors,
2 or 3 medium distributors,

several mediocre distributors,
and the remaining distributors are worthless.

Finding the good ones

Lists of distributors broken down by fields of activity are available for each country from the US Department of Commerce (good), from local chambers of commerce (usually not good), from local classified directories of various kinds (often too all-inclusive), and from other sources. But you don't want a list, you want the name of one distributor – the best one.

One or two firms may have contacted you, but the probability that they are the best is small. Don't waste your time contacting them all by mail and sending them forms to complete. Instead, follow these three steps toward finding a good distributor:

1. Go personally to the country, allowing ample time. Talk to the ultimate users of the equipment to find out from which distributors they prefer to buy and why. Two or three names will keep popping up in the replies you get.
2. Then go to those two or three distributors and see which one or ones you would be able to sign up.
3. But, before making the final choice, look for the distributor who has the key man for your line – as explained below.

Long ago, we used to travel around with a list on which we rated each distributor on a scale from one to ten in each of twenty-four different activities and abilities. Then we weighed these different matters in accordance with the importance of each one and arrived arithmetically at a single over-all rating for each distributor. This was done by taking into account his sales force, his coverage of the market, management ability, service personnel's capability, financial strength, connections, warehouse and service facilities, spare parts stocks, performance in related lines, technical ability to understand the equipment, and several other items.

Unfortunately, the final rating figure for the distributors we were supervising showed no correlation at all to their actual performance.

Then we threw away the list and looked for what was common to the few excellent distributors with which we had the privilege to be working. In this way, we discovered a single new factor which replaced the 24-point list and this new factor bore considerable correlation to success. We started to look for a distributor who had one capable man who would take the new line of equipment to his heart and make it his personal objective to make the sale of that line a success in his country. In some small distributorships, this key man was the owner. In others, he was the sales manager or a salesman. In one company, he was the service manager. In one case, there were two such men instead of one, but that was a rare distributor who somehow did three times what we considered to be the possible volume for his country.

In actual fact, it is not as easy to find a good distributor in some countries, especially in very small, less industrialized nations where you might find that there are:

zero excellent distributors,
zero medium distributors,
one or two mediocre distributors firmly tied to your competitors,
and the remaining distributors are worthless to you.

Suppose none of them shows any sign of having or getting the key man you are looking for. What do you do?

First, you can try to find a local businessman in a different field ... one who wants to fill the obvious need for a good distributor in your field. If that doesn't work, you can try to get one of the mediocre distributors to switch from the competitor to you. Occasionally you might get to him just when he has become angry at your competitor for some reason or another.

But failing that, you had better forget about appointing any distributor at all in that country – because having a worthless one will cost you time and money every year and possibly prevent a good newcomer in that country from asking for your line.

If everything else has failed, you may want to consider attending a local industrial exhibition in that country to ask further advice from the local prospective end users of your products. If there should be a near-by US trade center, it can help you mount a small exhibition of your products for the specific purpose of finding a distributor.

When you interview distributors, what they tell you is often revealing about them in ways they do not realize. Here is an example. We used to sell compressors and call on distributors in the heavy construction field. For some of them, their prime line was Caterpillar tractors, and for others International Harvester tractors. When asked how their business was, some would answer 'great' while others would say that it was impossible to compete against International Harvester or Caterpillar – whichever line they did not have.

Those who said it was impossible to compete raised one warning signal. Is this distributor going downhill? What has happened to him? Why can he not compete?

But those who said that the tractor business was great raised another equally important warning signal. Do they concentrate all of their efforts on their tractor line? Are they great in selling tractors and poor in selling everything else? Signing on distributors who are excellent for another manufacturer in an allied field does not always produce excellent results.

Keeping the good ones

The only way to keep a good distributor is to work closely and well with him, so that he can make money with your line.

View your business from the distributor's side. First of all, he must make money for himself. If that automatically makes him earn money for you, too, then fine. But if he does not make money with it for himself, any good distributor will quickly drop your line.

Even worse, he may put your line away and make it available only if one of his customers insists on getting some of your equipment ... but otherwise do nothing for your line.

Thus, you must not only keep the good distributor but also keep the distributor good. And the last part is not always easy because there are many demands on his time from other lines of equipment and from customers with interests and problems outside your field. Somehow, you must arrange through direct mail and visits to keep your line constantly in front of your distributor and among his daily duties and thoughts.

It is best, of course, if you can require that he have one or more full-time persons handling your line. But if the potential sales volume is not high enough to warrant this effort, do not ask for it. If you cause the distributor losses through excessive demands on him, it will backfire on you.

Above all, you must not be stingy in matters such as paying for the training of his men and going beyond your legal warranty obligations to your distributor. He goes beyond his legal warranty toward his customers, and he expects the same from you.

It is important that the rules be spelled out in advance concerning payment of commissions to the distributor or agent. Especially the conditions relating to non-payment of commissions must be clear. Nevertheless, when an unclear borderline case comes up, you should always rule in favor of your distributor. In the long run, the distributor's goodwill toward your company is more valuable than the commissions paid in borderline cases. The quickest way to destroy a distributor's goodwill is to make him feel cheated – even on a small matter.

Unless your sales volume with each distributor is very large, you cannot afford to run his business or remake a mediocre distributor into a good one.

One American company has an outstanding record of going against the above rule: Caterpillar. They will work so effectively with a distributor that they can make him good in many cases; but for most other companies, this method is too costly.

Instead, if a good distributor changes into a mediocre or bad one, the sooner you can replace him with an excellent alternative, the better. Of course, whether or not the new one will be excellent, you never know in advance. If the new distributor also turns out to be mediocre or worse, then you had better switch again as soon as you have found a third seemingly excellent prospect.

Some people argue that this switching shows a lack of stability and seriousness toward the ultimate users. Don't worry: the ultimate users are probably better aware of the shortcomings of your former distributor than you are. They appreciate your trying to find a good one: and your sales figures show it quickly when you succeed. Any good list of distributors is in constant change because the distributors themselves quickly change. It might be that the key man for your line has left his distributor-employer, and your sales drop forthwith to 10 per cent of what they previously were in that country. Unless you can get the distributor to replace the departed man with another excellent key man, or switch responsibility for your line to another one of his best men, don't keep that distributor – just hoping that things will improve.

Getting rid of the mediocre distributors

When you do change, do it totally, quickly, cleanly, and thoroughly, without worrying about being called ruthless by your old distributor. He will always feel that your cancellation is an affront to him personally, anyway. He will say that you are not loyal. Forget it. An active, aggressive, changing distributor list produces more sales. In addition, your aggressive policies tend to keep the medium distributors on their toes and doing their best.

The lengthy distributor contract has only one important clause: the cancellation clause. The remainder is mainly a listing of who does what, written in legalese. In most light industrial equipment businesses, it should be possible for either party to cancel any time after the first year, upon sixty days' notice to the other party.

What happens to the distributor's stock in case of cancellation by the manufacturer should be spelled out. It will vary considerably from country to country because of local laws, but in no case should the manufacturer be required to take back any obsolete or otherwise unsaleable inventory. If the manufacturer must agree to take back any other inventory, it should be at the net f.o.b., factory price, less a hefty restocking charge, unless local laws force him to do otherwise.

Prior to signing a distributorship contract, the cancellation clause should be checked by a local lawyer to minimize any local indemnification requirements to distributors upon cancellation.

Of course, some distributors may object to a strong cancellation clause, but it is well worth fighting for despite the natural hope that you will never need to use it.

In some countries, the indemnification to distributors upon cancellation depends on just how the business is conducted. In France, if the distributor has certain obligations to report names and addresses of purchasers to you, the indemnification risk increases to compensate the distributor for the market information. In Germany, there is no indemnification to a true distributor, 'Eigenhandler', but there is to a commission agent if he has certain reporting obligations.

Since the laws governing a distributor contract vary widely from country to country, their impact on cancellation of distributor contracts must be taken into account when choosing the country from which you want to service and supervise distributors. In an area such as Europe, you may prefer a country with favorable laws which you can invoke for governing the distributorship contracts.

To illustrate the opposite situation, assume that an American subsidiary to France supervises and supplies a distributor for Italy. In this case, the contract must be written so that either French or Italian law applies. Neither is particularly favorable, but Italian law is somewhat better than French law in case the distributor contract has to be cancelled.

But if the same Italian distributor had been supplied from an American subsidiary in Denmark, the contractor should get Danish law to apply, instead, in order to lower the risk of indemnification upon cancellation.

The cancellation of a distributor or licensee agreement can be a somewhat delicate transaction, and it must be handled carefully. If the distributor who is dropped is no good, then the remaining distributors in neighboring countries will understand and support the cancellation. But if the matter is not clear cut (e.g. for some business reason it should become necessary to drop a medium distributor), then the action must be thoroughly explained to the remaining distributors, customers, and others. An excellent distributor is never dropped. Any cancellation must, of course, always be thoroughly prepared under the applicable law.

Contrary to what distributors seem to feel, there is nothing morally wrong in terminating a distributorship which doesn't work out. And in the long run the true interest of a poor distributor will not be served by his representing your business anyway. Typically, the only economical way to improve upon an ineffective independent distributor is to change over to an effective one. Had it been your subsidiary instead, you could have eliminated the specific cause for the 'distributor's' ineffectiveness. Unfortunately, this is usually too difficult to do in an independent company.

Part Seven
Global Marketing in the Multinational Corporation

The large multinational corporation is the concern of Part Seven. The readings deal with two characteristic problems of global concern. The first problem is that of achieving coordination of the parts in the interest of the whole. An underlying issue is that of encouraging local initiative without harvesting gross national suboptimization. The second set of problems are those of organization at the national and headquarters levels. Both types of problems are perennial and call for continuous attention. The reason that no solutions are apt to be permanent is the constant change of the international business environment. As market structures change so do marketing strategies, sooner or later. Systems of coordination and organization will – or should – be adapted to the smooth implementation of whatever strategies are in effect at a given time.

Reading 28, by Keegan, examines the role of headquarters in the multinational corporation. Overall marketing planning, coordination to achieve 'multimarketing synergy' and control of operations are not only legitimate but inescapable functions of headquarters in any concern aspiring to a global outlook. Planning as well as performance evaluation demands a rich data base. The logic calls for a much greater involvement in the planning and monitoring of local marketing research than what is current custom. Reading 29, by d'Antin, discusses the product manager organization used in the local operations of Nestlé, one of the half-dozen most cosmopolitan concerns in the world. It also demonstrates how the activities of product managers around the world for a given good – say, instant coffee – are coordinated and supported by headquarters services units.

Reading 30, by Aylmer, accounts for a field survey of centralization and decentralization of marketing decisions in multinational firms. As one might expect, the degree of headquarters involvement varies greatly by type of decision. Product design, for instance, tends to be a great deal more centralized than advertising or the setting of price for local markets. Incidentally, the setting of export prices from local markets would typically be a rather centralized decision, as suggested by Reading 31. It should be added that, other circumstances equal, one should expect a greater degree of home office involvement (directly or at least in the shape of centrally trained local personnel) in a corporation aiming to be a change agent abroad than in one where unilateral adjustment to local environments is the rule. Similarly, a strategy of homogenization will tend to be reflected in greater centralization than one of heterogenization.

Reading 31, by Shulman, deals with the intricate problems of intracorporate marketing in multinational operations. It is focused on pricing as the single most critical variable, but it must be kept in mind that apart from the tax questions many analogous issues arise with regard to other marketing instruments (such as product and service) in transactions between national subsidiaries. A conclusion of the article is that the effects of different intracompany pricing policies on performance measurement and motivation of managements of subsidiary operations generally are more critical than any others, including tax effects.

28 W. J. Keegan

Headquarters Involvement in Multinational Marketing

Adapted from W. J. Keegan, 'Multinational marketing: the headquarters role', *Columbia Journal of World Business*, vol. 6, no. 1, 1971, pp. 85–90.

Headquarters should be directly involved in the multinational corporation's foreign marketing for several reasons. First of all, headquarters must be effectively informed to carry its responsibility for strategic planning. Marketing research is an important source of information and should therefore be monitored by headquarters. Secondly, certain market measures could be standardized so that results from each country would be comparable and allow international comparison of marketing performance. Of course, these comparisons would not justify simple, direct conclusions regarding the relative performance of one subsidiary to all others. Nevertheless, they could raise important questions regarding subsidiary performance and country potential. They would be a valuable input to the design of a marketing research program. A third justification for headquarters involvement is to insure that no country or area unknowingly undertakes research on a topic that has already been studied elsewhere in the international system. This could be avoided by simply monitoring the subjects and topics proposed and comparing them with completed research and projects underway.

The headquarters role has two explicit costs. One is the time of the person or people who plan the standardized research approaches and monitor the research activities of country and area organizations. A second is the one-time cost of switching countries over to a standardized research format. This switch would break the time series in each country's data base. The possibility of hidden costs in country and area companies should be carefully evaluated. One possible hidden cost would occur if headquarters involvement resulted in a decline in morale in country and area organizations. There is no reason why this must occur, particularly if each country and area is involved in formulating the standardized approach.

In a number of companies, there is a substantial amount of bias against efforts at systematic comparative analysis. This bias is greatest at the country operation level. As one headquarters executive put it, 'The more you know about a country, the more you think it is unique.' However, even in companies where there is little or no systematic comparative analysis of potential and operations, there is a considerable amount of ad hoc, 'seat of the pants' comparative analysis carried out by international managers whose travel places them in touch with different country operations. For example, a manager may suggest a new product for country B based on its success in country A, or he may question the value of a proposed study in country C based on knowledge from country D, or he may suggest a customer category or market segment for country E based on the success of this category or segment in country F.

Only a handful of companies engage in systematic comparative analysis of product performance and potential. Their success, however, has been noteworthy. One company in the computer field, for example, has discovered that industry applications for its products are comparable around the world and that its indexes of potential for the United States are applicable worldwide. In other areas, such as in conditions underlying levels of performance, it has developed a 'clustering' technique in which clusters of related countries are grouped for analytical purposes.

Company officials relying upon systematic comparative analysis of product performance and market potential argue that it is valuable to pinpoint areas where performance might be improved and to identify opportunity areas. They also claim that a comparative standard provides the supranational headquarters with an 'objective' and impersonal measure of performance. It enables the headquarters to evaluate subsidiary performance in a more objective atmosphere. As one manager explained:

'You might find a man who is hoarding people in his operations for some reason, and unless you have a comparative standard, you have no way to criticize him. If you have such a standard you can say, "Look, compared to other operations, you have twenty-five too many people." The value of this is that the criticism from the United States or from on top does not become personal. It's related to an objective standard: the performance of other operations that are similar in nature.'

Goals

Although the critical importance of objectives and goals to effective planning is recognized, many headquarters executives fail to participate in the formulation of objectives and goals. In country subsidiaries, there is a widespread view that international headquarters is not qualified to participate effectively in the process of selecting objectives and goals. Many country managers are convinced that executives at headquarters do not understand the relevant aspects of the conditions which prevail in their markets. This view is particularly pronounced in companies which dominate their US markets and have minor positions in foreign markets. In these cases, executives whose total experience has been in the management of products which dominate domestic markets attempt to apply their domestic experience to foreign markets. Unfortunately, the experience of a market leader is not always transferable to a market follower.

In one case, a company which held a major share of the US market for its product adopted for its domestic strategy the objective of increasing the demand for its product by expanding the occasions on which the product would be consumed. In order to do so, it added new flavors and products to its line. This worked well in the United States, where expansion in demand for the product class was synonymous with expansion in demand for the company's product. In Europe, the company held a minor share of the market. Under the influence of the company president, it extended its US product strategy. The result was a European product line that was, relative to sales volume, far too extensive. The company was spreading its limited resources in advertising and selling in Europe over a product line that would have been appropriate for an organization ten times its size.

The difficulty was the president's failure to understand the basic differences in the company's position in foreign markets. His lack of understanding should have been corrected by the joint efforts of headquarters and operating companies in the goal-setting process. This correction only occurs if (1) the country and headquarters managers are aware of their own limitations in knowledge and understanding, and (2) both the country and the headquarters managers assert themselves in the planning process. Each organizational location brings its own perspective to the planning process, and each is valuable. Problems develop whenever one location begins to dominate the others.

Product management

The differences between domestic and foreign market size, characteristics and regulation have led companies to create international divisions to achieve an organizational competence center which responds to global environmental differences. At the same time, this arrangement separates foreign country operations from the domestic centers of product knowledge and know-how. At the early stages of international development, this separation of foreign and domestic product competence is inevitable. The greater need is for an environmental response, and there is difficulty in getting domestic managers to devote their time to businesses which are relatively small compared to domestic operations.

Over time, if the foreign business grows relative to the domestic, the potential payoff for applying domestic competence to foreign problems grows. Eventually, the development of integrated product management is indicated, an integration that applies the total company competence to product management on a worldwide basis.

When does a company reach these crossover points? There is no general answer to this question. Each company must decide on the basis of its own situation. One force which may tend to delay the development of global product management is the existence of country organizations operating as profit centers. These organizational units are anxious to remain autonomous and independent of external influence. If they have been successful on a P and L basis, they can defend their position convincingly. However, the question management must decide is not whether country managers have done a good job, but rather whether interactive product management would produce better results.

Multimarketing synergy

The contrasting pull of the rich diversity and of the many basic similarities of international markets is striking. The diversity of world markets is perhaps more obvious than the similarities. It includes many factors which demand a response (different voltages in electrical appliances or country labeling laws in the food or drug business are just two of the many thousands of examples) from any company which is going to operate in a foreign country. This explains the almost universal use of the country subsidiary as an operating unit in the international company. A principal function of the country subsidiary is to respond to the diversity of the nation-state in which it is organized.

Less obvious than the diversity of world markets are the many similarities which exist in markets for the same product around the world. Response to these similarities is not mandatory; indeed, the purely local company operates within a national market without any explicit consideration of conditions outside its own market. Thus, response to similarities only occurs when management explicitly chooses to make such a response. An interactive marketing program, designed to respond not only to market differences but to similarities as well, can be the source of major international operating synergies. In this context, synergy occurs when the effectiveness of an integrated unit is greater than the sum of the capabilities of the individual operating units.

Marketing synergy in an interactive international company derives from many sources. Perhaps the most important is the ability of the interactive company to apply experience from operations in one country to similar or comparable situations in other countries. This requires that management become involved in comparative marketing. In order to cite an experience in country A as relevant to country B, it must be based on conditions in country A which are comparable to those in country B. This comparability is frequently established within a geographic region such as Europe.

A second important source of multinational marketing synergy is the application of knowledge generated in one market to problems in other markets. Any company must engage in a considerable amount of study and investigation to understand its markets. In an integrated multinational company, headquarters managers are involved in the management of marketing research. As a result, each subsidiary or country unit operates as part of an integrated organization. The unit conducts some studies which are unique to its market, but in areas where it faces conditions which are comparable to those in other markets, the unit draws on accumulated knowledge in the parent company, or it generates new knowledge which will be used in many countries in the system. The synergy of the integrated company in this area derives from the planned allocation of research resources and the avoidance of fragmented duplication.

Another major source of synergy in an integrated company comes from the better use of manpower. Instead of limiting all analytical and decision capabilities to a single country, an integrated company allows men to apply their analytical and creative energy to wider areas. The main development in this direction today is that of marketing management at the regional level, but a few companies are seeking to develop this capability on a world basis as well.

A fourth source of operating synergy in the integrated multinational company can be generated by experimentation in marketing. Instead of duplicating the marketing program in each country, a multi-country program can selectively adapt programs in each country to test the effectiveness of variations in the mix of marketing variables. If a manager questions the relative effectiveness of advertising versus personal selling, instead of splitting the communications budget between these two activities, he could run 75 per cent advertising and 25 per cent personal selling in country A and reverse these proportions in country B, where both countries were preselected as most nearly comparable in other marketing dimensions. Experimentation in marketing leads to greater program effectiveness because decisions are increasingly based on market facts as opposed to assumptions and estimates. International operations provide a unique opportunity to experiment because of the relative isolation of markets.

Finally, operating synergy is obtained from cost savings. If the same advertising theme can be used multinationally, the need to spend money on creative efforts in a fifty-country system might be reduced by from fifty times to perhaps four. The same kind of savings might accrue to product adaptation efforts. Instead of conducting fifty programs to adapt a product to local conditions, a company might place all of its efforts behind a program to develop three basic adaptations of its product to fit the needs of industrialized, developing and underdeveloped country markets. Except for the mandatory kinds of response demanded by basic differences, the response decisions faced by management are trade-off issues. Any response performance has a manpower time and money cost and is justified only if the gains from the response exceed its cost.

A major task of headquarters management is to design and staff an organization structure and an information system which will most effectively respond to market differences and similarities. This is a task which must be undertaken by top management or by top management's designate.

Given structure, staffing and information flows, the system must analyse, plan and control product design, price behavior, distribution and sourcing. These activities are the joint responsibility of each level of the system. This requires a degree of involvement from different levels that is related to the extent that markets for the company's product are differentiated. The greater the differentiation, the greater the need to rely upon inputs to the marketing management process at the country level. The greater the unification or similarity between markets, the greater the opportunity to increase the involvement of area, international and world headquarters units in the marketing management process.

Headquarters has an important role in marketing planning in the multinational company. Any company that wishes to take full advantage of the potential capabilities of the multinational company must commit itself to the development of an effective headquarters which will focus not only upon coordination, but upon integrating the company's planning effort to make the fullest possible use of operating experience and to apply on the widest possible basis the talents of the organization's most capable managers and analysts.

29 P. d'Antin

The Nestlé Product Manager as Demigod

P. d'Antin, 'The Nestlé product manager as demigod', *European Business*, no. 28, Spring 1971, pp. 44–9.

Nestlé marketing management devoted several years of adjustments and readjustments to finding a suitable marketing scheme. Such a painstaking function spends by far the greatest proportion of Nestlé's annual budget. The marketing of a new product, for example, may cost two to three times more than the plant that manufactured it.

Other reasons for Nestlé's organization around the product chief were the following factors in the firm's unique marketing situation:

1. The broad range of food products marketed.
2. The fact that foreign markets account for 97 per cent of total turnover.
3. The varying levels of development of the target countries.
4. Country-by-country taste differences – e.g. the French tend to prefer chicory in their coffee, while the Americans drink it straight.

In view of such complexities, it is understandable that Nestlé easily rejected the worldwide standardized marketing (including advertising) favored by such giants as Coca-Cola and Kodak, opting instead for a more intricate, product-oriented approach.

Two simple principles

The Nestlé scheme can be boiled down to two basic principles: centralization of method and decentralization of decision-making.

In centralizing method, the Swiss company has organized all country subsidiaries along the same lines. Each subsidiary, which lies within the domain of a regional manager (e.g. for the European region), is headed by a company official who is the equivalent of the *Président-Directeur général* in France. Under him are three managers – production, finance, and marketing. The marketing department, in turn, is subdivided into sales, market research, and publicity. The marketing manager, who heads the department, is assisted by a staff of product chiefs or managers. In the average Nestlé subsidiary, there is a product chief for Nescafé, milk, chocolate, and soup. For an item like coffee, there are sometimes two associate product specialists, one assigned to ordinary coffee and the other to decaffeinated coffee, which represents a wholly different market, since it appeals to different motivational groups. There are some 500 product managers in the company.

Although the product manager is nearly always a man with a university degree, he is considered to have virtually no practical experience, and must undergo a period of 'learning the ropes'. The ideal training period lasts at least a year and a half, with six months of selling on the road, six in market research, and six more in publicity. Not every trainee is afforded such extensive training, however, since he may be needed on the job right away. During each of the training periods, the future product chief is an apprentice who actively works rather than merely observes.

When the trainee is considered ripe for product responsibility, he is assigned a particular product in a particular country operation – e.g. coffee in Germany – and presented with the Nestlé marketing 'bible'. The bible is a loose-leaf volume in five parts:

1. A review of the Nestlé marketing framework and how it works.
2. An information section, subdivided into the general fact book and the product fact book.
3. Space for a provisional budget and a definitive budget.
4. Outline of a system for checking and evaluating marketing activities.
5. Briefing material for advertising agencies.

The product manager's first task is to fill in the information required for the general and product fact books. The general fact book is designed to provide general information on the market of the country to which the manager is assigned – surface area, population and its characteristics, family structure, household budgets, age groups, demographic growth, evolution of the cost of living, competition, income brackets, evolution of commerce, and public communications media, including the press, radio, television, cinema, and display advertising. In other words, the product chief must supply all the facts that apply to the market as a whole, without reference to any specific product. He can of course make use of the reference material available in the subsidiary or at the headquarters in Vevey (Switzerland).

Coffee as a source of rebellion

The product fact book contains all the country data concerning the manager's specific product. For coffee in Germany, the product manager must furnish answers to a number of questions: How does Germany rank in the hierarchy of the coffee consumers' market? Is Germany a high or a low consumption market? (These facts alone can be of enormous consequence. In Sweden, for instance, the annual per capita consumption of coffee is eighteen pounds, while in Japan it's half a gram!) How is coffee used – in bean form, ground, or powdered? If it is ground, how is it brewed? Which coffee is preferred – Brazilian Santos blended with Colombian coffee, or robusta from the Ivory Coast? Is it roasted? Do the people prefer dark roasted or blond coffee? (The answer to this question is likewise important: the color of Nestlé's soluble coffee must resemble as closely as possible the color of the coffee consumed in the country.) Do the Germans drink coffee after lunch or with their breakfast? Do they take it black or with cream or milk? Do they drink coffee in the evening? Do they sweeten it? (In France, the answer is clear: in the morning, coffee with milk; at noon, black coffee – i.e. two utterly different coffees.) At what age do people begin drinking coffee? Is it a traditional beverage, as in France, or is it a form of rebellion, as in England and Japan, where the younger generation has taken up coffee drinking in order to defy their tea-drinking parents?

The questions in the product fact book obviously probe much more deeply than those in the general fact book. The product manager hence may not be able to answer them with mere documentary research. He may have to resort to motivational surveys, using non-directive interviews that bring out the consumers' true motivations. Such motivational research pinpointed the identical motivations of young coffee drinkers in England and Japan, and Nestlé now uses practically the same advertising plugs in both countries.

When the product manager has completed both fact books, he must tackle the third part of his bible – drafting the budget, which is also referred to as product planning. First of all, he must draft a six-year budget. Using both past figures and data for the current year, he projects sales for the coming six years in terms of pounds or cases of coffee, and estimates turnover based on probable price increases or decreases due to competition and to estimated contingency factors within Germany. He must also deal with the expense factor, allowing for an evolution in tax rates, social security charges, and labor costs. For this purpose, the production manager supplies him with the necessary information.

Nestlé requires the product manager to make the six-year plan mainly so that he will get into the habit of living in the future. It is considered unimportant if events ultimately contradict his forecast. The important thing is that the product manager – and consequently everyone else in the marketing framework – has had to think far ahead.

When the six-year budget has been presented, the product manager proceeds with his most important report, the one on which he will be judged – i.e. the budget for the coming year. This exercise is not merely a simple bookkeeping forecast, but must include a general review of all the data for mixed marketing – products, brands, packaging and appearance, distribution channels, prices, sales, advertising, market research, and after-sales follow-up. The budget must, of course, contain figures. But the product manager's method of arriving at such figures requires him to ask some rather basic questions: Is the product formula the best? Is the product attractively wrapped? Would there be any advantage in smaller or larger packages? Is this the most suitable brand label? Are the prices too high or too low?

The debate with headquarters at Vevey

Although the product chief is finally responsible for the annual plan, he must consult the marketing manager and the head of his subsidiary before submitting the plan to Vevey. The plan is written up in two stages: in the spring of the year, he submits to the head office a summary budget or plan containing the main figures. After review, the plan is returned to him, and he is then expected to prepare a detailed budget by October.

The following review at Vevey involves a tripartite discussion among the head office's marketing division, the regional management concerned (in this case, European area management), and a representative of the subsidiary, who may be the product manager himself if he is not located too far away from headquarters. Once the two- to three-day debate is over, the finalized annual plan is accepted.

Headquarters usually manages to review the approximately 500 product budgets or plans of the seventy subsidiaries by the end of November. It then enters on a master sheet a résumé of the German subsidiary's total activity for coffee in the coming year. The model for this report is contained in the product manager's bible. Its condensed form makes it possible for the head office to know at a glance, for example, what advertising campaign is being planned for coffee in Germany.

Here is where the centralization of method ends and the decentralization of decision-making begins.

After the final budget has been approved, the product manager alone is the boss. There is no further discussion with headquarters unless some significant change has occurred in the targets. Vevey expects only to receive a monthly report in which the reasons for advances or delays are explained.

Not only is the product manager generally free to implement his product plan, but he has also played a major role in shaping that plan and its objectives in the first place. Vevey officials are quick to point out that planning and budgeting for the entire range of products – even on a six-year scale – are merely the sum total of all the computerized budgets of all the product managers. In both planning and implementation of plans, then, the product chief is the key man in the Nestlé marketing framework.

The product manager is ultimately judged on the success of his product – not just its sales success, but also its profits. It is from the ranks of the product managers that the marketing managers of all subsidiaries are recruited, and very often the president of a subsidiary is a former product chief.

Where do innovations come from?

According to top marketing management, one chief advantage of the Nestlé network is its open-endedness, allowing for product innovations to be initiated either through the product manager (from the bottom up) or by Vevey (from the top down). The following case examples based on some facts illustrate the two means by which changes are introduced.

At the outset, a fairly standard Nescafé is released on the English market – i.e. the product in the form in which it is appreciated by the average consumer, but with a few alterations geared to the English market. This particular Nescafé happens to be similar to the one sold in the United States, which is not too astonishing. The English were generally accustomed to drinking only tea, until the presence of American troops led them to discover coffee. The coffee they tried was the Nescafé from the States, with the American taste – a relatively light, almost blond coffee.

A few years pass. Gradually the accumulated data on the market and on consumer attitudes indicate that Britons who have traveled in Italy and France have acquired a taste for a more fully roasted coffee, one that is blacker and somewhat more bitter. A market survey then reveals that a segment of the population – a small but affluent segment – is definitely interested in a product with a fuller-bodied taste made from a darker roasted coffee.

At this point, change is initiated at the product manager level. The product chief queries the subsidiary's production department: 'We could sell 100,000 cases of stronger coffee a year. Any suggestions?'

The production manager writes Vevey requesting the manufacturing processes for a coffee that would be more like the Italian and French coffees. By return mail (ideally), he receives the data on roasting temperatures and the blends to use. He and the product chief approve this sample, and write again to Vevey, this time requesting that a pilot plant in Switzerland produce 10,000 jars of one, two, or three varieties of this kind of Franco-Italian coffee. These jars are shipped to England and distributed to 1,000 families, mixed, of course, with other kinds of coffee. In this way, a wide sampling is obtained, which is backed up by a serious market survey.

A decision is then reached – a decision for which the product manager is mainly responsible, though of course with the backing of the English marketing manager and the subsidiary manager. The product chief describes in detail how the new product is to be launched, including the details in his annual budget.

The launching of a special coffee requires greater publicity than ordinary Nescafé. To attract a more affluent segment of the consumer population, a novelty container will be necessary, with a gold-colored top and an engraved label. In settling all these details, the product manager confers with the production department. If he and the production chief disagree on the specifications – e.g. the height of the Nescafé jar – subsidiary management steps in to arbitrate.

When the top marketing manager steps in

As stated earlier, one of the duties of the top marketing manager at Vevey HQ is to discuss the figures for all the product budgets during October and November. Once this task is out of the way, he has time for reflection. From the reports submitted to him, he may discover, for example, that there is a demand in several countries for a higher quality coffee, possibly more expensive, which would lend itself to being drunk black rather than with cream.

Dropping into his production colleague's office, the Vevey marketing manager presents his findings. The production manager may reply in one of several ways. A better blend may be found. Better coffees may be discovered in Colombia, Venezuela, or Costa Rica or – and this has happened – a new lyophilization technique may be developed, by which a frozen product is dried.

If lyophilization seems the most attractive solution, laboratory tests are undertaken with the various blends and roasts, and also with the various cold temperatures for lyophilization. Such research may take a year or two. It does not end with an *ex-cathedra* verdict. The production manager may produce a number of samples – as actually happened in this case – that are subjected to taste tests before the final choice of the coffee to be launched.

Matters do not end here. The production manager claims that he is going to consider building a new plant, and that this plant will be more expensive than the one that performs the traditional drying process. Hence, the financial manager must be consulted. His reply can be readily anticipated: it will be necessary to fix the price of a jar of lyophilized coffee at 2.50 Swiss francs as against 1.85 Swiss francs for standard Nescafé.

At this juncture, the Vevey marketing manager confers with the European regional manager, and his remarks go something like this: 'We have a new and more expensive coffee, for which a market exists. It means building a plant that will cost X Deutsche marks. Why don't we try this coffee out in Germany?'

The regional manager may possibly disagree with the marketing manager. In this case, the deputy administration is consulted, and he arbitrates. If he approves, discussions are begun with the president of the German branch, who consults his marketing manager and his coffee product manager, and the machinery goes into motion.

The Vevey marketing manager is not without influence in this machinery. Lyophilized coffee in its initial German version bore no faint resemblance to ordinary coffee. Since people are usually reluctant to change their habits, there was some resistance. Some customers even commented that although they liked this coffee better, it 'looked funny'. The firm considered processing it differently so that it would look like ordinary Nescafé.

But the head marketing manager gave this advice: 'Don't change the processing. Test the market again, taking a different advertising tack. Plug the product as a new coffee produced by revolutionary methods. The proof of its novelty is the fact that it doesn't even look like coffee!'

Retesting was undertaken, with the result that the public declared the coffee to be much better than normal coffee.

Besides contributing much creativity to the development and marketing of products, the head office marketing department is responsible for seeing that the brand name and image are uniformly maintained. It also pays close attention to the uniformity of containers and packaging. The brand image is considered particularly important in an age when many people travel widely. Apart from breaking into the decentralized system to impose its will on such general matters, however, the Vevey marketing department bends over backward to maintain the sovereignty of its product managers.

Appendix: so this is paradise?

That 'demigod', the product chief, is in an extremely delicate position in the company structure. To recapitulate: the product chief is in neither a line nor a staff position. He must be able to call on all the marketing resources – market research, sales, technical services, advertising and promotion – and yet he has no authority to demand information or cooperation. His only tool is persuasion. His duty is to determine how each of these functions will contribute to the profitability of his product during the

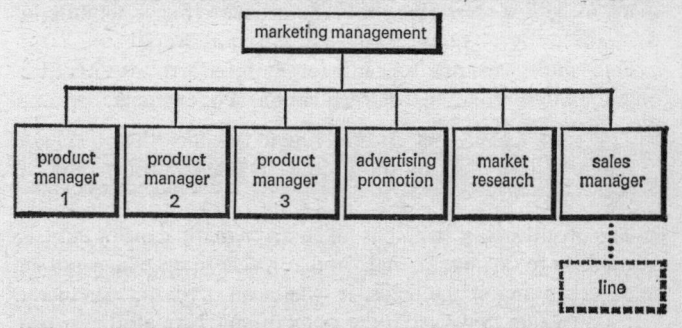

Figure 1 The product manager on an equal level with the functional team

coming year – and even how much money will be spent, for example, on various types of advertising. But, although he may have spent a few months on the publicity side of the business, the product chief is no advertising expert. Similarly, he can request technical innovations for the product, but he is no technical expert, etc.

Further complicating the situation is the rather intricate organizational structures that have evolved as corporations have grown larger and their product ranges wider. Figure 1 shows that comparatively Eden-like structure of bygone, simpler times, when the product manager was on a level with the functional personnel he had to deal with every day, and few intermediary levels existed to hamper efficient functioning. However, as Figure 2 reveals, the product manager in today's more elaborate framework is on a different level from the technical marketing services that he must try to guide and coordinate.

Another factor not to be overlooked is that if the product chief is given a great degree of autonomy to plan the entire year's activities for his product, he may well begin to believe in his own demigodhood. He may just conceive of himself as a technical expert, an old advertising hand and sales genius combined.

However outstanding in diplomacy and creativity a product chief may be, he is very likely to become a friction point within the company because of the autonomy granted to him.

Although the structure is described by Nestlé as the perfect solution to many marketing problems, it may well prove to be the source of other, unforeseen difficulties. In Figure 2, we see that the marketing team has become less homogeneous and that several marketing technicians have moved to different levels. Since work seems to be done less efficiently, the product chief is tending to take into his own hands the duties of the various marketing technicians. Such intrusions can cause tensions (see arrows in Figure 2 for the 'hottest' zones in the organization). For example:

1. The staff technicians bitterly resent the fact that they are rendered powerless by the product manager's usurpation of their tasks.

2. The product chief, who has taken up so many reins of duty, is unlikely to do any job really well, especially since he is not an expert in any of the fields. It is as if an orchestra conductor tried to step down from the podium and play all the instruments at once.

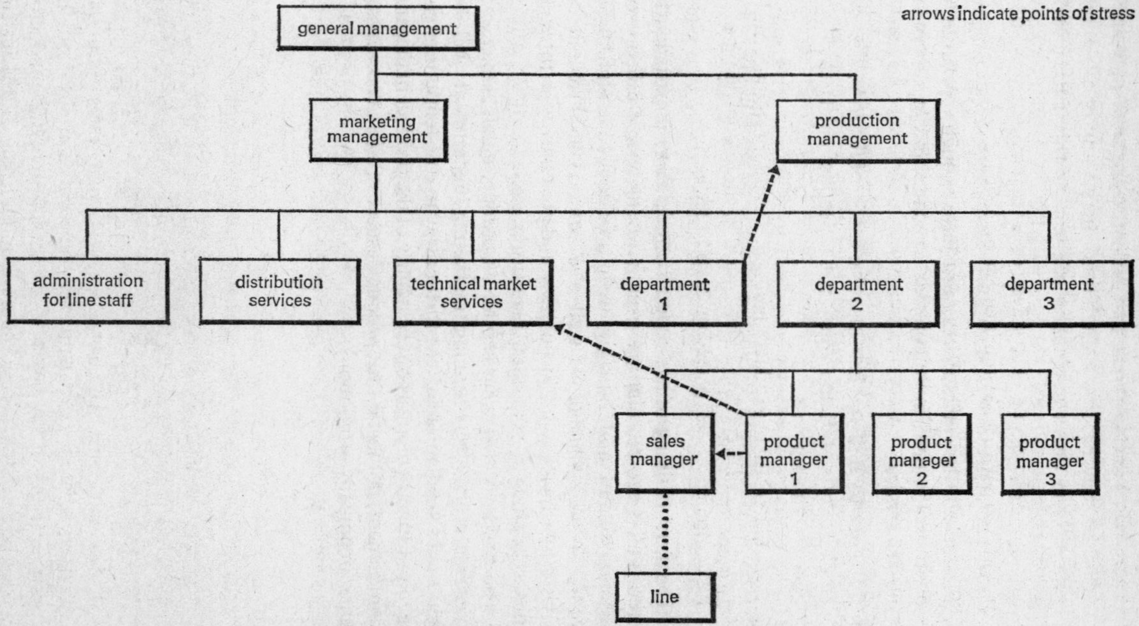

Figure 2 When the product manager functions on different levels

arrows indicate points of stress

P. d'Antin 299

3. Costs and delays multiply.
4. There is a growing threat that an entire sector of marketing activities may become immobilized due to any of the above aggravations or a combination of them. So this is paradise?!

How can these problems be solved or at least minimized so that work gets done with a reasonable degree of efficiency?

1. First of all, the staff services must have enough specialists to adapt to the new, more complex structure and to supply all needed services.
2. Recourse to staff services must be made obligatory. For example, only a staff specialist (not a product chief) could request outside services.
3. The role of each product manager should be more clearly defined, so that certain limits – ideally, those coinciding with his competence – are placed on his powers.

The strict defining of the product chief's tasks is particularly important, since recruits are usually young men fresh out of business school and bursting with unconcealed ambition. It would be advantageous as well if a work program could be devised by which the product chief would periodically go through another training cycle in sales, advertising, etc.

The company that can keep all its product chiefs happy and maintain a smoothly-running marketing department will be achieving a small miracle. One further way to ease tensions might be to put strong emphasis on the quality of the product manager's management, not just on his product's success, when considering him for company promotions.

30 R. J. Aylmer

Who Makes Marketing Decisions in the Multinational Firm?

R. J. Aylmer, 'Who makes marketing decisions in the multinational firm?', *Journal of Marketing* October 1970, pp. 25-30 (some footnotes deleted).

The problems of mounting marketing programs on a multinational scale have begun to command more of management's attention, as international markets have assumed a more important overall role in the multinational firm's future and as national markets have become more interdependent. Generally such attention is centered on the pros and cons of standardizing marketing decisions across national markets, given various environmental forces. Less attention seems to be devoted to locating authority for these decisions within a particular firm. Normally, marketing is considered an 'operating' rather than a 'planning' function, and primary authority for marketing decisions is decentralized to local management in each country. Yet, to a large extent the ability to transfer, coordinate, or otherwise standardize marketing decisions among national markets may be linked to the location of authority adopted for these decisions. It would seem worthwhile, therefore, to examine more closely who makes marketing decisions in the multinational firm.

The following analysis reports such behavior, as observed for the Western European operations of nine US-based manufacturers from October 1966 to June 1967. First, the extent of local management's autonomy for marketing decisions is determined. Then, certain internal forces are identified which in part appeared to lead the firm to adopt its particular patterns for the location of authority. Each analysis is carried out for several different decisions, reflecting the variety of elements in a typical marketing 'mix'.

With the exception of automobiles, the nine firms include almost all major US-based manufacturers of consumer durable goods with manufacturing investments in Western Europe at the time of field research. Eight different products are represented, ranging from refrigerators and toasters to movie cameras and electric razors. Twenty-six local affiliates are represented, an average of about three affiliates per firm. These affiliates are located in France, the UK, West Germany, Italy, Switzerland, and Sweden. All but two of them are wholly-owned subsidiaries.

The observations for the location of primary authority are based on marketing programs employed by the local affiliates for particular products during the time of the study. As each local affiliate competed in several of the eight product categories, a total of eighty-six separate marketing programs were recorded. Frequently, marketing programs were observed for several firms competing in one national market in the same product category. Four different decisions were recorded for each marketing program; i.e. design of product, principal advertising approach, 'going' retail price, and number of distribution outlets purchasing directly from the local affiliate. For each decision, the primary location of authority was determined. These observations provide the basis for this analysis.

Local management's autonomy

In the nine firms, to what extent was local management's traditional authority for marketing decisions supplemented or replaced by authority located in organization levels with a more multinational perspective? Table 1 reports the degree of local management's autonomy observed, classified according to the four different marketing decisions. The field observations were categorized in regard to whether *local* management (1) retained primary authority; (2) *shared* this authority with other organization levels, such as the regional office or corporate headquarters; or (3) whether primary authority rested elsewhere so that, in effect, the decision was *imposed* upon local management. These field observations were determined from several sources. Fifty corporate executives at all management levels in both the United States and Europe were interviewed. Marketing plans, operating procedures, and files were also reviewed. In every instance, the primary location of authority was determined for the more strategic components of a particular decision. For example, a product's basic performance features and overall appearance generally had more strategic connotations than, say, the specification of 110/220 electrical systems or foot-pound/metric measurement systems. Basic copy theme and overall design fulfilled similar functions for the advertising-approach decision.

The most striking pattern reported in Table 1 is the vital role played by local management in the development of marketing programs. Local management was primarily responsible for

Table 1 **Degree of local management autonomy classified according to type of local marketing decision**[a]

	Local Marketing Decision			
Degree of local management autonomy	Product design	Advertising approach	Retail price	Distribution outlets per 1000 population
Primary authority rested with local management	30%	86%	74%	61%
Local management shared authority with other levels in organization	15%	8%	20%	38%
Decision primarily imposed upon local management	55%	6%	6%	1%
	100%	100%	100%	100%
N (Marketing programs observed)	N = 86	N = 84[b]	N = 84[b]	N = 86

a For Western European affiliates of 9 US-based manufacturers.
b Classification information not available in two cases.

86 per cent of the advertising decisions, 74 per cent of the pricing decisions, and 61 per cent of the channel decisions. As a result, only on rare occasions did higher organization levels become involved in the design of overall marketing programs. The final task of developing viable local strategy was left to local management.

Even where other organization levels were involved, local management often retained a strong *say* in a decision's final outcome, as illustrated by the 'shared' decisions in Table 1. Authority was shared for 15 per cent of the product design decisions, 20 per cent of the pricing decisions, and 38 per cent of the channel decisions. In effect, local management collaborated with one or more higher organization levels in such a fashion that neither dominated the decision-making process. Only product-design decisions were imposed upon local management in 55 per cent of the instances observed.

Certain environmental forces which differed among the eight product categories appeared to encourage standardization of particular marketing decisions, and indirectly may have influenced the location of their authority. For example, greater standardization in product designs was observed for movie cameras and toasters. This was apparently due, in part, to marketers' needs to achieve longer production runs in order to be competitive. In addition, three of the eight products studied – movie and still cameras and electric razors – were more likely to be shipped across national boundaries, particularly by members of the distribution channel. Within the European Economic Community, where tariffs largely had disappeared, channel members had begun to realize significant price reductions or to upstage local competitors by 'shopping around' outside their national markets. Marketers of these three products felt obliged to 'harmonize major marketing activities' throughout Western Europe, particularly for product design and pricing decisions.

On the other hand, differences among market-share positions of local affiliates and national channel traditions appeared to discourage standardization for other marketing decisions. Market positions were remotely similar across four countries in only three of twenty-three instances, rendering the standardization of promotional and pricing decisions particularly difficult. For example, where the local position was commanding, the advertising message typically sought to enlarge total demand for that product category. Where it was merely competitive, the message usually promoted allegiance to the particular product. For eight of the nine firms, channel of distribution decisions were almost totally a function of local traditions and existing institutions. Camera manufacturers, for example, employed wholesalers and maintained retail prices in Western Germany, with a trade margin of almost 40 per cent. In France, they distributed directly to camera dealers and allowed a 28 per cent trade margin which then was discounted.

Partly as a result of such forces, certain decisions in the marketing mix were standardized more often across countries than were other decisions, and these patterns were more pronounced for some products. Examples are product designs for cameras and electric razors which evidenced far greater standardization than designs for refrigerators and washing machines. Such patterns indirectly influenced the location of authority within the firm for the decisions effected (Table 1). However, differences in the location of authority often were observed in firms competing in the same national markets within the same product categories. Reactions to environmental forces such as described above could not explain these differences. Rather, they seemed influenced by forces at work within the firm.

Organization forces within the firm

What were the organization forces which appeared to affect the location in primary authority for marketing decisions within the firm? The most important seemed to be (1) the relative importance of the firm's international operations, and (2) the relative importance of the local affiliate's position within the firm. Corporate management's desire to participate in local marketing decision making differed greatly among the nine firms, apparently according to the relative importance of international operations. Where this desire existed, it took different forms for each local affiliate. Management of major affiliates, for instance, shared authority with corporate management for the development of key marketing decisions more often than did management of the less important affiliates.

Relative importance of international operations

For many US-based firms, corporate management's interest in its international activities appears to grow as the perceived importance of these operations increases relative to domestic operations. At some point, this interest becomes so great that management adopts a global or 'multinational' approach when directing the company's affairs. 'Foreign operations are no more one distinct part of activities. Operations are organized in such a way that the entire top management is involved in worldwide operations' (Aharoni, 1967). Such thorough involvement encourages greater high-level participation in local decision making, including marketing decisions.

An overall look at the frequency of higher level involvement in local decision making is presented in Table 2. Firms were classified into three groups according to the percentage of total 1966 sales accounted for by international operations. For Group 1, such operations accounted for less than 15 per cent of total sales; the figure for Group 2 was 15 per cent to 25 per cent, and for Group 3 over 25 per cent. The same field observations reported in Table 1 were reclassified into these three groups. For simplicity of presentation only the 'shared' and 'imposed' observations are reported and combined in the table. The resulting total in each column is expressed as a percentage of all observations obtained for that particular group of firms. Thus, higher level management either imposed the decision upon local management or shared authority for 44 per cent of eighteen product-design decisions observed in Group 1.

Table 2 reports a fairly strong relationship between the firm's share of total sales derived from international operations and the frequency of higher level participation in local decision making.

Table 2 **Frequency of higher level management participation in local decision making**[a]

Classified by Firm's International Sales as Percentage of Total Sales and Marketing Decision

Local marketing decision	Firm's international sales as % of Total sales		
	Group 1 under 15	Group 2 15–25	Group 3 over 25
Product Design	44[c]	73	78
Advertising Approach[b]		22	17
Retail Price[b]		40	43
Distribution Outlets/'000 Population		4	70
N (Marketing programs observed)	100 = 18	100 = 22	100 = 46
N (Firms)	3	3	3

a For 26 Western European affiliates of 9 US-based manufacturers.
b Necessary assessments not available in two instances: $\Sigma N = 84$.
c Read: in 44 per cent of product designs observed in Group 1 higher level management either shared authority or imposed decision upon local management.
Note: Instances where primary authority rested with local management have been omitted from this table.

This is found more or less across the board for all decisions observed and is particularly evident when firms in Group 1 are contrasted to the other two groups. For that group, local management developed channel, pricing, and advertising decisions autonomously. It also developed product designs independently in 56 per cent of the instances observed, while three of every four remaining design decisions were imposed upon local management. Such patterns seemed representative of the traditional, decentralized or 'arm's length' approach to decision making. For Group 3, on the other hand, higher level executives frequently participated in local decision making with the exception of advertising decisions. They participated in 78 per cent of product-design decisions and in 70 per cent of channel decisions.

Perhaps more important, this involvement was less often of an 'arm's length' nature and included more frequently executives from corporate headquarters, although this analysis is not reflected directly in Table 2. Group 3 accounted for eleven of thirteen shared product-design decisions and the seven shared advertising decisions observed. Executives from corporate headquarters were involved with 74 per cent of Group 3's product-design decisions, 22 per cent of Group 2's decisions, and none of Group 1's decisions.

Differences in the location of authority were important. They could affect the degree of standardization in marketing decisions and hence the firm's reactions to the various environmental forces described in the previous section. For example, Alpha and Epsilon[1] competed directly in many European washing machine markets. At Alpha, where international operations accounted for over half of total sales, top management was directly involved with the major marketing decisions of all European affiliates, as described by the worldwide vice-president, marketing:

We've moved toward more centralization in marketing planning, particularly during the past two years. The European new products committee, which I chair, is one example. Its members include representatives from each of our major European affiliates plus regional and area offices. Its first major project was the development of a Pan-European washing machine design suitable for most of our European companies. Product development required about two years and was the primary responsibility of our UK company, working to design criteria established by our committee. We convened in London every two or three months to review progress. In this way, management from the other countries could effect whatever design alterations were advisable in order to facilitate acceptance in their markets. As a result, we expect this product to capture sizable market shares in a number of European countries.

Epsilon, where international operations accounted for less than 10 per cent of total sales, employed a different procedure, as described by the manager of its overseas appliance division:

Our basic policy is to delegate authority of product planning and other elements of the marketing program to local 'plant' (affiliate) management. Our function in New York is a staff one, to review and advise. For example, each plant's new product proposals are submitted to us for approval. This consists of an engineering review for the introduction date, the brand name treatment, cost feasibility, and production and technical specifications. Each plant's proposals are reviewed solely on their own merits as each designs and produces primarily for its local market.

As a result, Alpha marketed one line of washing machines throughout Europe, and Epsilon marketed a different line in most

1. To protect the proprietary nature of much of the information included in this study, the names of the nine firms have been disguised.

European countries. Alpha's promotional programs were somewhat similar across countries, whereas Epsilon's evidenced no apparent relationship. In the end, faced with competition from the 'Italian Invasion' of Europe's appliance markets and by firms such as Alpha, Epsilon was in full retreat throughout Europe. It preferred to close plants rather than alter its decentralized operating procedures. The author believes that Epsilon's response was largely a reflection of top management's relative indifference to international operations.

Local affiliate's position

Each local affiliate occupies a different position within the multinational firm. Where the firm desires to depart from decentralized operating procedures, these differences may require management to fulfil different decision-making roles at each affiliate. The sheer number of such affiliates often renders equal treatment unfeasible. Even within the limited confines of this study, Eta's European division included seventeen wholly-owned subsidiaries; Beta's, even more. Also, affiliates have vastly diverse scales of operations and capabilities due to the size and development of the local market, their position in the market, and the existence of manufacturing facilities. Alpha UK operated seven plants. Its annual turnover approximated $115 million which represented over one-third of the firm's worldwide turnover. Alpha Germany, on the other hand, performed primarily a distributive function as it had no manufacturing facilities; its turnover was approximately $13 million. Management at more important affiliates such as Alpha UK had evolved new and potentially important working relationships with corporate management, particularly for key marketing decisions.

Figure 1 reports a reclassification of the same observations for the degree of local autonomy employed previously, this time according to each affiliate's percentage of its firm's 1966 sales under or over 1·5 per cent. Absolute figures are employed and 'local' observations again have been omitted for simplicity of presentation. Figure 1 points out the difference that the relative size of the local affiliate seemed to have upon the type of established working relationship. Although frequency of higher level involvement was similar for the two groups, this involvement took different forms for each group. At the smaller affiliates, higher level management more often imposed decisions upon local management; this was true for twenty-eight product designs and six

local marketing decision	local affiliate's sales/firm's sales		
	under 1·5%	over 1·5%	
product design	2 shared, 28 imposed	11 shared, 19 imposed	
advertising approach	7 shared, 6 imposed	3 shared, imposed	
retail price	6 shared, 6 imposed	16 shared, imposed	
distribution outlets per thousand population	9 shared, imposed	22 shared, 1 imposed	
N (marketing programs observed)	42	42	84[a]
N (local affiliates)	11	15	26

a Classification information not available for two marketing programs.

Figure 1 Form and frequency of higher level management participation in local decision making, classified by marketing decision and local affiliate's percentage of firm's total sales

price and advertising decisions. At the larger affiliates, such higher level involvement more often took the form of authority shared with local management, as happened for eleven product designs, sixteen pricing decisions, and twenty-two channel decisions.

The many nuances observed among local management roles, according to the affiliate's position, could not be reported justly in a bare figure. Several examples may help. At Eta, according to the assistant vice-president, marketing – Europe, '"The Big Four" – UK, France, Italy, and West Germany – enjoy more autonomy than do our other companies.' One very sensible explanation was offered by the product manager at Eta, France:

Our recently formed European marketing group has scheduled semi-annual planning meetings. At the last one, we were eighteen. Too many!

It was bedlam. Each argued for his local problems and nothing was accomplished. For the next meeting, I and my counterparts from the other 'Big Four' countries plus our European product manager will meet beforehand to develop detailed plans.

Shared decision making, as reported in Table 1 and Figure 1, was observed only in firms of Group 3. Although each practiced some shared decision making: Beta's worldwide marketing committee was the furthest advanced in its procedures. To some extent, they had evolved to meet specific needs, as described by the corporate vice-president, marketing:

In the early 1960s, US R and D developed a significant technological innovation, a new product concept, following the expenditure of large amounts of funds and time. A worldwide launch was needed to effect the preferred financial payback. A committee was formed and given the planning responsibility. Its members were the Marketing Directors from Beta Canada, Australia, UK, France, West Germany, International, and the US. Over a period of three years, this Committee supervised the innovation's transition from concept to a *set* of products and supporting marketing programs. The US operation developed most of the line originally recommended, incorporating modifications suggested by the other marketing directors. The UK operation developed an economy-priced model, the line's eventual sales leader. And the German operation developed variations in the line featuring more sophisticated and technical components in the European tradition.

This committee had developed multinational price-harmonization policies. Subcommittees were investigating the harmonization of advertising programs, marketing information systems, and research techniques, and even the feasibility of Pan-European marketing programs. In each instance, the members of these subcommittees were the executives responsible for the given activity at the various local affiliates; for example, advertising managers formed the advertising subcommittee. At Beta and the two other firms, such committees seemed to operate with enough flexibility so as to be able to depart from the 'centralization means standardization' axiom when they chose to. More and more, they were searching for mutually acceptable harmonized decisions.

At the same time, other Beta affiliates, who had no management representative on the worldwide marketing committee (all but the five largest), had less *say* in major marketing decisions. For the product-design decisions described above the role of the Swiss general manager is illustrative. One year after the committee had begun preparations for the new products' introduction:

I, and my colleagues from other Beta 'houses' (affiliates), attended a meeting at (headquarters). We were presented with the product concept and various models. We were told the line would be introduced the following spring. Each manager then selected those he desired, from the American, British, and German models available, and submitted his sales estimate.

These diverse roles played by local management according to their particular affiliate's position could have been etched more sharply had the sample included a larger number of firms similar to those in Group 3. Generally, the two other groups failed to differentiate among local affiliates, treating each in a similar 'arm's length' fashion.

Conclusion

Local management was usually responsible for developing viable overall local marketing strategies for these nine firms. Its autonomy, however, varied greatly among the various marketing decisions. These patterns seemed to be influenced, in part, by forces within the firm, particularly by the relative importance of its international operations and by each local affiliate's position. These findings suggest that the problem of locating authority for marketing decisions in the multinational firm is quite complex. It is not likely that this problem is amenable to overly simple generalizations, which fail to differentiate among the various marketing decisions, or ignore important forces at work within the firm. The specific responses of the Western European operations of these nine firms are probably not directly applicable to other firms, industries, or parts of the world. Nevertheless, similar types of forces may arise in many instances, particularly for US-based firms competing in other consumer goods industries. The variations in collaborative or shared decision making observed in the firms of Group 3 seem particularly worthy of further attention by management and researchers. They appear to be the logical outcome of the need these firms expressed to strike a careful balance between the roles of local and higher level managements in multinational marketing decision making.

Reference

AHARONI, Y. (1967), *The Foreign Investment Decision Process*, Division of Research, Harvard Business School, pp. 180–81.

31 J. S. Shulman

Transfer Pricing in the Multinational Firm

Adapted from J. S. Shulman, 'Transfer pricing in the multinational firm', *European Business* January 1969, pp. 46–54.

The spread of decentralized corporate operations has been accompanied by widespread utilization of the profit center concept to measure, evaluate, and motivate divisional management. As the implications of the profit center idea have been recognized, the need has arisen for rational systems to price intra-company transfers of goods at varying stages of production.

The aim, in general, has been to devise methods that would satisfy the goals of divisional managers to earn adequate profit for their divisions, while simultaneously furthering corporate profit goals. In single country operations, the system is meant to function for this purpose and to provide a foundation for a properly operating control system.

But when a company operates across national borders and exports its practice of decentralized management, with all the accompanying apparatus, new complicating dimensions are added. In international business, there are opportunities to maximize profits that may override the significance of a control system and the transfer pricing mechanism. Likewise, this environment contains threats to international firms, often unforeseen and, even when perceived, seldom factored into control systems.

This article deals with the characteristics which attach to and compound the problem of transfer pricing *when a decentralized firm expands its operations into the international environment*. It is based upon field interviews with various officers responsible for control, pricing, and taxation functions in the international divisions of several large United States firms.

As might be expected, transfer pricing practices vary widely. Each different policy is justified on a reasonable basis – on some special variable which is considered critical by the individual company. Therefore, by looking into the basic argument justifying each specific transfer pricing policy, we may study some of the variables that are critical to transfer pricing policies.

Taxes

It has been observed that the pervasiveness of taxation clouds the entire background of transfer pricing in international firms, and that taxes represent the touchstone by which all transfer pricing is judged. Tax considerations lurk in the background of so many decisions in modern management that the impression of all-importance is understandable.

Evidence indicates that headquarters management often considers international income tax costs in setting transfer prices. But this practice evokes two kinds of problems – one external and one internal. The external problem relates to the counteraction taken by government tax authorities in both the United States and foreign countries. Faced with the minimizing methods practiced by taxpayers, revenue departments throughout the world attempt to take steps which will maximize tax revenues. Despite the fact that international auditing is still relatively new, American government auditors are familiar with corporate tax-minimizing practices. It is also a fact that foreign auditors are expanding their awareness of these problems, and are increasingly taking steps to overcome the long-standing advantages of corporate tax practices. In other words, tax minimization by corporations runs head-on into tax maximizing of government treasury departments.

Internally, pricing for tax savings causes aberrations in divisional operating results. The resulting conflicts in goals lead to dysfunctional decisions. Many control systems in international use do not make allowances for aberrations in price caused by tax minimizing schemes. When allowances are made, they are not always effective or satisfactory. The same problem holds true in other facets of the environment detailed below.

Corporate costs and profits are affected also by import duties assessed by countries of import. A change in a transfer price may cause a change in the duty, both as to amount and as to rate. Therefore, it adds to a company's profit to send goods at low prices into countries with high rates of duty. It may also be advantageous to ship goods at high prices into countries with low import tax rates.

The source of the end product may thus be affected if production processes may be performed on transferred materials equally well, and at no cost differential, in two or more countries with different rates of import taxes.

The impact of income and import taxes upon transfer prices leads to additional problems for management, and again one of these problems occurs externally and the other internally. Externally, the goals of income tax administrators and customs officials to maximize revenues for their respective departments are in conflict, because the increased revenue of the one tends to reduce the revenue of the other. The higher the import tax assessed to the importer, the lower the profit remaining as a basis for income taxes. To add to the tax manager's headache, he finds virtually no coordination of the two revenue collecting departments in any country, and a tax-paying firm has to bear the brunt of the two taxing divisions' conflicting goals. Internally, the problems have to do with the effect of import tax pricing upon divisional operating results and upon the motivation of divisional managers. But an added twist results from the attempt of the firm to balance the added cost of duty resulting from a high import price against the lower cost of income taxation in the country of importation as well as the potentially higher income tax in the exporting division.

Notwithstanding the importance of taxation, many firms consider it only one among other factors. One company attitude is summed up in the words of its Vice-President of International Operations: 'We could connive on taxes, but the savings would be trivial. We prefer to give full attention to operating our company and let the tax liabilities fall where they may.' This company considers anything but a straightforward application of tax laws as morally improper. Another company neglects the impact of taxes on pricing entirely, arguing that simple and consistent pricing practices tend to minimize tax investigation problems.

Another reason for neglecting the tax considerations is given by an electronics firm. While this company is aware of the impact of taxes on income, the importance of greater harmony among divisional managers has eliminated tax-motivated transfer price changes. In the past, moves designed to minimize taxes have caused interpersonal conflicts to such an extent as to discourage any further tax-minimizing practices. It is also observed that the narrowing gap among world tax rates makes it less possible to effect significant tax savings, and therefore the sacrifice to greater managerial harmony continually becomes less costly.

Currency fluctuations

In most cases, the respondents of our survey use generally recognized practices to mitigate the deleterious effects of inflation in host countries. A preferable method among some firms is to withdraw funds to a safer haven. But, generally, countries that are suffering from rapid inflation are also hard pressed to maintain an adequate balance of foreign exchange. Therefore, in such countries foreign exchange is often restricted by government order to necessary materials purchased, while being withheld from profit transfers.

These problems have triggered apparently opposite pricing practices in two companies operating in Brazil, where excessive inflation is a continuous threat. Because the inflationary condition has made it nearly impossible to show a profit, one firm ships goods in at low prices as a subsidy to its Brazilian division to assist it in profitable operation. Also, the Brazilian government requirement to post a cash deposit equal to six months' projected imports is costly because the cash deposits continually lose value. Resultant side effects of the low pricing practice not only reduce this deposit, but also reduce the inflationary loss of value of the deposit over the six-month period. On the other hand, another company preferred to ship materials into Brazil at extra high prices, in order to remove as much cash as possible to the United States. In this instance, the firm was willing to show a higher profit and pay higher taxes in the United States, but at least, the controller reported, the cash asset, even after taxes and deposit erosion, was safe from further loss of value.

Thus transfer prices can be, and actually are, used as a device to counteract inflationary erosions of assets.

Economic restrictions

Under this heading we include three areas of concern to multinational corporations, the effects of which may be mitigated by adjustments to transfer prices. The first of these has to do with currency rationing. Some countries (notably Israel and several South American nations) have adopted regulations that rigidly restrict the conditions under which profits of foreign-owned corporations may be transmitted out of the country. At the same time, governments such as these ration currencies available to corporations' imports. This system provides close supervision by the host country over the outflow of its vital foreign exchange. To some extent, it is possible to circumvent such restrictions by increasing the prices of imports from parent or related companies. High prices paid by a restricted division to related companies can result in a repatriation of profits despite the desires of a host government. Thus, when one avenue is closed alert managements seek other ways to achieve their goals.

Secondly, as a way of increasing manufacturing activity locally, some governments impose restrictions on the number and kinds of components that may be imported into a larger unit. In Mexico, the systematic action of the government in forcing United States parents to ship fewer components, and causing more parts to be manufactured by local sources of supply has had impact on many firms – notably in the automotive industry.

Finally, some governments restrict allocation against local taxable income for expenses incurred and services performed in the country. Thus, for example, head office expenses such as administrative and general, R and D, marketing, and other costs may not be charged to subsidiaries in Venezuela, for example, if the services are performed (as they usually are) elsewhere. In one country, a respondent found himself forbidden to remit royalties, his method of operation in many other countries of the world. In such a case, costs may be recouped by increases in the transfer prices of goods shipped to the foreign subsidiary. At times, the subject foreign government may suspect the compensating use of transfer prices, and local managements are forced to devote time and effort to justify their actions to local government officials.

Unstable governments

When a company operates in a country in which there has been a tendency for the government to be overthrown (or shaken) with recurring regularity, it is to the interest of the company to keep as little cash as possible in that country. The high feelings of nationalism which often accompany a revolutionary regime further endanger assets of foreign businesses, and expropriation is a risk in such situations.

The fact that a government has been in power for many years does not always call for confidence either. Cuba and Nigeria are two cases in point, in which comparatively stable governments (one of them of long standing) were overthrown much to the shock of managements which were not sensitive to local politics, and were not prepared to deal with the consequences of revolution. In such environments, low prices on transfers out of the country can facilitate transmittal of excess cash, since exports at low prices tend to reduce cash flowing into such countries. High prices on imports may also have the same effect.

Competitive advantages

Transfer prices are used to strengthen the competitive position of a company, or to control or weaken the competitive position of others in a foreign environment. In the case of integrated oil companies, for example, it seems apparent that producers enjoy substantial profit on the raw product. When competing refiners and refining divisions of the producing company enter the market at this stage, raw material costs have already provided a large measure of profit to the producers. The small spread remaining in refining, processing and marketing tends to leave the producers in control of final market prices for finished products throughout the world.

In the firms of our experience this situation does not prevail to any noticeable extent. Some companies do manufacture basic products in bulk (pharmaceutical and chemical firms are cases in point), and they do sell such products to competing manufacturers which process and refine the raw or basic ingredients into competing end products. Attempts are made to maintain resale prices of bulk products at a level which will cause prices of end products to be high enough for competitive advantage. The attempts are not wholly successful. In spite of a limited number of bulk processors, competition at the bulk level keeps the access cost to competitors low enough to cause competition at the level of finished goods.

In another respect, however, transfer prices are used to mitigate the internal effects of outside competition. When competitive forces in a foreign country cause external prices to be lowered by a particular division with resultant damage to the profits, consideration is usually extended to reduce transfer prices into that division. If the local competitive squeeze is beyond the control of the damaged division, the local managers in many countries request the parent – or other divisions – to share its losses by changing transfer prices. It is recalled that in some firms, transfer prices are a function of external prices. In such cases, then, downward changes in external prices beyond local control will, in time, cause changes in transfer prices to strengthen competitive action.

Foreign partners

Incentive exists for companies to charge higher transfer prices to jointly-owned than to wholly-owned divisions. At the same time, in counteracting such a tendency, the jointly-owned subsidiary has incentive for a directly opposite action. In the field a higher degree of circumspection seems to surround transfer pricing practices where joint ownership exists. In other words, regardless of the locus or the method used to set transfer prices, real arm's length bargaining takes place to a greater extent. Because it also happens, not accidentally we are sure, that jointly-owned subsidiaries are usually more fully integrated, they have a measure of autonomy over outside purchasing and selling beyond the permissible limit for wholly-owned subsidiaries. This freedom is reflected in transfer prices which are acceptable by both sides.

Public relations

Under this heading we include several effects of importance which may be attributed to or which accompany transfer pricing systems and concepts. Since external pricing exerts some influence on transfer prices, there is a secondary effect on transfer prices caused by a desire for 'good citizenship'. The sample companies do consider this effect in their desire to pay a fair share of taxes to host governments.

An overriding constraint to the allocation of income to foreign divisions is a desire to show some measure of good faith to host governments by submitting profits to local taxation.

Along similar lines, we report here the practice of one company with a manufacturing subsidiary in Mexico. In that country the law requires a sharing of profits with employees (currently at the rate of 10 per cent of profits with a rise in the offing). As a result this firm sets transfer prices to leave a 'reasonable' profit in that country. In addition, an attempt is made to show year-to-year earnings in a gradually ascending amount.

Finally, while possible effects on transfer prices might be brought about by the right of labor unions in Italy to audit company profits and by the right of labor representatives to sit on the boards of directors of corporations in France and Germany, the firms appear to consider the possible consequences too slight to affect their transfer prices.

Interpersonal reactions

The findings discussed so far have been strictly from the point of view of the corporate officers who devise and administer the transfer pricing systems under review. Since interviews were not conducted with overseas managers we cannot report specific personal attitudes or perceived reactions of such individuals. However, it seemed to us that headquarters personnel attempted to consider the perceived needs of overseas personnel. Even if it were intended to ignore managers of foreign divisions, modern management methods coupled with today's speedy communication and easy intercontinental travel make regular interpersonal contacts between management personnel an integral part of corporate life.

In the case of a company whose highly directive transfer pricing system causes a disproportionate share of income to arise overseas, its international managers are sometimes tempted to boast about their 'contributions' to corporate profits at periodic meetings of corporate executives. The fact that their profits are in effect allocated rather than earned does not deter their proprietary self-glorification, much to the frustration of domestic managers, not to mention the dismay of headquarters executives.

In all companies whose transfer prices are a function of environmental influence some method of adjustment is used to give appropriate credit to divisions for their real contribution. The method may be credit-backs, or 'dual' sets of books, or some other form of memorandum allowance, or compensation in budgets and profit plans. But regardless of the intent, 'some things get lost in the wash', and dissensions result in dysfunctional upsets among all such firms at one time or another. It is a rare manager who waits patiently for a headquarters controller to adjust for profit or costs which are put out of line by headquarters directives. In one company, it was reported, the United Kingdom division was directed to lower its price to a new French subsidiary so as to improve startup operating results; but a good deal of ill-feeling was generated when headquarters seemed to forget that the resulting poor performance in the United Kingdom was not at all a reflection of local management.

When freedom to purchase and sell outside is sharply limited, divisional managers chafe for two reasons. First, they feel they are being discriminated against by having to overpay and subsidize a fellow division. Second, they complain about lack of interest for the company as a whole, because higher internal costs may at times reduce total corporate profit. If headquarters seems to be cavalier about corporate profits, local management frustrations may cause dysfunctional attitudes and action in the field. In those companies which present a uniform price to the world, the managers of more efficient plants sometimes complain of having virtually to subsidize less efficient members by reason of their own economies.

These kinds of reactions are sometimes evident in purely domestic operations, but for the most part the far-reaching influence of the multinational environment, when coupled with differences in national temperament and cultural backgrounds, causes complaints of a more serious nature to a greater extent than in a single-country operation.

Conclusions

The establishment and operation of a functional control system to measure, evaluate, and motivate management in purely domestic surroundings is difficult enough by itself. In the case of multinational companies, however, the need for feasible control systems is rendered more urgent by the additional complexities of the larger environment. An executive has emphasized that the risks in international business are larger in number and different in kind than in the domestic environment. He was referring mostly to the problems enumerated here. Regardless of the risks, however, there is wide recognition among our sample that the rewards of the international environment – at least to date – have offered ample incentive to United States firms to expand in this direction. Nevertheless, any actions which affect the control mechanism are likely to be more dangerous to the firms engaged in multinational business; and when adaptations to new conditions cause alterations to an existing system, management must be careful not merely to substitute one problem for another.

Accordingly, the first criterion of a transfer pricing method in multinational business should be that it does not cause destructive changes in the existing control system, unless adequate adjustments compensate for the changes, and keep the system operational. In other words, unless a price change is called for by functional needs of managers, first attention should be directed at its effect on the control system. For example, if transfer prices have to be recast in response to changes in cost of production inputs, the control system, such as it is, ought not to be changed. If it has been providing useful information in the first place, it will now reflect the new conditions (the causes, or inputs) as well as the resultant changes (the effects, or outputs).

But when a transfer price change is introduced in order to counteract, or take advantage of, circumstances external to the usual routine, then the system will reflect results which are not necessarily the result of the operations it is designed to measure.

And if measurements are false, then resultant decisions are likely to be wrong. We consider the three basic requirements of *measurement*, *evaluation*, and *motivation* to be so vital to the promotion of corporate effectiveness that changes in the control system should not be tolerated which may react at cross-purposes to these requirements.

Our recommendation is that the transfer pricing system must primarily be compatible with the operational goals of the control system, and must reinforce its regulatory functions. But when external conditions are of such substance that they either expose the firm to grave threats or make available opportunities for material gains, then the transfer price system may be revamped to accord the greater return to the firm. The magnitude of threat or gain is of relevance to the proposal, since it is not intended to disturb control systems for every minor circumstance. Under such a practice systems would soon cease to operate effectively. In each firm, criteria should be established for selection (or elimination) of matters for consideration.

Quantitative limits would point up the particular relevance in each case. For example, one might use as measures a relative or absolute profit contribution, or a change in market share. Appropriate measures should be apparent in each case. Qualitative rules also have to be established, although they do not lend themselves to precise measurements. For example, one might consider interpersonal effects among managers (at all levels), reaction of public opinion, or changes in attitude of host or parent governments, to mention just a few. And again, the special conditions in each firm and its environment would dictate the criteria.

In proposing what may be thought of as a flexible approach to transfer pricing in multinational business, we are at the same time rejecting a simplistic approach to the problems. There is simply no one easy solution to the problems. We also regard a willingness to tinker incessantly with transfer prices to be equally dysfunctional, because incessant adjustment to the changing world without quantitative or qualitative tests represents too mechanistic and narrow an approach in a complex and changing world.

International business has grown by leaps and bounds, and problems have grown apace; but managers have not always been aware of them. When they have perceived the problems, they have not always responded with suitable solutions. Empirical evidence indicates that interest is high but attention is uneven.

We therefore advise extra care in approaching the concept of transfer pricing in the multinational firm. We recommend a multinational outlook, which includes consideration of regional problems. We suggest that greater effectiveness and, it should follow, greater profit will be the reward for those managements which recognize the multi-faced problems, and achieve solutions which reconcile the differences.

Part Eight
**The Marketing Plan:
Marketing and Economic Development**

In the final part of the book an attempt is made to pull the threads together. The object of the marketing plan is seen as harmonizing market structure and marketing strategy while retaining a requisite minimum of international coordination.

Reading 32, by Buzzell, provides a backdrop by an incisive discussion of the extent to which it is feasible – or advisable – to standardize strategy in multinational marketing. The exhibit of structural factors which may place limits on attempts at homogenizing strategy is particularly instructive. The conclusion that both the pros and cons of standardization in multinational marketing programs should be considered is very much in tune with the ecologic approach of this book.

In Reading 33 we have tried to apply the ecologic view to the task of marketing planning. A step-by-step procedure is sketched out, comprising the original commitment decision as well as an initial plan of operations.

It is befitting that a book on international marketing strategy should end with some thoughts on the broader social and economic significance of the marketing process. Ecology teaches us that marketing institutions and practices as we know them will survive only as they serve a useful purpose in the broader environment. As indicated in Part One, the development of affluescent society and customer-oriented marketing have gone hand in hand – and surely not by accident. Reading 34, by Drucker, points to the vast and sadly neglected contribution potential of modern marketing to economic development in the LDCs.

In reading Drucker one is reminded of Paul Hoffman's statement about the most important lesson he learned during his thirteen years as head of the UN Development Programme: 'One illusion is that you can industrialize a country by building factories. You don't. You industrialize it by building markets.'

(As quoted in *Time*, 17 January 1972.) Here is indeed a challenge for the Second Development Decade: a challenge for planners at the national governmental and international technical assistance levels to make room for, and prevail upon, the greatest change agent as yet devised in non-dictatorial cultures, and a challenge to international marketers to demonstrate the power of their tools.

Looking beyond the LDCs, we note that international marketing is the vehicle by which is implemented the international division of labor based on the differential advantages of countries and firms, and it is the means of bringing economies of scale to bear in such incredibly resource-demanding industries as petroleum, drugs, computers and aircraft. What is more, in our age the multinational corporation has proven a far more effective torch-bearer of a global outlook and inter-cultural understanding than either national governments or the United Nations. Many have reasons to envy the mission of the international marketer.

32 R. D. Buzzell

Can You Standardize Multinational Marketing?

Adapted from R. D. Buzzell, 'Can you standardize multinational marketing?', *Harvard Business Review* November–December 1968, pp. 102–113.

Is it practical to consider the development of a marketing strategy, in terms of *all* of its elements, on a multinational scale? The conventional wisdom suggests that a multinational approach is *not* realistic, because of the great differences that still exist – and probably always will exist – among nations. For example, George Weissman, President of Philip Morris, Inc., has concluded that 'until we achieve One World there is no such thing as international marketing, only local marketing around the world' (1967). Apparently most other marketing executives agree with this view. Thus, Millard H. Pryor, Jr, Director of Corporate Planning for Singer Company, writes:

Marketing is conspicuous by its absence from the functions which can be planned at the corporate headquarters level. The operating experience of many international firms appears to confirm the desirability of assigning long-range planning of marketing activities to local managers (1965).

The prevailing view, then, is that marketing strategy is a local problem. The best strategy for a company will differ from country to country, and the design of the strategy should be left to local management in each country.

Two-sided case

But is the answer this simple? The experiences of leading US-based companies in recent years suggest that there may indeed be something to be said in favor of a multinational marketing strategy. This article is intended to outline some of the possibilities – and limitations – of an integrated approach to multinational marketing. My thesis is that although there are many obstacles to the application of common marketing policies in different countries, there are also some very tangible potential benefits. The relative importance of the pros and cons will, of course, vary from industry to industry and from company to company. But the benefits are sufficiently universal and sufficiently important to merit careful analysis by management in virtually any multinational company. Management should not automatically dismiss the idea of standardizing some parts of the marketing strategy, at least within major regions of the world.

Benefits of standardization

As a practical matter, standardization is not a clear cut issue. In a literal sense, multinational standardization would mean the offering of *identical* product lines at identical prices through identical distribution systems, supported by identical promotional programs, in several different countries. At the other extreme, completely 'localized' marketing strategies would contain *no* common elements whatsoever. Obviously, neither of these extremes is often feasible or desirable.

The practical question is: Which *elements* of the marketing strategy can or should be standardized, and to what degree? Currently, most multinational companies employ strategies that are much closer to the 'localized' end of the spectrum than to the opposite pole. If there are potential benefits of increased standardization, then they would be achieved by incorporating *more* common elements in a multinational strategy. Each marketing aspect of policy should be considered, first, in its own right, and second, in relation to the other elements of the 'mix'.

Let us examine the most important potential benefits of standardization in multinational marketing strategy.

Significant cost savings

Differences in national income levels, tastes, and other factors have traditionally dictated the need for local products and corresponding local marketing programs. The annals of international business provide countless examples, even for such apparently similar countries as the United States and Canada. Philip Morris, Inc., for example, tried unsuccessfully to convert Canadian smokers to one of its popular American cigarette brands. The Canadians apparently would rather fight; they preserved their traditional preference for so-called 'Virginia-type' tobacco blends. Examples of this kind suggest that to attain maximum sales in each country, a company should offer products, as well as packages, advertisements, and other marketing elements, which are tailored to that country's distinctive needs and desires.

However, maximizing sales is not the only goal in designing a marketing strategy. Profitability depends ultimately both on sales *and* costs, and there are significant opportunities for cost reduction via standardization. The most obvious, and usually the most important, area for cost savings is product design. By offering the same basic product in several markets with some possible variations in functional and/or design features, a manufacturer can frequently achieve longer production runs, spread research and development costs over a greater volume, and thus reduce total unit costs.

The 'Italian invasion'

The lesson of mass production economies through standardization, first demonstrated by Henry Ford I, has been dramatically retaught during the 1960s by the Italian household appliance industry.

In the mid-1950s, total combined Italian production of refrigerators and washing machines was less than 300,000 units; there were no strong Italian appliance manufacturers. In 1955, only 3 per cent of Italian households owned refrigerators, and around 1 per cent owned washing machines.

Starting in the late 1950s, several companies began aggressive programs of product development and marketing. Ironically, some of the Italian entrepreneurs were simply applying lessons learned from America. One member of the Fumagalli family, owners of the appliance firm, Candy, had been a prisoner of war in the United States and brought back the idea of 'a washing machine in every home'.

The Italian appliance firms installed modern, highly automated equipment, reinvested profits, and produced relatively simple, *standardized* products in great numbers. By 1965, refrigerator output was estimated at 2·6 million units, and washing machine output at 1·5 million units. Much of this volume was sold in Italy; home ownership of the two appliances rose to 50 per cent and 23 per cent respectively. But the Italian companies were aggressive in export marketing, too; by 1965 Italian-made refrigerators accounted for 32 per cent of the total French market and for 40 per cent to 50 per cent of the Benelux market. Even in Germany, the home market of such electrical giants as AEG, Bosch, and Siemens, the Italian products attained a 12 per cent market share. The export pattern of washing machines has followed that of refrigerators; by 1965 Italian exports had accounted for 10 per cent to 15 per cent of market sales in most other Western European countries (from Castellano, 1965, and *Marketing In Europe*, 1966 and 1967).

The success of the Italian appliance industry has been a painful experience for the traditional leaders – American, British, and German – as well as for the smaller French companies that had previously had tariff protection. Whirlpool Corporation, which acquired a French refrigerator plant in 1962, subsequently leased the facility to a French competitor. Even Frigidaire decided, in mid-1967, to close down its refrigerator production in France.

In competition with other European appliance makers, the Italian companies have benefited from some natural advantages in terms of lower wage rates and government export incentives. But mass production of simple, standardized products has been at least equally important. And, according to *Fortune*, 'refrigerators have begun to look more and more alike as national tastes in product design give way to an international "sheer-line" style.'

Turnabout at Hoover

To compete with this 'Italian invasion' in appliances, some of the established manufacturers have tried new approaches. An interesting example is the recent introduction of a new line of automatic washing machines by Hoover Ltd, the market leader in the United Kingdom. Hoover's previous automatics, introduced in 1961, were designed primarily for the British market. The company's new 'Keymatic' models featured:

An exclusive 'pulsator' washing action.
A tilted, enamelled steel drum.
Hot water provided by the home's central hot-water heater.

In contrast, most European manufacturers, including the Italian producers, offered front-loading, tumble-action washers with stainless steel drums and self-contained water heaters. Either because these features were better suited to continental needs, or because so many sellers promoted them, or perhaps both, Hoover saw its position in the major continental markets gradually decline.

When the Hoover management set out to design a new product line, beginning in 1965, it decided to look for a *single* basic design that would meet the needs of housewives in France, Germany, and Scandinavia as well as in the United Kingdom. A committee including representatives of the continental subsidiaries and of the parent company, Hoover Worldwide Corporation (New York), spent many weeks finding mutually acceptable specifications for the new line.

The result, which went on sale in the spring of 1967, was a front loading, tumble-action machine, closer in concept to the 'continental' design than Hoover's previous washers, but with provisions for 'hot water fill' and enamelled steel drums on models to be sold in the United Kingdom. By standardizing most of the key design elements in the new machine, Hoover was able to make substantial savings in development costs, tooling, and unit production costs.

Other economies

The potential economies of standardization are not confined solely to product design decisions. In some industries, packaging costs represent a significant part of total costs. Here, too, standardization may offer the possibility of savings. Charles R. Williams cites the case of a food processor selling prepared soups throughout Europe in eleven different packages. He observes, 'The company believes it could achieve a significant savings in cost and at the same time reduce consumer confusion by standardizing the packaging' (1967).

Still another area for cost savings is that of advertising. For some of the major package goods manufacturers, the production of art work, films, and other advertising materials costs millions of dollars annually. Although differences in language limit the degree of standardization that can be imposed, *some* common elements can often be used. To illustrate: Pepsi-Cola is bottled in 465 plants and sold in 110 countries outside the United States. Part of its foreign advertising is done by films. According to one of the company's top marketing executives, 'We have found that it is possible to produce commercial films overseas in one market, if planned properly, for use in most (but not all) of our international markets.' According to company estimates, the added cost of producing separate films for each market would be $8 million per year (Heller, 1966).

All of these examples illustrate the same basic point: standardization of product design, packaging, and promotional materials *can* offer important economies to the multinational marketer. Even if these cost savings are attained at the expense of lower sales in some markets, the net effect on profits may be positive.

Consistency with customers

Quite apart from the possibilities of cost reduction, some multinational companies are moving toward standardization in order to achieve consistency in their dealings with customers. Executives of these companies believe that consistency in product style, in sales and customer service, in brand names and packages, and generally in the 'image' projected to customers, is a powerful means of increasing sales.

If all customers lived incommunicado behind their respective national frontiers, there would be no point in worrying about this matter; only diplomatic couriers and border-crossing guards would ever notice any inconsistencies in products, services, or promotion. But in reality, of course, this is not the case. The most visible type of cross-border flow is international travel by tourists and businessmen. Especially in Europe, with its relatively high income levels and short distances, the number of people visiting other countries has reached flood proportions in the 1960s, and shows no sign of abating. If the German tourist in Spain sees his accustomed brands in the store, he is likely to buy them during his visit. More important, his re-exposure to the products and their advertising may strengthen his loyalty back home or, at least, protect him from the temptation to change his allegiance to a competitor.

Then there is the flow of communications across boundaries. Magazines, newspapers, radio and television broadcasts – all including advertising – reach international audiences. For example, according to estimates by Young and Rubicam International (1966):

German television broadcasts are received by 40 per cent of Dutch homes with TV sets.

Paris Match has a circulation of 85,000 in Belgium, 26,000 in Switzerland, and substantial readership in Luxemburg, Germany, Italy, and Holland.

On an average day, over four million French housewives tune to Radio Luxemburg; the same broadcast reaches 620,000 Belgian housewives, 30,000 in Switzerland, and 100,000 in Holland.[1]

The possibility of reaching multimarket audiences with common advertising messages, and the risk of confusion that may result from reaching such audiences with different brand names and promotional appeals, has led some of the major consumer

1. 'When is a frontier not a frontier?', (pamphlet), Brussels, May 1966.

goods producers to explore ways and means of standardizing at least the basic elements of their European campaigns. For instance, the Nestlé Company, Inc. and Unilever Ltd, probably the most experienced multinational consumer goods firms, have both moved in the direction of more 'unified' European advertising during the 1960s. When Nestlé launched 'New Nescafé' in 1961–1962, for example, the same basic theme ('fresh-ground aroma') and very similar creative treatments were used not only throughout Europe, but also in other markets such as Australia. The value of this approach is, perhaps, reflected in the fact that several years ago Nescafé was the leading brand of instant coffee in every European country.

Balanced appraisal needed

To summarize, then, many companies have found real benefits in a multinational approach to marketing strategy. The gains have included greater effectiveness in marketing, reduced costs, and improved planning and control. Moreover, especially in Western Europe but also in some other parts of the world, social and economic trends are working in favor of more, rather than less, standardization in marketing policies. Tourism, international communication, increased numbers of multinational customers, and other forces are all tending toward greater unification of multinational markets.

But this is just one side of the story. It would be a mistake to assume, as at least a few companies have done, that marketing programs can be transferred from one market to another without careful consideration of the *differences* which still exist. Let us turn next to that side of the picture.

Common barriers

Despite the potential benefits of standardization, the great majority of companies still operate on the premise that each national market is different and must therefore be provided with its own, distinctive marketing program. For instance, after a careful study of the marketing policies of US appliance and photographic manufacturers in Europe, Richard Aylmer concluded: 'In over 85 per cent of the cases observed, advertising and promotion decisions were based on *local* product marketing objectives' (1968).

Why is diversity still the rule of the day in multinational marketing? In many cases, differences simply reflect *customary* ways of doing business which have evolved in an earlier period when national boundaries were more formidable barriers than they are today. But even if tradition did not play a role, it must be recognized that there are and will continue to be some important obstacles to standardization.

A comprehensive list of these obstacles would fill many pages, and would include many factors that affect only one or two industries. The most important and generally applicable factors are summarized in Table 1. The rows of this table represent the major *classes* of factors which limit standardization in multinational marketing strategies. The columns correspond to different elements of a marketing program, and the 'cells' in the table illustrate the ways in which the various factors affect each program element. In effect, each cell represents a condition or characteristic which *may* differ sufficiently among countries, and *may* require variations in marketing strategies. As we shall see presently, the experiences of multinational companies afford numerous examples of these barriers to standardization. Let us look briefly at each of the four major factors limiting standardization that are listed in Table 1.

Marketing characteristics

Perhaps the most permanent differences among national markets are those arising from the physical environment – climate, topography, and resources (see the top left of Table 1). Climate has an obvious effect on the sales potential for many products, and may also require differences in packaging. Topography influences the density of population, and this in turn may have a strong influence on the distribution system available to a manufacturer.

The cell in Table 1 labeled 'Product use conditions' includes a wide variety of environmental factors affecting marketing strategies. Differences in the size and configuration of homes, for example, have an important bearing on product design for appliances and home furnishings. European kitchens are typically small by US standards, and there is seldom any basement space available to apartment dwellers for laundry facilities. As a result, there is a great emphasis on compactness of design in automatic washers, for they must somehow be fitted into a small and already crowded area. As noted in the example of Hoover Ltd washing machines must also be equipped with self-contained water heating systems to compensate for the lack of central hot-water heaters in most continental homes.

Table 1 Obstacles to standardization in international marketing strategies

Factors limiting standardization	Elements of marketing program				
	Product design	Pricing	Distribution	Sales force	Advertising and promotion, branding and packaging
Market characteristics					
Physical environment	Climate		Customer mobility	Dispersion of customers	Access to media
	Product use conditions				Climate
Stage of economic and industrial development	Income levels	Income levels	Consumer shopping patterns	Wage levels, availability of manpower	Needs for convenience rather than economy
	Labor costs in relation to capital costs				Purchase quantities
Cultural factors	'Custom and tradition'	Attitudes toward bargaining	Consumer shopping patterns	Attitudes toward selling	Language, literacy
	Attitudes toward foreign goods				Symbolism
Industry conditions					
Stage of product life cycle in each market	Extent of product differentiation	Elasticity of demand	Availability of outlets	Need for missionary sales effort	Awareness, experience with products
			Desirability of private brands		
Competition	Quality levels	Local costs	Competitors' control of outlets	Competitors' sales forces	Competitive expenditure messages
		Prices of substitutes			
Marketing institutions					
Distributive system	Availability of outlets	Prevailing margins	Number and variety of outlets available	Number, size, dispersion of outlets	Extent of self-service
			Ability to 'force' distribution	Effectiveness of advertising, need for substitutes	
Advertising media and agencies					Media availability, costs, overlaps
Legal restrictions	Product standards	Tariffs and taxes	Restrictions on product lines	General employment restrictions	Specific restrictions on messages, costs
	Patent laws	Antitrust laws	Resale price maintenance	Specific restrictions on selling	Trademark laws
	Tariffs and taxes	Resale price maintenance			

Industrial goods manufacturers also frequently encounter differences in product use conditions. To illustrate:

1. A US producer of farm equipment found that one of his pieces of machinery could not be moved through the narrow, crooked streets of French and Belgian farm villages.
2. Concluding that there is more dissimilarity than similarity in industrial markets in Europe, a chemical industry marketing researcher writes: '(A factor) which would severely affect the market for surface coatings is the fact that materials used in building construction are vastly different in various parts of Europe. Brick, mortar, and tile are used predominantly in Southern Europe, whereas this is not the case in Northern Germany and in Benelux' (Gerunsky, 1967).

Many similar examples could be cited of differences in the environment which call for variations in product design and other aspects of marketing policy.

Development stage

Differences among countries in stages of economic and industrial development (second item under 'Market characteristics' in Table 1) also have a profound influence on marketing strategies. Because of the wide gaps in per capita income levels, many products or models which are regarded as inexpensive staples in the United States or Western Europe must be marketed as 'luxuries' elsewhere. Even among the industrialized countries income differences are substantial: appliance manufacturers such as Philco-Ford Corporation and Kelvinator of Canada, Ltd find themselves with little choice but to position their products as deluxe, relatively high-priced items. This, in turn, implies a very different marketing strategy from that used in the United States.

For industrial products, differences in economic development are reflected in variations in relative costs of capital and labor. Thus, General Electric Company and other companies have sold numerical controls for machine tools to US factories primarily on the basis of labor cost savings. The same approach may be suitable in Germany, where there is a critical shortage of labor. But in most other countries it would be far more difficult to justify numerical controls on the basis of labor substitution.

Cultural factors

This category is a convenient catchall for the many differences in market structure and behavior that cannot readily be explained in terms of more tangible factors. Consider, for example, the figures in Table 2, which are taken from a recent survey made by the European Economic Community's Statistical Office. Why do French households consume more than fifty times as much wine as Dutch households, but only two-thirds as much milk? No doubt these differences could be explained historically in terms of variations in water, soil, and so on. But for practical purposes, it is usually sufficient and certainly more efficient simply to take differences in consumption patterns and attitudes *as given*, and to adjust to them.

There are many examples of cultural differences that have affected marketing success or failure. One cultural factor is the attitude of consumers toward 'foreign' goods. To illustrate: Princess Housewares, Inc., a large US appliance manufacturer, introduced a line of electric housewares in the German market. The company's brand name was well known and highly regarded in the United States, but relatively unknown in Germany; and the brand had a definitely 'American' sound. The company discovered that the American association was a real drawback among German consumers. According to a survey, fewer than 40 per cent of German individuals felt 'confident' about electrical products made in the United States, compared with 91 per cent who were 'confident' of German-made products.

Lack of brand awareness, coupled with suspicion of the quality of 'American' products, required the company to adopt a very different marketing strategy in Germany than that employed in the United States, where both awareness and a quality image were taken for granted.

Industry conditions

A convenient framework for comparing industry and competitive conditions in different national markets is that of the 'product life cycle'. The histories of many different products in the United States suggest that most of them pass through several distinct *stages* over a period of years, and that marketing strategies typically change from stage to stage.

Some products are in different stages of their life cycles in different national markets. For example, in late 1965 the Polaroid Corporation introduced the 'Swinger' Polaroid Land camera in the United States. The Swinger, with a retail list price of $19.95, was Polaroid's first camera selling for less than $50. The introductory promotion for the new model in the United States placed very heavy emphasis on price; there was no need to explain the basic concept of 'instant photography', since millions of Polaroid Land cameras had already been sold over a seventeen-year period. Surveys indicated that over 80 per cent of US consumers were aware of the name 'Polaroid' and of the company's basic product features.

The Swinger was introduced in Europe during 1966. Prior to that time, Polaroid cameras had been extremely high-priced, owing in part to high tariffs, and the company's sales had been at a very low level. Distribution of Polaroid cameras and film was spotty. Most important, fewer than 10 per cent of consumers were aware of the Polaroid instant photography concept.

Table 2 **Average household consumption of beverages, 1963–1964** (in litres).

Country	Milk	Wine	Beer
France	103	116	28
Germany	100	7	46
Holland	153	2	11
Italy	87	95	2

Source: Le Monde 15–21 February, 1968, p. 7.

Under these circumstances, a very different marketing strategy was needed for the Swinger in Europe. Polaroid advertising had to be designed to do a more basic educational job, since awareness of the instant picture principle could not be taken for granted. The promotional program also had to be aimed at building retail distribution, which was also taken for granted in the United States.

If products are in different stages of their life cycles in different countries, then it is tempting to conclude that marketing strategies used in the past in the more 'advanced' countries should be used in other 'follower' nations. There is some evidence to support this conclusion. For instance, as described earlier, the Italian appliance manufacturers have successfully employed strategies similar to those of Henry Ford in the early 1900s; similarly, Polaroid in the 1960s in Europe can profitably use many of the same approaches that it employed in America in the early 1950s. However, history does not repeat itself exactly, and past marketing strategies cannot be reapplied without some modifications.

Competitive practices

Another important industry condition, partly but not entirely related to the product life cycle, is the extent of competition in each national market. Differences in products, costs, prices, and promotional levels may permit or even require differences in the strategies used by a multinational company in various markets. Even within the European Common Market, there are still substantial variations in prices of many products, reflecting in part traditional differences in the degree of competition. A survey made in 1967 by the European Economic Community's Statistical Office showed that price variations are still substantial even with the Common Market. Typical prices were compared for some 125 different consumer products by country; on the average, the difference between prices in the countries with the highest and lowest prices was 58 per cent. Even the price of a staple item such as aspirin varied from a high of 38 cents in Germany to a low of 22 cents in Holland.

The growth of multinational companies in itself has tended to reduce traditional differences in competitive practices. For example: advertising expenditures have traditionally been lower in France than in the United States and other European countries; on a per capita basis, total French advertising outlays are around one-eighth those of the United States and one-third those of Germany. However, according to M. André Bouhebent, a top French advertising agency executive, the entry of foreign competitors is changing the situation: 'When German advertisers sell in France, they have the habit of spending at the same rate (as at home), which is three times that of their French competitors...' (*Advertising Age*, 1966). As an example, it was noted that the German Triumph bra and girdle company spends three to four times as much as a French undergarment company to promote its products.

Marketing institutions

The combination of continued differences in marketing institutions *now* with the prospect of greater similarities in the *future* creates some difficult problems for multinational marketers. One such problem may be timing. The experience of Princess Housewares in Germany, previously mentioned, is a case in point.

When Princess Housewares went into the German market, the company had a basic choice to make regarding channels of distribution. In the early 1960s, the predominant system of appliance distribution was independent wholesalers selling to retail stores. Small specialty retailers still dominated the market. However, department stores, mail-order firms, and discounters were growing in importance. Most of these large retailers were able to obtain *gross-handler* (wholesaler) discounts from manufacturers, and many of them sold at substantial discounts from 'suggested' retail prices. The suggested prices, in turn, were often set at artificially high levels (so-called 'moon' prices) to permit the appearance of large price cuts at retail. At the same time, because of public confusion and discontent over artificial list prices and equally artificial discounts, the resale price maintenance law was under increasing attack.

Princess Housewares, as a relatively unknown brand, felt that its first task was to obtain distribution. To do this, the company decided to establish maintained prices and enforce them, so that small retailers' margins would be protected. But this put the company at a disadvantage in selling to the large discounters. It also meant that the company had to sell direct to retailers, since wholesalers could not be relied on to enforce resale prices.

In some ways, the Princess Housewares case boils down to a choice between a traditional distributive system, similar to that used in the United States in the early 1950s, and an emerging but still undeveloped system. US experience suggests that the emerging system will become the dominant one. But can a manufacturer afford to be ahead of the trend?

Legal restrictions

Different countries require or permit very different practices in the areas of product design, competitive practices, pricing, employment, and advertising. They also impose differing taxes and tariffs, and multinational companies often follow devious paths in the attempt to minimize the total cost effects of these levies. Obviously, such practices can be stumbling blocks for the would-be standardizer.

Some product standards, though ostensibly designed for purposes of safety, are used by governments as a device for protecting home industries. A notable case in point was the imposition of new regulations for electrical appliances by France in 1967, along with delays in issuing approvals. This was generally regarded as a deliberate move to slow down the onslaught of competition by the Italian companies and thus give the domestic industry a breathing space.

Conclusion

Traditionally, marketing strategy has been regarded as a strictly local problem in each national market. Differences in customer needs and preferences, in competition, in institutional systems, and in legal regulations have seemed to require basically different marketing programs. Any similarity between countries has been seen as purely coincidental.

There is no doubt that differences among nations are still great, and that these differences should be recognized in marketing planning. But the experiences of a growing number of multinational companies suggest that there are also some real potential gains in an integrated approach to marketing strategy. Standardization of products, packages, and promotional approaches may permit substantial cost savings, as well as greater consistency in dealings with customers. The harmonization of price policies often facilitates better internal planning and control. Finally, if good ideas are scarce, and if some of them have universal appeal, they should be used as widely as possible.

All of this adds up to the conclusion that both the pros *and* the cons of standardization in multinational marketing programs should be considered.

References

AYLMER, R. (1968), 'Marketing decision-making in the multinational firm', unpublished doctoral thesis, Harvard Business School.

BOUHEBENT, A. (1966), quoted in *Advertising Age*, 29 August, p. 218.

CASTELLANO, C. (1965), *L'Industria Degli Elettrodomestici in Italia*, Universita Degli Studi di Genova.

GERUNSKY, W. (1967), 'International marketing research' in N. H. Giragosian (ed.), *Chemical Marketing Research*, Reinhold Publishing Corporation, p. 258.

HELLER, N. (1966), 'How Pepsi-Cola does it in 110 countries', in J. S. Wright and J. L. Goldstucker (eds.), *New Ideas for Successful Marketing*, American Marketing Association, p. 700.

Le Monde (1968), weekly overseas edition, 15-21 February, p. 7.

Marketing in Europe, October 1966 and September 1967.

PRYOR, M. H. Jr (1965), 'Planning in a worldwide business', *Harvard Business Review*, January-February, p. 137.

WEISSMAN, G. (1967), 'International expansion', in L. Adler (ed.), *Plotting Marketing Strategy*, *A New Orientation*, Simon and Schuster, p. 229.

WILLIAMS, C. R. (1967), 'Regional management overseas', *Harvard Business Review*, January-February, p. 89.

YOUNG and RUBICAM INTERNATIONAL, 'When is a frontier not a frontier?' (pamphlet), May 1966.

33 H. B. Thorelli

The International Marketing Plan: A Checklist Approach

A Reading originally written for this collection.

To conduct any activity in an orderly fashion one needs a plan. There is no science of planning. However, ever since Henri Fayol defined planning as consisting of the two elements of forecasting the future and providing for it there is a fairly broad consensus of what is involved. Rather than adding another essay on planning to an already large body of literature, the approach taken here is that of condensing a great number of writings into a summary checklist form. This is done in an attempt to serve the needs of the busy executive.

This Reading serves the dual purpose of integrating the materials in this volume. Thus it is natural that we shall apply the ecologic view in presenting our checklists. For a detailed restatement of the ecologic concept of marketing the reader is referred to Reading 1. Briefly, it admonishes the planner to look at the firm's resources ('what are we good at?') and objectives ('what do we want to become?') and to analyse the environment for opportunities and restrictions ('what current or potential customer needs could our firm most effectively satisfy?'). The means of relating the environment (and in it notably the market structure) to the firm's objectives and resources is marketing strategy. We claim that the key challenge in business planning is to harmonize market structure and marketing strategy.

It should be clear against this background that these checklists are illustrative, not normative. They make no pretense of restating 'principles of international marketing management', but they should serve well as bases of reference to practical decision-makers. In any given business situation some of the factors referred to will almost surely seem irrelevant, and some variables not even mentioned here may be highly important. The checklists are not substitutes for executive judgement and experience.

Three comments about the checklists are in order. First, while there is hopefully a logical ordering among the various steps indicated on the lists we are not implying that they should necessarily be handled in numerical order. For instance, in a given instance it may be preferable to begin by an examination of objectives rather than of resources. Second, while the order between the steps is not so important it is indeed vital that there is feedback among all of them. For instance, it would clearly be suicidal to define a set of objectives without any reference to the operating environment. Third, it will be desirable at many junctures in the planning process – especially if it relates to an LDC – to include an estimate of the reliability and likely error margins of data employed.

Of the two checklists presented, Checklist A relates to the commitment decision. Before a serious planning effort for an operation in any given country can be undertaken it seems logical to assume that a commitment decision of some kind has to be made, based on a preliminary analysis of various candidate countries. Assuming this has been done, Checklist B provides guidelines for the initial marketing plan of the new international venture. The word 'initial' is admittedly vague; the appropriate time horizon in short-term planning will depend on type of product, extent of the commitment made, the financial strength of the firm, and other variables. Typically, the initial plan would comprise a year.

Checklist A: the commitment decision

1. Reasons to enter markets abroad
    11. Domestic market saturation
        (follow international product life cycle)
    12. Greater profitability
        (margin greater and/or strong demand)
    13. Preempt competition
    14. Excess liquidity
    15. Going international as means of growth preferable to product diversification, acquisitions, etc. at home
    16. Better utilization of current resources and differential advantage (capitalizing on synergy)
    17. Temporary overcapacity or excess inventory
2. Own resources
    21. Domestic operations 'under control'
        (going international rarely a good escape from domestic problems)

22. Sources of differential advantage:
    221 cost leadership
    222 manpower skills
    223 patents
    224 high liquidity
    225 marketing knowhow
3. Own objectives and philosophy (see also Reading 1)
    31. Growth rate
    32. Means of growth (growth in current products vs unrelated products, finance growth from within, attitude to acquisitions)
    33. Desirable sources of differential advantage
    34. Profitability, return on investment required
    35. Risk preferences
    36. Liquidity preferences
4. Type of country preferred
    41. Industrialized West, Japan
    42. LDC
    43. East block

Predictability, relatively low risk, excellent infrastructure, firm-to-firm transactions, relative absence of government intervention in individual transactions, stiff competition and moderate to good profits are signposts of the industrialized democracies. The LDCs typically evidence lower predictability; fairly high risk, poor infrastructure, high rates of inflation, a dual economy (large primitive, smaller modern sector), frequent government intervention in individual transactions, an environment of regulations which is somewhat flexible (negotiated concessions, tariff exemptions, etc.), modest competition, good to excellent profit perspectives to firms really understanding local conditions, and the challenge of contributing to human welfare more than elsewhere. East Block countries are highly unpredictable until a contract is signed but thereafter traditionally very reliable trading partners, they offer low after-sales risk, poor infrastructure (but distribution is the buyer's problem), firm-to-state transactions, no contact with end consumers, great demands for credit, a highly legalistic bureaucracy, typically either very heavy or almost no competition (you are the chosen instrument), somewhat unpredictable profitability (especially due to impossibility of predicting pre-contract selling costs), at least in the past high risks of piracy or grossly insufficient compensation for patents, designs and other industrial property rights, interest thus far essentially in industrial products and technical knowhow.

Some firms prefer to limit their initial search to countries where English or some other world language is widely spoken in business circles.

5. Specific country analyses

Unless there are special circumstances pointing to a given country, several candidate nations of the type preferred should be separately examined by means of a comparative framework such as that indicated below.

51. International environment
    511. Relations between home office country and country X
    512. Tariffs in country X
    513. Non-tariff barriers
    514. Currency controls
    515. Transportation costs
52. Local marketing environment
    521. Government stability
    522. Predictability of public policy
    523. Economic development, growth rate, development policies
    524. Sensitivity to business cycles, rate of inflation
    525. Government controls
        5251. Regulation of competitive practices
        5252. State marketing bodies
        5253. Health and safety
        5254. Product labeling, standardization
    526. Local business culture
        5261. Philosophy of competition and cooperation
        5262. Extent of cartelization
        5263. Respect for contracts
        5264. Business ethics
    527. Marketing infrastructure
        5271. Data availability and reliability
        5272. Marketing research agencies
        5273. Literacy
        5274. Advertising media
        5275. Advertising agencies
        5276. Public warehousing facilities
        5277. Extent and reliability of postal and telephone systems
        5278. Transportation facilities and costs

53. Market structure and demand analysis
    Re market structure details, see Reading 1
    531. Consumer buying behavior
    532. Distributors and margins
    533. Price range
    534. Product variations
    535. Competitors by size and type
    536. Competitive strategies
    537. Potential competition
    538. Local stage of product life cycle
    539. Market potential, short and long term
54. Financial estimates
    541. Short term
        5411. Investment need
        5412. Sales volume
        5413. Profitability, return on investment
    542. Long term

Checklist B: the initial marketing plan

It is essential that a plan incorporate the general assumptions and specific forecasts on which it is based. It is also essential that the plan – especially an initial one – be prepared in written form. Without these essentials there is no built-in signal system for if and when the plan needs to be revised, nor can a plan lacking in these prerequisites rationally be used as an instrument of delegation, coordination and evaluation of managerial performance.

If there is anything behavioral science has proven it is that, in Western cultures at least, enthusiastic execution of decisions presupposes some degree of involvement in the preceding decision-making process. Thus, planning cannot be simply delegated to a staff specialist in an obscure corner of the organization. Line executives will rarely have the time to do much of the data-gathering job; however, it is essential that they regularly partake in the actual shaping of the plan.

For the sake of simplicity we shall assume that the decision has been made to begin marketing operations in an LDC on a modest scale (no local production). Once an ongoing operation has been established the preparation of a marketing plan would be similar to that of making a domestic marketing plan; the main difference would be the incorporation of matters involving relationships with headquarters and any operations in third countries.

10. Objectives
  101. Sales volume expected during initial period
  102. Profitability, return on investment
       Note: the larger the scale of operations, the more likely negative profits during a build-up period.
  103. Permissible risk exposure
  104. Going in for a fast profit and then leave vs aiming for a lasting commitment
  105. Philosophy on ownership
  106. Complete adaptation vs acting as local change agent
  107. Data feedback for future decisions
       Test marketing or other marketing research, acquisition of data to determine desirability and form of long-term commitment – all the while keeping costs of data generation and analysis in mind.
  108. Justification of local objectives in terms of overall company objectives

20. International environment
    See Checklist A item 51.

30. Local marketing environment
  301. See Checklist A item 52.
  302. Local government view of our kind of product
  303· Could we – and should we – obtain favored treatment from the government?

40. Market structure and demand analysis
  401. See Checklist A item 53.
  402. Detailed industry and company sales forecast

50. Resources
  501. Expected sources of differential advantage (See Checklist A item 22)
  502. Local validity of own patents and trademarks
  503. Availability of company personnel with prior local experience
  504. Tasks to be performed by us, tasks to be contracted out
       Marketing research, advertising, distribution may all be contracted out, if desired, given sufficient local marketing infrastructure.
  505. Available sources of supply relative to expected sales volume. Supply from headquarters or from other subsidiaries or from outside firms. Adequacy of sources and their ability to adjust to possible fluctuations in demand.

60. Mode of entry
    See Reading 24
70. Strategy
    701. Overall concept (Gestalt) of our strategy
        Strategy should be explicitly related to local objectives and to our notion of differential advantage. Include definition of market niche, if nichemanship is sought. Deluxe image vs mass marketer. Low profile vs beating the drum, etc.
    702. Rationale for contemplated differentiation from domestic strategy, if any
        Such deviations are often inevitable or desirable. As they do lessen synergy their justification should, however, be made explicit.
    703. Homogenization and heterogenization of local demand
    704. Marketing mix implications of strategy
        7041. Product
            Models to be marketed, modifications for local market (if any)
        7042. Price
            Skimming vs penetration. Price relative to current and potential competition. Price relative to our policies elsewhere. If price very high relative to domestic due to tariffs, freight, high distributor margins, etc., justify belief that it will be accepted locally. If planned local price is very low, contemplate side-effects on company operations elsewhere.
        7043. Promotion and intelligence
            Budget, theme, media, timing. If major resources to be committed, include plan for measurement of promotion effectiveness. Feedback from the marketplace, marketing research.
        7044. Distribution
            70441. See above under 60. Mode of entry
            70442. Functions to be performed
            70443. Margins, promotional allowances, if any
            70444. Short term vs long term commitments
                Note possible need for future flexibility
        7045. Post-transaction service
            70451. Service and warranty system
            70452. Spare parts

7046. Trust
Plan for the build-up of goodwill and customer confidence. The larger the operation and the longer its time perspective the more important is trust. See also Reading 1.

80. Headquarters services and coordination
801. Manpower allocation at headquarters and overseas
802. Organizational adjustments at HQ, if any
803. Identification of areas of HQ direction, assistance and consultation. Areas of local autonomy.
804. Reporting arrangements
805. Pricing and other policies for intra-company transactions

90. Schedules
901. Step-by-step timing of activities and the attainment of subtargets
PERT or flow diagram techniques may be helpful here.
902. Budgeting
9021. Master budget
9022. Projected profit and loss statements for each reporting period
9023. Proforma balance sheets for each reporting period
9024. Cash flow in each reporting period

100. Action potential at the end of the planning period
This is an advance audit of operational performance, assuming full realization of the plan. At the end of the period a post-audit should be undertaken, including a re-evaluation of the commitment decision and its future implications. These management audits should comprise items of the type indicated below:

1001. Resource profile, including personnel skills
1002. Differential advantage
1003. Data about the market structure
1004. Trust and goodwill
1005. Patents and trade-marks
1006. Standing arrangements with suppliers or customers
1007. Competitive position
1008. Performance relative to budget
1009. Performance relative to other aspects of objectives and plan

110. Contingency plan
Contingency planning is the stand-by plan for emergencies. It may be a strike, an import prohibition, a currency

devaluation, failure to obtain local financing if planned for, or simply the fact that some vital assumption about the future might be mistaken. Take a cue from the military, and put down some ideas on how to meet likely contingencies.

120. Long-term plan

Assuming that the substance of the initial plan will be realized, the long-term plan should at least present a sketch of the next three to five years. In abbreviated form the framework suggested above would be equally suited to the long-term plan.

34 P. F. Drucker

Marketing and Economic Development

Excerpt from P. F. Drucker, 'Marketing and economic development', *Journal of Marketing*, vol. 22, 1958, pp. 252–259

Marketing is generally the most neglected area in the economic life of developing countries. It is manufacturing or construction which occupies the greatest attention in these economies. Yet marketing holds a key position in these countries. Its effectiveness as an engine of economic development with special emphasis on its ability to develop rapidly much-needed entrepreneurial and managerial skills needs hardly any elaboration. Because it provides a systematic discipline in a vital area of economic activity it fills one of the greatest needs of a developing economy.

Marketing as a business discipline

A distinguished pioneer of marketing, Charles Coolidge Parlin, was largely instrumental in developing marketing as a systematic business discipline: in teaching us how to go about, in an orderly purposeful and planned way, to find and create customers; to identify and define markets; to create new ones and promote them; to integrate customers' needs, wants and preferences, and the intellectual and creative capacity and skills of an industrial society, towards the design of new and better products and of new distributive concepts and processes. It is in marketing that we satisfy individual and social values, needs, and wants – be it through producing goods, supplying services, fostering innovation, or creating satisfaction. Marketing has its focus on the customer, that is, on the individual making decisions within a social structure and within a personal and social value system. Marketing is thus the process through which economy is integrated into society to serve human needs.

The role of marketing

Marketing occupies a critical role in respect to underdeveloped 'growth' countries. Indeed marketing is the most important 'multiplier' of such development. It is in itself in every one of these areas the least developed, the most backward part of the economic system. Its development, above all others, makes possible economic integration and the fullest utilization of whatever assets and productive capacity an economy already possesses. It mobilizes latent economic energy. It contributes to the greatest needs: that for the rapid development of entrepreneurs and managers, and at the same time it may be the easiest area of managerial work to get going. The reason is that, thanks to men like Parlin, it is the most systematized and, therefore, the most learnable and the most teachable of all areas of business management and entrepreneurship.

International and interracial inequality

For the first time in man's history the whole world is united and unified. This may seem a strange statement in view of the conflicts and threats of suicidal wars that scream at us from every headline. But conflict has always been with us. What is new is that today all of mankind shares the same vision, the same objective, the same goal, the same hope, and believes in the same tools. This vision might, in gross over-simplification, be called 'industrialization'.

It is the belief that it is possible for man to improve his economic lot through systematic, purposeful, and directed effort – individually as well as for an entire society. It is the belief that we have the tools at our disposal – the technological, the conceptual, and the social tools – to enable man to raise himself, through his own efforts. And this is an irreversible new fact. It has been made so by these true agents of revolution in our times: the new tools of communication – the dirt road, the truck, and the radio, which have penetrated even the farthest, most isolated, and most primitive community.

This is new, and cannot be emphasized too much and too often. It is both a tremendous vision and a tremendous danger in that catastrophe must result if it cannot be satisfied, at least to a modest degree. But at the same time we have a new, unprecedented danger, that of international and interracial inequality. What we are engaged in today is essentially a race between the promise of economic development and the threat of international worldwide class war. The economic development is the opportunity of this age. The class war is the danger. Both are new. Both are indeed so new that most of us do not even see them as yet. But they are the essential economic realities of this industrial age of ours. And whether we shall realize the opportunity or succumb to danger will largely decide not only the economic future of this world – it may largely decide its spiritual, its intellectual, its political, and its social future.

Significance of marketing

Marketing is central in this new situation. For marketing is one of our most potent levers to convert the danger into the opportunity. To understand this we must ask: what do we mean by 'underdeveloped'?

The first answer is, of course, that we mean areas of very low income. But income is, after all, a result. It is a result first of extreme agricultural overpopulation in which the great bulk of the people have to find a living on the land which, as a result, cannot even produce enough food to feed them, let alone produce a surplus. It is certainly a result of low productivity. And both, in a vicious circle, mean that there is not enough capital for investment and very low productivity of what is being invested – owing largely to misdirection of investment into unessential and unproductive channels.

The essential aspect of an 'underdeveloped' economy and the factor, the absence of which keeps it 'underdeveloped', is the inability to organize economic efforts and energies, to bring together resources, wants, and capacities, and so to convert a self-limiting static system into creative, self-generating organic growth. And this is where marketing comes in.

Lack of development in underdeveloped countries

First, in every 'underdeveloped' country, marketing is the most underdeveloped – or the least developed – part of the economy, if only because of the strong, pervasive prejudice against the 'middleman'. As a result, these countries are stunted by inability to make effective use of the little they have. Marketing might by itself go far toward changing the entire economic tone of the existing system – without any change in methods of production, distribution of population, or of income.

It would make the producers capable of producing marketable products by providing them with standards, with quality demands and with specifications for their product. It would make the product capable of being brought to markets instead of perishing on the way. And it would make the consumer capable of discrimination, that is, of obtaining the greatest value for his very limited purchasing power.

In every one of these countries, marketing profits are characteristically low. Indeed the people engaged in marketing barely eke out a subsistence living. And 'mark-ups' are minute by our standards. But marketing costs are outrageously high. The waste in distribution and marketing if only from spoilage, or from the accumulation of unsaleable inventories that clog the shelves for years, has to be seen to be believed. And marketing service is by and large all but non-existent.

What is needed in any 'growth' country to make economic development realistic, and at the same time produce a vivid demonstration of what economic development can produce, is a marketing system: a system of physical distribution; a financial system to make possible the distribution of goods; and actual marketing, that is, an actual system of integrating wants, needs, and purchasing power of the consumer with capacity and resources of production.

This need is largely masked today because marketing is so often confused with the traditional 'trader and merchant' of which every one of these countries has more than enough. It would be one of our most important contributions to the development of 'underdeveloped' countries to get across the fact that marketing is something quite different.

It would be basic to get across the triple function of marketing: the function of crystallizing and directing demand for maximum productive effectiveness and efficiency; the function of guiding production purposefully toward maximum consumer satisfaction and consumer value; and the function of creating discrimination that then gives rewards to those who really contribute excellence; and that then also penalize the monopolist, the slothful, or those who only want to take but do not want to contribute or to risk.

Utilization by the entrepreneur

Secondly, marketing is also the most easily accessible 'multiplier' of managers and entrepreneurs in an 'underdeveloped' growth area. And managers and entrepreneurs are the foremost need of these countries. In the first place, 'economic development' is not a force of nature. It is the result of the action – the purposeful, responsible, risk-taking action – of men as entrepreneurs and managers. Certainly it is the entrepreneur and manager who alone can convey to the people of these countries an understanding of what economic development means and how it can be achieved.

Marketing can convert latent demand into effective demand. It cannot, by itself, create purchasing power. But it can uncover and channel all purchasing power that exists. It can, therefore, rapidly create the conditions for a much higher level of economic activity than existed before, can create the opportunities for the entrepreneur. It then can create the stimulus for the development of modern, responsible, professional management by creating opportunity for the producer who knows how to plan, how to organize, how to lead people, and how to innovate.

In most of these countries, markets are of necessity very small. They are too small to make it possible to organize distribution for a single-product line in any effective manner. As a result, without a marketing organization, many products for which there is an adequate demand at a reasonable price cannot be distributed; or worse, they can be produced and distributed only under monopoly conditions. A marketing system is needed which serves as the joint and common channel for many producers if any of them is to be able to come into existence. This means in effect that a marketing system in the 'underdeveloped' countries is the creator of small business, is the only way in which a man of vision and daring can become a businessman and an entrepreneur himself. This is thereby also the only way in which a true middle class can develop in the countries in which the habit of investment in productive enterprise has still to be created.

Developer of standards

Thirdly, marketing in an 'underdeveloped' country is the developer of standards – of standards for product and service as well as of standards of conduct, of integrity, of reliability, of foresight, and of concern for the basic long-range impact of decisions on the customer, the supplier, the economy and the society.

Rather than making theoretical statements let me point to one illustration: the impact Sears, Roebuck has had on several countries of Latin America. To be sure, the countries of Latin America in which Sears operates – Mexico, Brazil, Cuba, Venezuela, Colombia and Peru – are not 'underdeveloped' in the same sense in which Indonesia or the Congo are 'underdeveloped'. Their average income, although very low by our standards, is at least two times, perhaps as much as four or five times, that of the truly 'underdeveloped' countries in which the bulk of mankind still live. Still, in every respect, except income level, these Latin American countries are at best 'developing'.

It is also true that Sears in these countries is not a 'low-price' merchandiser. It caters to the middle class in the richer of these countries, and to the upper middle class in the poorest of these countries. Incidentally, the income level of these groups is still lower than that of the worker in the industrial sector of our economy. Still Sears is a mass-marketer even in Colombia or Peru. What is perhaps even more important, it is applying in these 'underdeveloped' countries exactly the same policies and principles it applies in this country, carries substantially the same merchandise (although most of it is produced in the countries themselves), and applies the same concepts of marketing it uses in Indianapolis or Philadelphia. Its impact and experience are, therefore, a fair test of what marketing knowledge and marketing techniques can achieve.

The impact of this one American business which does not have more than a mere handful of stores in these countries and handles no more than a small fraction of the total retail business of these countries is truly amazing. In the first place, Sears' latent purchasing power has fast become actual purchasing power. Or, to put it less theoretically, people have begun to organize their buying and to go out for value in what they do buy.

Secondly, by the very fact that it builds one store in one city, Sears forces a revolution in retailing throughout the whole surrounding area. It forces a different attitude toward the customer, toward the store clerk, toward the supplier, and toward the merchandise itself. It forces other retailers to adopt modern methods of pricing, of inventory control, of training, and of window display.

The greatest impact Sears has had, however, is in the multiplication of new industrial business for which Sears creates a marketing channel. Because it has to sell goods manufactured in these countries rather than import them (if only because of foreign exchange restrictions), Sears has been instrumental in getting established literally hundreds of new manufacturers making goods which, a few years ago, could not be made in the country let alone be sold in adequate quantity. Simply to satisfy its own marketing needs, Sears has had to insist on standards of workmanship, quality, and delivery – that is, on standards of production management, of technical management, and above all of the management of people – which, in a few short years, have advanced the art and science of management in these countries by at least a generation.

I hardly need to add that Sears is not in Latin America for

reasons of philanthropy, but because it is good and profitable business with extraordinary growth potential. In other words, Sears is in Latin America because marketing is the major opportunity in a 'growth economy' – precisely because its absence is a major economic gap and the greatest need.

Marketing the catalyst

Marketing is obviously not a cure-all, not a paradox. It is only one thing we need. But it answers a critical need. Indeed without marketing as the hinge on which to turn, economic development will almost have to take the totalitarian form. A totalitarian system can be defined economically as one in which economic development is being attempted without marketing. Indeed as one in which marketing is suppressed. Precisely because it first looks at the values and wants of the individual, and because it then develops people to act purposefully and responsibly – that is, because of its effectiveness in developing a free economy – marketing is suppressed in a totalitarian system. If we want economic development in freedom and responsibility, we have to build it on the development of marketing.

In the new and unprecedented world we live in, a world which knows both a new unity of vision and growth and a new and most dangerous cleavage, marketing has a special and central role to play. This role goes beyond 'getting the stuff out the back door'; beyond 'getting the most sales with the least cost'; beyond 'the optimal integration of our values and wants as customers, citizens, and persons, with our productive resources and intellectual achievements' – the role marketing plays in a developed society.

In a developing economy, marketing is, of course, all of this. But in addition, in an economy that is striving to break the age-old bondage of man to misery, want, and destitution, marketing is also the catalyst for the transmutation of latent resources into actual resources, of desires into accomplishments, and the development of responsible economic leaders and informed economic citizens.

Further Reading

A high-quality source of many publications in international marketing is *Business International*, 12–14 Chemin Rieu, Geneva and 757 Third Avenue, New York. Excellent surveys of international markets are continuously prepared by the *Economist Intelligence Unit*, 27 St James' Place, London. The UN, the OECD and the EEC have many useful publications. The ministries of commerce (in the UK, the Department of Trade and Industry) and the consular services of most countries will furnish advice about governmental services and sources of information and may also be helpful in handling specific trade enquiries. For major transactions and commitments even seasoned executives request the advice of commercial banks and international consulting or accounting firms.

For further reading the journals and books from which our Readings were selected, as well as the works referenced in the Readings, are recommended in addition to the writings listed below.

R. E. Baldwin, *Nontariff Distortions of International Trade*, Brookings Institute, Washington, 1970.

R. Bartels, *Comparative Marketing: Wholesaling in Fifteen Countries*, Irwin, Illinois, 1963.

H. Deschampsneufs, *Marketing Overseas*, Pergamon, London, 1967.

S. W. Dunn, *International Handbook of Advertising*, McGraw-Hill, New York, 1964.

D. Evans, ed., *Destiny or Delusion: Britain and the Common Market*, Gollancz, London, 1971.

GATT, *A Bibliography of Market Surveys by Products and Countries*, GATT, Geneva, 1967.

W. P. Glade and others, *Marketing in a Developing Nation*, Heath Lexington Books, Massachusetts, 1970.

E. T. Hall, 'The silent language in overseas business', *Harvard Business Review*, May–June 1960.

T. R. Heatley, *How to Start Selling Consumer Goods Abroad*, Business Books, London, 1969.

R. L. Kramer, *International Marketing*, South-Western Publishing, Ohio, 1970.

L. L. Lewis, ed., *International Trade Handbook*, Dartnell, Chicago, 1965

G. E. Miracle and G. S. Albaum, *International Marketing Management*, Irwin, Illinois, 1970.

R. Moyer and S. C. Hollander, *Markets and Marketing in Developing Economics*, spons. by the American Marketing Association, Irwin, Illinois, 1968.

D. F. Mulvihill, *Domestic Marketing Systems Abroad: An Annotated Bibliography*, Kent State University Press, Ohio, 1967.

National Industrial Conference Board, *Policies and Problems in Piggyback Exporting*, The Conference Board, New York, 1968.

S. Pisar, *Guidelines for Transactions Between East and West*, McGraw-Hill, 1970.

Reader's Digest Association, *A Survey of Europe Today*, RDA, London, 1970.

K. Simmonds and H. Smith, 'The first export order; a marketing innovation', *British Journal of Marketing*, Summer, 1968.

H. B. Thorelli, 'The multinational corporation as a change agent', *Southern Journal of Business*, July, 1966.

G. Wills and R. Hayhurst, 'Marketing in socialist societies', *British Journal of Marketing*, Spring, 1971.

M. Y. Yoshino, *The Japanese Marketing System*, MIT Press, Massachusetts, 1971.

Acknowledgements

Permission to reproduce the readings in this volume is acknowledged to the following sources:

2. Her Majesty's Stationery Office
3. OECD Development Centre, F. Kahnert, P. Richards, A. Stoutjesdijk and P. Thomopulos
4. *Columbia Journal of World Business* and J. A. Ramsey
5. *American Review of East–West Trade* and M. W. Duncan
6. British Institute of International and Comparative Law, and D. Thompson and M. S. Massel
7. *Business International*
8. *Columbia Journal of World Business* and C. D. Edwards
9. European Communities Press and Information Service, Washington and E. M. J. A. Sassen
10. *Journal of Development Studies* and L. E. Preston
11. *Journal of Marketing*
12. McGraw-Hill, G. Katona, B. Strumpel and E. Zahn
13. *Business Horizons*, W. T. Anderson, Jr. and L. K. Sharpe
14. *Journal of Marketing*, H. A. Lipson and D. F. Lamont
15. *Journal of Marketing Research* and R. Moyer
16. *Journal of Marketing* and L. T. Wells, Jr
17. *European Business* and W. J. Keegan
18. *British Industry Week* and P. Stone
19. *International Marketing*, P. R. Cateora and J. M. Hess
20. *Business Week*
21. *Columbia Journal of World Business* and J. K. Ryans, Jr
22. *Management Japan* and Y. Ikeda
23. *Harvard Business Review* and J. K. Sweeney
24. *Business International*
25. Organization for Economic Cooperation and Development
26. *Business Europe*
27. American Management Association and G. Beeth
28. *Columbia Journal of World Business* and W. J. Keegan
29. *European Business* and P. d'Antin
30. *Journal of Marketing* and R. J. Aylmer
31. *European Business* and J. S. Shulman
32. *Harvard Business Review* and R. D. Buzzell
34. *Journal of Marketing* and P. F. Drucker

Special thanks are due the authors represented in this volume who gracefully consented to have excerpts and abridgements of their original contribution made in the interest of the kind of compact treatment desirable in a readings collection of broad coverage.

We are also grateful to Mr Alan P. Strom who assisted materially in the selection of articles.

Author Index

Adler, L., 339
Aharoni, Y., 305, 311
Aliber, R., 213, 221
Almond, G. A., 137, 145
Anderson, W., 146–53
Ansoff, H. I., 40
d'Antin, P., 290–300
Aylmer, R. J., 301–11, 331, 339

Bahrdt, H. P., 142, 145
Bauer, P. T., 120, 128
Beeth, G., 273–9
Bouhebent, A., 337, 339
Buzzell, R. D., 325–39

Castellano, C., 328, 339
Cateora, P., 209–21
Chenery, H., 169–71, 179
Clee, H., 247–8, 256

Drucker, P. F., 349–55
Duncan, M. W., 64–70

Edwards, C. D., 89–103
Elinder, E., 228, 236
Erickson, L. G., 172, 179

Fatt, A. C., 228, 236
Faucett, J. G., 176, 178, 179

Galbraith, J. K., 147, 153
Gerunsky, W., 334, 339
Gilbert, M., 179
Giragosian, N. H., 339
Goldstrucker, J. L., 339
Goldthorpe, J. H., 141, 145
Gomberg, W., 145
Gosser, D. M., 177, 179

Hamilton, R. F., 143, 145
Helleiner, G. K., 120, 128
Heller, N., 329, 339
Hess, J., 209–21
Hirsch, S., 182, 191
Hufbauer, G. C., 185, 191

Ikeda, Y., 237–43

Jures, E. A., 142, 145

Kastens, M. L., 173, 179
Katona, G., 135–45
Keegan, W. J., 195–203, 283–9
Kelley, E. J., 146, 153
Kesting, H., 142, 145
Kurtis, C., 229, 236

Lamont, D. F., 154–61
Lenormand, J. M., 229, 236
Levitt, T., 40
Lipson, H. A., 154–61
Lockwood, D., 141, 145

Maizels, A., 167, 174, 179
Massel, S., 71–82
Moyer, R., 162–79

Ord, L. C., 138, 145

Papitz, H., 142, 145
Peacock, A. T., 177, 179
Preston, L. E., 116–28
Pryor, M. H., 325, 339

Ramsey, J. A., 58–63
Rosenberg, M., 137, 145
Ryans, J. K., 227–36

Sassen, C. M. J. A., 104–15
di Scipio, A., 247–8, 256
Seakwood, H. J., 211, 221
Sharpe, L., 146–53
Shostak, A. B., 145
Shulman, J. S., 312–21
Stein, H., 213, 221
Stone, P., 204–8
Stoutjesdijk, A., 47–57
Strumpel, B., 135–45
Sweeney, J. K., 247–56

Thorelli, H. B., 11–40, 129–32, 340–48

Verba, S., 137, 145

Weissman, G., 325, 339
Wells, L. T., 180–91
Whyte, W. H., 147

Williams, C. R., 329, 339
Wright, J. S., 339

Yamey, B. S., 120, 128

Zahn, E., 135–45

Subject Index

Advertising, 227–36, 329–31, 337
　agencies, 229–31
　collective, 264
　consumer categories, 233–6
　in LDCs, 159–60
　media, 230–32
　product, 232–3
Agent, *see* Distributor
American Selling Price, 73
Andean Group, *see* LAFTA
Anti-dumping, 73, 83–6, 94
　duty, 83–5
　East Bloc, 85
　EEC code, 83–6
Antitrust, 89–103, 104–15
　dual liability, 99–101
　joint venture, 93–5
　jurisdiction, 95–7, 99–101
　patents, 92–3
　price maintenance, 98
　restraint of trade, 91–5
　Sherman Act, 99
　Treaty of Rome, 98–9
　US law explained, 90–91
Apartheid, 129–32
　border industries, 129–30

Bilateral trade, *see* Trade
Boycott, 77
Brand, 264, 334–5
'Buy American' Policy, 78–9

CACM, 49–50, 54, 55
Cartels, 58–63, 82, 91–2, 94–8, 131
Cash flow planning, 347
Central planning, *see* East Bloc,
　LDC, Organization
Channels, *see* Distribution
Commitment decision, 245–56,
　341–4
Common economies, 28, 36–7,
　286–7
Communication, 15–16, 341
　regional, 55–6
Comparative marketing, 13
Competition, 29–33, 342–4

Competition policy, 89–103,
　104–15, 316–17
Consignment, 272
Consumer
　credit, 158
　style of life, 146–53, *see also*
　Socioculture
Control, *see* Market;
　Government; Organization
Convertibility, 222–3, 315–16
Cooperative agreements, 58–63
　East–West trade, 58–63
　inter-nation, 266–7
　marketing, 60–63
　tourism, *see also* Cartels, 59–60
Counterculture, 151–2
Credit, 69, 158
　competitive, 65
　under inflation, 224–6; *see also*
　Hire-purchase; Installment
　buying
Culture, *see* Socioculture
Currency, 223–4, 314–16
　regional, 51; *see also* Exchange
Customer
　orientation, 23–5
　satisfaction, 25–6, 29; *see also*
　Consumer

Decision-making, 25, 344
Demand, 29–32, 38–9, 345–8,
　352–3
　analysis, 133
　patterns, 163–6
Developing country, *see* LDC
Differential advantage, 30, 32,
　38–9, 41, 288–9
Distribution, 31, 213–14, 246,
　253–4, 257–9, 261–4, 270–72,
　346, 352–5
　Japanese trading companies,
　237–43
Distributor
　contract, 277–9
　goodwill, 276–7
　selection criteria, 273–6

Subject Index 367

Domain, 28–9
Dual economy, 88, 177–8
Dumping, see Anti-dumping
Duty, 313–14; see also Tariff; Anti-dumping

EAEC, 49–50
ECSC, 110–11
EEC, 15, 43–6, 72, 83–6, 98–9, 102–3, 104–15, 123, 162, 304
 Anti-Dumping Code (features), 83–6
 antitrust, rules of competition, 104–15
 exclusive dealing, 107–8, 110–15
 mergers, 108–10
 Treaty of Rome, 98–9, 102, 105, 109–15
EFTA, 43–4
East Africa
 Currency Board, 55
 Development Bank, 53
East Bloc, Eastern Europe, 58–63, 64–70, 342
East–West trade, 58–63, 64–70
 cooperative agreements, 58–63
 credit, 70
 demonstrations, exhibits, seminars, shows, 67–8
 exchange shortage, 65
 FTO, 65–8
 joint ventures, 58–63
 LDCs, 60
 marketing, 60–63
 reciprocity, 66–7
 technology sales, 64, 68–70
 tourism, 59–60
 Turn-key project, 69
 Union Carbide case, 64–70
Ecologic marketing, 25–39, 340
Economic
 cooperation, 47–9
 development, 58–63, 129–30, 349–55
 integration, 47–9, 51–5

Economies of scale, 183–4, 187
 regional, 47
Entrepreneur, 352–3
Environment, 135–45, 340, 343
 inter-nation, 36, 343
 layers of, 33–6
 local marketing, 35–6, 343
 socioculture, 135–45
Equity participation
 East–West, 58, 62–3
Exchange, 156–7
 controls, 156–7, 223, 314–16
 East–West trade, 65
 rates, 214–16
 shortage, 65
Exclusive dealing, 107–8, 110–15
Export controls
 'voluntary', 77
Export marketing
 cooperation, 261–9
 foreign partners, 266–7
 groups, see Marketing
Export sales, 257–60
Expropriation, 316

FTO, 65–8
Finance, financing, 214–16; see also Credit; Exchange; Inflation
Foreign exchange, see Exchange
Foreign trade, see International marketing

GATT, 36, 83, 85, 213
Government
 agencies, 126–7
 competition policy, 89–103, 316–17
 controls, 89–90, 313–14
 marketing agencies, 65–8, 119–21, 125–8, 160
 officials, 253
 regulation, 35–6, 343
 stability, 316; see also Market control

Headquarters, *see* Organization
Health regulations, 74–6
Heterogenization, 15, 346
Hire purchase, 158
Homogenization, 15, 38, 346

Import permits, 76–7
Import substitution, 56, 164–5, 168–71
Income elasticity, 166–71
Industrial marketing, 64–70, 247–56, 273–9
Industrialization, 47, 51–2
Inflation, 121–3, 214–16, 222–6
  hedges against, 223–6, 314–15
Infrastructure, *see* Marketing
Input–Output, 176–7
Installment buying, 145, 158
International marketing, 11–13
Interpersonal relations, 318–20
Intracompany pricing, *see* Transfer pricing
Inventory, 277–8
Investment
  regional policies, 53, 56–7
Invisible trade barriers, 36, 71–82; *see also* Trade barriers, 35

Japanese trading companies, 237–43
Joint ventures, 58–63, 93–5, 260, 317–18
  antitrust, 93–4

LAFTA, 49–55
  Andean Group, 54
LDCs, 16–17, 27, 37, 87–8, 341–2, 349–55
  as exporters, 185–6
  defined, 154
  East–West trade, 60
  economic cooperation, 47–56
  market analysis, 162–79
  market control, 116–28
  market infrastructure, 154–61, 341–3
  role of marketing, 349–55

Labelling, 75
Labor, 250, 318–19
Languages, 156, 254–5
Legal environment, 33–6, 89–103, 116–28, 338, 343, 347
Licensing, 92–3, 259–60
Local content, 316
Low profile strategy, 346

MAGHREB, 49, 50, 53
Management, *see* Organization
Management audit, 347
Manpower management
  conflicts, 314
  expatriots, 254–6
  managers, 318–20
  nationals, 254–6
  sales force, 253–4
Margin, 215–16
Market
  defined, 117
  plan, 323–4, 340–48
  regional, 49–56
  regulations, 130–31, 156
  selection, 264–6
  services, 346–7
  structure, 14–15, 21, 26, 31, 87–8, 133–4, 340–48
  testing, 294–300; *see also* Socioculture
Market analysis, 135–45, 146–53, 154–60, 162–79, 180–86, 201–2, 264–6
  income elasticity, 166–71
  Input–output analysis, 176–7
  regression analysis, 173–6
  segmentation, 155–6, 162, 189–90
Market control
  appraisal, 127–8
  government agencies, 95–7, 119–23, 125–8, 156–60
  inflation, 121–3
  product quality, 123–4
  public corporation, 125–7
  redistribution, 124–5

Subject Index 369

Market control–*contd*
  South Africa, 130–32
  welfare goals, 125
Market structure, *see* Market
Marketing
  channels, *see* Distribution
  concepts, 23–39, 284–5
  cost savings, 326–7, 329
  East–West, 59–63
  groups, export, 258–9, 261–9
  in LDCs, 159–60, 349–55
  infrastructure, 35–6, 146–61, 333–4
  mix, 28, 32, 346–7
  multinational, 325–39
  plan, 344–8
  risks, 266–7
  social changes in US, 146–53
  standardization, 325–39
  timing, 337–8; *see also*
    Piggyback strategy
Marketing research, *see also*
  Market analysis, 30, 35–6
Marketing strategy, *see* Strategy
Marketization, 119–20
Mergers, 108–10
Middleman, *see* Distributor
Monopoly, 65, 104, 131
  FTO, 65
Most favored nation, 64–5
Motivation, 17
Multinational firm, *see*
  Organization
Multinational marketing, *see*
  Marketing

Nationalism, 16
Niche, nichemanship, 28, 37–8, 346
Non-tariff barriers, *see* Trade barriers

Organization, 17, 27–9, 281–2, 347
  central planning, 64–8
  centralized, 28, 283–5, 290–300

conflicts, 314
decentralized, 285–6, 294, 301–11, 312
Export Marketing Groups, 261–9
multinational, 283–9, 290–300, 301–11, 312–21
structure, 283–9

Participation, *see* Equity participation
Patents, 73–4, 92–3
Personnel, *see* Manpower management
Piggyback, 258, 270–72
  defined, 270
Planning, international agencies, 56–7; *see also* Central planning
Political environment, 16, 41–2, 87–8, 154–61, 350, 355
Price, pricing, 120–21, 209–21, 337
  cost, 209–16
  escalation, 216–21
  in LDCs, 160, 353–4
  maintenance, 98
  objectives, 209
  transfer, 211–12, 312–21
  under inflation, 223–6, 314–15
Producer orientation, 23
Product
  quality, 123–4
  management, 285–6, 290–300
  manager, 290–97
  selection, 262–6
  simplification, 204–8, 304
  strategy, 195–200, 292–3, 297–8
Product life cycle, 134, 180–91, 335–6, 341, 344
Productivity, 30
Profit, profitability, 30
  centers, 286, 312
  distortions, 319
  repatriation, 315
Promotion, 261–4

Public corporation, 125–7
Public relations, 318

Quota, 85, 104

Reciprocity, 67
Regional markets, 47–57
  economic integration, 47–8, 51–5
  economies of scale, 47
  import substitution, 56
  industrialization, 49, 51–5
  investment policies, 53, 57
  trade, intra-regional, 49–51, 54–5
  transport, 54–5; *see also* EEC
Research and Development, 45
Resources, 345
Risk, 266, 341–3

Safety rules, 74–5
Sales force, *see* Manpower management
Socioculture, 135–45, 334–5
  changes in marketing, 146–53
  class differences, 139–45
  installment buying, 145, 158
  leisure, 144
  trust and self-reliance, 33, 136–40
Specialization, 45
Standardization, 326–31
Strategy, 14–15, 21, 27–9, 32–5, 193–208, 326–7, 340, 346–7
  defined, 32
  market entry, 247–56, 261–72, 326–7
  price escalation, 216–20
  product, 198–200
  selection of, 201–3
  uniformity, 195–8
Structure, *see* Market, Organization
Style of life, *see* Consumer
Suboptimization, 284
  defined, 31
Subsidiaries, 286–8
Synergy, *see* Common Economies

TVA, 194, 219–20; *see also* Tax
Tariffs, 104, 212–13
  ad valorem, 73
  barrier, 71–82, 338
  concession, 52
  most favored nation, 64–5
Tax, 76, 212–13, 313–14
  regional systems, 53–4
  transfer, 50
  turnover, value-added, 194, 219–20; *see also* Tariffs
Technology sales, 64, 68–70
Timing, *see* Marketing
Tourism
  East–West, 59–60
Trade
  associations, 268–9
  bilateral, 65
  discrimination, 50
  free, 54
  intra-regional, 49–51, 54–5
  liberalization, 50–51
  regulation, 130–32
  shows, centers, 68, 275
Trade barriers, 71–82, 338
  anti-dumping laws, 73
  customs administration, 73
  government purchases, subsidies, 75–6
  health, safety rules, 74–5
  labeling, 75
  patents and trademarks, 73–4
  quotas and embargoes, 72, 96, 104
  taxes, *see* Tariffs, 76
Trademarks, 73–4
Trading companies, 67
  Japanese, 237–43
Transfer pricing, 83, 282, 312–21
  competitive advantage, 316–17
  inflation, 314–15
  intracompany, 211–12
  project distortions, 318–20
  public relations, 318
  taxes, 313–14

Transportation, 54–5
Treaty of Rome, *see* EEC
Trust, 33, 347
Turn-Key project, 69
Turnover tax, *see* Tax

UDEAC, 49–50, 53
UNCTAD, 54

Underdeveloped country, *see* LDC

Value added tax, *see* Tax

Webb-Pomerene Export Trade Act, US, 258
Welfare goals, 125

Country Index

For regional groupings such as EEC and LAFTA, see subject index.

Africa, 159
　Central, 51, 55
　East, 51, 55
Algeria, 53
America
　Central, 51, 54, 55
　South, 165, 353–5
Argentina, 54, 74, 185
Austria, 98

Belgium, 102, 196
Biafra, 155
Brazil, 54, 172, 178, 222–6, 315

Cameroon, 53
Canada, 89, 102, 138, 326
Central African Republic, 53
Chad, 53
China, 196
Congo (Brazzaville), 53
Cuba, 316
Czechoslovakia, 60, 85

Denmark, 98

Egypt, 124
El Salvador, 54
Europe
　Eastern, 58–62, 64–70, 85
　Western, 140, 144, 247–56, 285, 330

France, 254–5, 337–8

Gabon, 53
Germany, 61–2, 83, 98, 136–8, 140–43, 145, 270–72, 294–7, 337
Great Britain, see United Kingdom
Guatemala, 158

Holland, 11, 96, 98, 102, 139, 142–5

Honduras, 54
Hungary, 62

India, 154–6, 158, 160
Israel, 123
Italy, 129, 136–8, 327–8

Japan, 77, 102, 237–43

Kenya, 51, 53

Lebanon, 123

Mexico, 54, 154–5, 157, 159–60, 316, 318
Morocco, 53

New Zealand, 97
Nigeria, 154–5, 158, 206, 316

Poland, 62

Rumania, 62

Scandinavia, 62
South Africa, 129–32
Soviet Union, see USSR
Spain, 98, 197
Sweden, 37
Switzerland, 98, 102

Tanzania, 50, 51, 53
Tunisia, 53

Uganda, 50, 53
United Kingdom, 43–5, 98, 102, 137–8, 140–43, 197, 199, 205–7, 214, 249–53
USA, 59, 72–4, 87, 89–102, 136–40, 142–3, 146–53, 180–91, 197–8, 214, 284–5, 313
USSR, 62–3, 64, 67–9, 255

Venezuela, 316

West Germany, see Germany

Yugoslavia, 62–3

Country Index 375

Company Index

AEG, Germany, 327
Alliance de Constructeurs francaise de Machine-outils, France, 114
American Cyanamid, USA, 271–2
Armco, USA, 156
Associated Products (AP), USA, 271
S.A. Ateliers de Constructions Electriques de Charleroi (ACEC), Brussels, 114–15
Avis Rent-A-Car, USA, 196

Bamletts, UK, 207
Bantu Investment Corporation, South Africa, 129
Barnängens Tekniska Fabriker, Sweden, 270
Bosch, Germany, 327
Butyl Products, UK, 206

Campbell Soup Company, USA, 214
Candy, Italy, 327
Carnation, USA, 160
Caterpillar Tractor Company, USA, 275, 277
Chrysler Corporation, USA, 159, 197
Coca-Cola, USA, 14, 32, 33, 159, 196, 232, 290
Colgate Palmolive, USA, 200
Computer Machinery Corporation, USA, 247–56
Corn Products (CPC), USA, 222–6
Csepel Machine Tool Factory, Hungary, 58

Danube Iron Works, Hungary, 59
Datsun, Japan, 159
duPont, USA, 95

Eastman Kodak, USA, 290
Eimco Corporation, USA, 211

Ericsson Telephone Corporation, Sweden, 37
Esso, USA, 160, 199, 227, 229
Esso Petroleum, UK, 207

Fiat, Italy, 58, 62
Ford Motor Company, USA, 159
Frigidaire, Div. General Motors, USA, 328

General Electric Company, USA, 95, 334
General Electric Company, Ltd, UK 256
General Motors, USA, 159, 188
Gillette, USA, 271
Grey Advertising, USA, 228

Hindustan Antibiotics, India, 156
Hoover, Ltd, UK, 328, 332
Hoover Worldwide Corporation, USA, 329

IBM, USA, 250
Imperial Chemical Industries, (ICI), USA, 62, 95–6
Inter-Continental Hotels, USA, 59
International Harvester Company, USA, 275
International Nickel, Canada, 27

John Holt, UK, 158

Kelvinator of Canada, Ltd, 334
Kerns, USA, 158
Komplex, Hungary, 60
Krupp, Germany, 58, 62

McCann-Erickson Europe, 229
Merck, Sharpe and Dohme, USA, 156
Mitsubishi, Japan, 239
Mitsui and Company, Ltd, Japan, 62, 239
Montecatini, Italy, 62

Company Index 379

National Housewares Manufacturers Association, USA, 218
National Lead, USA, 95
The Nestlé Company, Inc., Switzerland, 28, 199, 203, 281, 290–300, 331

Olivetti, Italy, 62

PepsiCo, USA, 196–8, 329
Peugeot, France, 190
Philco-Ford, Corporation, USA, 334
Philip Morris, Inc., USA, 325–6
Philips, Holland, 95–6
Polaroid Corporation, USA, 335–6
Princess Housewares, Inc., USA, 335, 338

Renault, France, 190
Rheinstahl, Germany, 59
Rolls-Royce, UK, 32

Schick Safety Razor, USA, 270–72
Sears, Roebuck and Company, USA, 17–18, 39, 157, 353–5
Siemens, Germany, 27, 327
Simmering–Graz–Pauker, Austria, 60
Simmons Machine Tool Corporation, USA, 58

Simmons-Skoda, Czech–USA, 59, 62
The Singer Company, USA, 325
Skoda, Czechoslovakia, 58
Socemas, France, 114
Societe Automobile Berliet, France, 114–15
Steyr–Daimler–Puch, Austria, 58
Swedish Sales Institute, Sweden, 228

Tata, India, 156
J. Walter Thompson Company, USA, 172
Toyo Kogyo, Japan, 204
Toyota, Japan, 27

Unilever, Ltd, UK, 27, 331
Union Carbide, USA, 64–70
United Africa Company (UAC), UK, 158

Voest, Austria, 60
Volkswagen, Germany, 159, 190
Volkswagen of America, USA, 28, 37, 202
Volvo, Sweden, 190

Whirlpool Corporation, USA, 328

Young and Rubicam International, USA, 330

International Investment
Edited by John H. Dunning

This volume gives the reader access to the main stream of research and writing on international investment since the Second World War. The emphasis is largely on direct investment, that is investment undertaken by companies in foreign ventures in which they have a controlling and managing interest.

Part One traces the growth of international capital movements from the beginning of the nineteenth century to the present day. The two main issues in the theory of foreign investment are discussed in Part Two: the effect of international capital movements on the economic welfare of importing or exporting countries and the determinants of foreign investments. Part Three analyses portfolio investment and the growth of new forms of international securities, while Part Four is devoted to the impact of foreign investment on industrial organization. Parts Five and Six deal in turn with the relationship between trade, balance of payments and foreign investment and then the latter's effect on economic development. The book ends with Harry Johnson's cogent analysis of the welfare implications of the international corporation.

John H. Dunning is Professor of Economics at the University of Reading.

International Trade and Economic Development
G. K. Helleiner

This book describes and analyses the issues of world trade as they relate to the less developed countries. The tools of international economic theory are employed in a practical fashion to illuminate the options available to trade policymakers in rich and poor countries. Special emphasis is placed upon the strategy and policies which may be pursued by the less developed countries themselves.

Chapter One summarizes the disputes about the historical role of international trade. Chapters Two and Three analyse international commodity markets and policy for their modification or control. Chapters Four and Six consider industrial export expansion and import substitution. In Chapter Five the causes, costs and possible remedies for export instability are discussed. Chapters Seven to Ten provide an analysis of the various instruments of commercial and exchange-rate policy, including the measurement of effective protection, the devaluation decision, and economic integration.

G. K. Helleiner is Professor of Economics at the University of Toronto.